love & death in kathmandu

love & death
in
kathmandu

a strange tale of royal murder

Amy Willesee
& Mark Whittaker

ST. MARTIN'S PRESS ✦ NEW YORK

www.stmartins.com

ISBN 0-312-32994-6

First published in Australia in Macmillan
by Pan Macmillan Australia Pty Limited

First U.S. Edition: July 2004

10 9 8 7 6 5 4 3 2 1

contents

family tree*

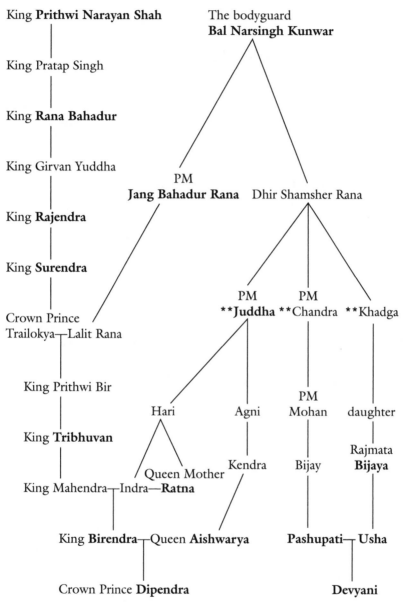

King **Prithwi Narayan Shah**

King Pratap Singh

King **Rana Bahadur**

King Girvan Yuddha

King **Rajendra**

King **Surendra**

Crown Prince
Trailokya—Lalit Rana

King Prithwi Bir

King **Tribhuvan**

King Mahendra—Indra—**Ratna**

King **Birendra**—Queen **Aishwarya**

Crown Prince **Dipendra**

The bodyguard
Bal Narsingh Kunwar

PM
Jang Bahadur Rana   Dhir Shamsher Rana

PM   PM
**Juddha **Chandra **Khadga

Hari   Agni   PM
                        Mohan   daughter

Queen Mother   Kendra   Bijay   Rajmata
                                                Bijaya

Pashupati— Usha

Devyani

* This is an edited family tree.
(**Juddha, Chandra and Khadga Shamsher Rana were born in
reverse order to that shown)

vii

juddha's descendants*

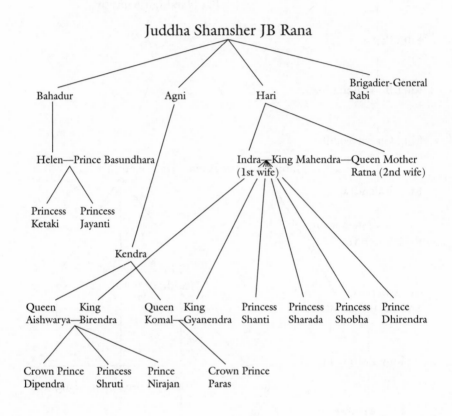

Juddha Shamsher JB Rana

Bahadur   Agni   Hari   Brigadier-General
                                       Rabi

Helen—Prince Basundhara   Indra—King Mahendra—Queen Mother
                               (1st wife)   Ratna (2nd wife)

Princess   Princess
Ketaki   Jayanti

        Kendra

Queen   King   Queen   King   Princess   Princess   Princess   Prince
Aishwarya—Birendra   Komal—Gyanendra Shanti   Sharada   Shobha   Dhirendra

Crown Prince   Princess   Prince   Crown Prince
Dipendra   Shruti   Nirajan   Paras

* This is an edited family tree.

cast of characters

Nepalese royal family

King Birendra	King of Nepal from 31 Jan 1972 to June 2001; father to Crown Prince Dipendra, Princess Shruti and Prince Nirajan.
Queen Aishwarya	Married King Birendra in Feb 1970.
Crown Prince/ King Dipendra	Son of King Birendra and Queen Aishwarya; born 27 June 1971.
Princess Shruti	Dipendra's sister; born 15 Oct 1976; married Gorakh Shamsher Rana in May 1997; mother of Surangana and Girwani.
Prince Nirajan	Dipendra's younger brother; born 6 Nov 1978.
Prince/Regent/ King Gyanendra	King Birendra's brother; crowned king as a 3-year-old during King Tribhuvan's escape to India in 1950–51; became regent then king following massacre.
Princess/Queen Komal	Queen Aishwarya's sister; Gyanendra's wife.
Prince/Crown Prince Paras	Gyanendra and Komal's son; Dipendra's first cousin.
Princess Prerana	Gyanendra and Komal's daughter.
Princess Himani	Paras's wife.
Prince Dhirendra/ Dhirendra Shah	Youngest brother of Birendra and Gyanendra.
Queen Mother Ratna	Sister of King Mahendra's first wife, Indra, became Mahendra's second wife; stepmother of Birendra.
Princess Shanti	Birendra's sister.
Princess Sharada	Birendra's sister; married to Kumar Khadga Bikram Shah.
Princess Shobha	Birendra's sister.

Palace insiders/royal relations

Princess Helen	Wife of Prince Basundhara; mother of Princess Jayanti and Ketaki.
Gorakh Shamsher Rana	Dipendra's brother-in-law; Princess Shruti's husband.
Princess Ketaki/ Ketaki Chester	Granddaughter of King Tribhuvan; daughter of Prince Basundhara and Princess Helen.
Maheshwar Kumar Singh	Royal in-law; married King Tribhuvan's daughter Bimala in 1952.
Kumar Khadga Bikram Shah	Married to Princess Sharada.
Rabi Shamsher Rana	Son of Juddha; married King Tribhuvan's daughter Tika in 1941; brigadier-general.
Dr Rajiv Shahi	Dhirendra's son-in-law; army doctor.
Suraj Shamsher Rana	Queen Aishwarya's brother.
Anju Shamsher Rana	Wife of Suraj Shamsher; cousin of Queen Aishwarya.
Princess Prekshya	Aishwarya's sister; married to Prince Dhirendra until 1988; died in helicopter crash in 2001.
Binod Singh	Son of Princess Shanti; the Raja of Bajhang.
Pramod Singh	Younger son of Princess Shanti; Binod's brother.
Prabhakar Rana	Gyanendra's cousin; in charge of royal business interests.
'Krishna'	One of Dipendra's cousins.
'Kiran'	One of Dipendra's cousins.
'Shyam'	One of Dipendra's cousins.
'Tej'	One of Dipendra's closest friends from school.
Alan Chester	English helicopter pilot; Ketaki's second husband.
Colonel Sundar Pratap Rana	Palace ADC during Dipendra's childhood; later King Birendra's senior ADC.

'Bim'	ADC; became one of King Birendra's senior aides.
Major Gajendra Bohra	Dipendra's ADC.
Major Raju Karki	Dipendra's ADC.
Ananta Simha	Instructor during Dipendra's time at the military academy; major, as Queen Aishwarya's ADC, in 2001.
Captain Chakra Shah	Queen Mother Ratna's ADC.
Pawan Khatri	Palace ADC.
Dr Mangal Raj Joshi	Royal astrologer.
Mohan Bahadur Pandey	Palace principal press secretary.
Ramesh Prasad Pandey	Chief royal priest.
Nayan Raj Pandey	Former royal guru.
Dr Khagendra Shrestha	Royal physician.
Dr Bal Kumar K.C.	Dipendra's geography tutor.
Major-General Bharat Simha	Member of royal staff; later ambassador to London and one of Dipendra's three guardians.
Dharmapal Thapa	Undercover history teacher at Budhanilkantha; later commander-in-chief of the army.

Nepalese history

Jaya Prakash Malla	Eighteenth-century king of Kathmandu.
Ram Shah	Gorkha king; ancestor of Prithwi Narayan Shah.

Prithwi Narayan Shah	First Shah king of Nepal (reigned 1768 to 1775); tenth Shah king of Gorkha (from 1742).
Goraknath	Holy man/guru; foretold of Shah dynasty's rule.
Rana Bahadur Shah	Third Shah king of Nepal (1777–1806); married Brahmin widow Kantawati; ruled as regent after placing Girvan Yuddha on the throne.
Sher Bahadur Shah	King Rana Bahadur's half-brother; allegedly murdered his brother.
Bal Narsingh Kunwar	King Rana Bahadur's bodyguard; killed Sher Bahadur and led 1806 palace massacre; Jang Bahadur's father; ancestor of Birendra, Aishwarya and Devyani.
Bhimsen Thapa	King Rana Bahadur's adviser; organised 1806 palace massacre; 'ruled' Nepal for 31 years.
Girvan Yuddha Shah	Fourth Shah king of Nepal (1799–1816); son of Rana Bahadur and Kantawati.
Rajendra Shah	Fifth Shah king (1816–1847).
Rajya Laxmi	King Rajendra's second wife; junior queen.
Gagan Singh	Junior queen Rajya Laxmi's lover; shot dead in Sept 1846.
Jang Bahadur Kunwar/Rana	Son of Bal Narsingh; began hereditary dictatorship of the Ranas in 1846 after Kot massacre.
Putali	Rajya Laxmi's chambermaid; Jang Bahadur's spy and later his wife.
Bijay Raj Pandey	Palace priest; acted as spy for Jang Bahadur.
Jagat Jang Rana	Son of Jang Bahadur.
Mathbar Singh Thapa	Prime minster; killed by his nephew Jang Bahadur in May 1845.
Surendra Shah	Troublemaking crown prince; became sixth Shah king when Jang Bahadur dethroned his father, Rajendra, in 1847; died 1881.

Trailokya Shah — Crown prince; son of Surendra; married two of Jang Bahadur's daughters in 1857, beginning Rana descent in Shah line; died in 1878 without ascending throne.

Prithwi Bir Shah — Seventh Shah king (1881–1911).

Ranaudip Rana — Younger brother of Jang Bahadur; third Rana prime minister; murdered by his nephews in 1885 coup d'etat.

Dhir Shamsher Rana — Youngest brother of Jang Bahadur; father of Bir, Chandra, Kadga and Juddha; died 1884.

Bir Shamsher Rana — Eldest son of Dhir Shamsher; became prime minister by coup d'etat in Nov 1885; died 1901.

Khadga Shamsher Rana — Son of Dhir Shamsher; took part in Nov 1885 coup d'etat; ancestor of Devyani.

Chandra Shamsher Rana — Son of Dhir Shamsher; took part in Nov 1885 coup d'etat; prime minister for 28 years; ancestor of Devyani.

Tribhuvan Shah — Eighth Shah king of Nepal (1911–55); grandfather of Birendra; fled to India and brought down Rana regime in 1951.

Juddha Shamsher Rana — Son of Dhir Shamsher; born 1875; prime minister from 1932 to 1945; great-grandfather of Queen Aishwarya and King Birendra.

Mohan Shamsher Rana — Last Rana prime minister; Devyani's great-grandfather.

Mahendra Shah — Ninth Shah king of Nepal (1955–72); father of Birendra; married Indra in 1940; widowed then married sister-in-law Ratna.

Basundhara Shah — Youngest brother of King Mahendra; married Helen; had relationship with Barbara Adams; died 1977.

part one

From forth the fatal loins of these two foes
A pair of star-crossed lovers take their life.

Romeo and Juliet
William Shakespeare

Part One

prologue

In the Nepalese hill village of Dolakha, a tolling bell calls frightened townsfolk to their famous temple. An old man with high cheekbones and a white, whiskery goatee joins the crowd pressing through the ancient, narrow streets.

As he reaches the temple, one of Nepal's holiest for 550 years, he finds villagers bowing and praying with a quiet desperation. The god, a black, wedge-shaped rock, is sweating again. The old man wonders what upheaval awaits his poor country this time.

When Domber Bahadur Shrestha was a boy, the village elders told him that when the idol sweated, something bad always happened. It sweated, they recalled, shortly before the 1934 earthquake that killed 8519 people. No one had bothered writing such things down, though, and so the curious child, lucky to be literate in a country where few were, decided he would become the record keeper of these bouts of perspiration.

The boy grew to be a schoolteacher and public servant. During his lifetime, the idol has sweated eight times – and eight times disaster has followed. From catastrophic landslides to the fall of dictatorships and the death of kings, it has foreseen them all.

The temple priest takes a swab from the sweating idol and sends it to the royal palace, eighty kilometres away in the nation's capital, Kathmandu. The king must always be informed when the idol sweats. His Majesty will send a sacrificial he-goat and an emissary to perform the correct *puja* (ritual worship). But they are slow in coming.

News of Dolakha's weeping idol is not the only menacing portent filtering into the royal bureaucracy. Across the tiny mountain kingdom there is a sense of unease. From the royal family's ancestral palace at Gorkha comes a report of water falling from the sky on a clear night. It is construed as an omen directed at the king. In a dark-wooden house opposite the old Kathmandu palace, a perfect ring of pimples circles the face of the child goddess, Kumari. A sure sign the deity is about to leave the girl's body. Then in late May, Saturn moves into a new constellation and astrologers predict disturbances. An earthquake, perhaps.

The signs are there. The palace has people to handle such things. There should be no surprises. But no one foresees what happens next.

On 1 June 2001, the heir to the throne, the impeccable Crown Prince Dipendra, picks up several guns and blows his family away.

It is a story delivered to us in Australia by the breakfast-table newspapers, a curiosity from a faraway land. A demigod dons military fatigues and kills his parents – King Birendra and Queen Aishwarya – along with his brother, sister and a collection of aunts and uncles, before turning the gun on himself. He is declared king while lying in a coma, as the world speculates on why he did it. The most consistent story to emerge centres on a rift between the queen and the twenty-nine-year-old crown prince over the woman he loved, an arrestingly beautiful aristocrat named Devyani Rana.

Three days later, the homicidal crown prince is dead. We are glued to the story, watching as the Himalayan kingdom wedged between China and India struggles to survive.

Eleven days after the massacre, we are struck by reports of a death ritual performed for the late King Birendra. As part of the elaborate *katto* ceremony reserved for Hindu monarchs, a Brahmin priest representing the dead king defiles himself by eating meat laced with ash from Birendra's funeral pyre. The Brahmin, dressed in heavy gold brocade and wearing a replica of the king's plumed crown, then mounts a lavishly adorned elephant and crosses the sacred Bagmati River, ensuring a safe passage into heaven for Birendra's spirit. The old priest, having lost his caste – his position in the strict Hindu social system – is then expected to leave the Kathmandu Valley, forced into exile for the rest of his life.

Three days later, a similar ceremony is held for the murderous Crown Prince Dipendra. But this time, the elephant will only leave under a barrage of rotten fruit and a beating that leaves blood streaming down its face. It is an inauspicious sign for Dipendra's soul.

Sitting in a kitchen in Sydney, it is this image that persuades us to come to Nepal. To discover both the madness and the magic in which the massacre has taken place, to understand what happened that dark night, and to immerse ourselves in this enigmatic land.

Aside from the crime, we find ourselves captivated by the idea of Nepal. We know little about the country, but it is a place we've always wanted to visit. What we do know has been pieced together from friends' trekking snaps, documentaries of Mount Everest conquests, news reports of an emerging guerilla war in the hills, and stories of the courage and ferocity of the Gurkha soldiers.

The rest is a mystery. That's part of the allure. We imagine a mystical, vibrant land of ancient tradition. The more we read in the massacre's wake, so it seems to be. A nation where living gods and goddesses, untouchables and kings are guided by superstition and karma. Where each man's fate is written at birth on his forehead.

Finding a patch of sunlight out of the shadow of the old Kathmandu palace, we take a seat on the worn temple step. It is chilly, despite the sun, but from here we can watch the monkeys as they lope across the palace rooftop.

Around us, the sprawling Durbar Square is going about its business. Where sunshine lights the winter cobblestones between temples, ragged women nurse their babies, and bored rickshaw drivers loll in empty carriages. A *saddhu* (Hindu holy man) wanders over, all saffron robes, long white beard and skinny legs. He gestures to us with an empty begging tin: 'You want photo?' We are soon distracted by the soldier marching past in heavy boots. Across the square, a circle of old women in vibrant saris chant and sing.

It is January 2002. It has taken us six months to quit our newspaper and magazine jobs and come to Nepal. We flew in only a few days ago, but already realise there is so much about the country we need to understand before we can begin to delve into the massacre: the protocol and traditions of the royal Shah dynasty; the long, capricious history between Crown Prince Dipendra's ancestors (the Shahs) and those of his lover (the Ranas); the culture of royal violence; and an age-old belief system, fiercely protected and so very different from our own. This is a country where the twenty-first and fourteenth centuries come together in a strange, brilliant patchwork, where belief systems are often more important than facts.

Few Nepalis we meet believe their crown prince is guilty. There is an air of quiet resignation in Kathmandu, both in the few who believe the apparent evidence, and among the majority who cling to what they know in their hearts. Their beloved Crown Prince Dipendra, they tell us, simply cannot have killed his parents. Indeed, in the world's only Hindu kingdom, many believe he was a living incarnation of the god Vishnu.

We soon understand that, more than just one violent night in the royal palace, this story is an intricate web of family feuds, mysticism, conspiracy theories and fact. It is also a story of place. We decide we will begin by exploring Kathmandu and Nepal itself. From there our journey will spiral inwards to the heart: a portrait of Crown Prince Dipendra, his love affair with Devyani Rana, and the events that may yet lead to the end of a dynasty.

chapter 1

the goddess and the king

Our first week in Kathmandu was, for the most part, spent in a crush of wide-eyed wonder as we struggled to contain the onslaught to our senses. We found ourselves on a wonderful, eccentric ride in a city where cows ruled the streets, and baby marijuana plants sprouted by the side of the road.

On dirty pavements, cross-legged women sat bundled in brilliant crimsons. They sold fried fish, pieces of coconut, chewing gum and nylon bras. Or they would read your palm, bargaining to the last rupee with a smile, while above them fluorescent lights announced supermarkets and department stores – the face of new Kathmandu – all white, bright and fixed price.

Bumping through the city's pock-marked streets in the back of a cab, we passed a motorcycle dealership advertising 'Honda – the family bike'. And it was, too. Middle-class families of Dad, Mum, two kids and a baby would zip by on their motorbike, nonchalantly dodging wheezing tuk-tuks and tinny buses belching black smoke.

Billboards spruiked cigarettes 'Inspired by Nepal' and bargain-price health care – 'Now you can afford open heart surgery and angioplasty' – while lepers, widows and small children lined New Road, tugging at your clothes with withered and filthy fingers in the hope of a few rupees.

In the bazaars of old Kathmandu's warren of rickety lanes, the pace slowed. We looked up to admire the handsome shutters and elegant woodwork of the old-style houses. Women and children hung out of windows to watch the activity in the alley below, where pregnant hessian sacks spilled lentils and rice, and jostled with a spectrum of silk and pashmina. Neat piles of offerings from that morning's *puja* dotted the path, and the sizzle of frying mustard-seed oil stung our nostrils over the spicy warmth of incense. And just when we were completely transported, a family bike would honk its horn a metre behind and we'd jump out of its way, right back into the twenty-first century.

It was here in the heart of ancient Kathmandu, by the old royal palace, that our journey really began.

'Ladies and gentlemen,' our guide, Rama, addressed us, although there were only two of us, 'this is the home of the child goddess Kumari.'

We were standing outside a dark little doorway in Durbar Square, finishing Rama's hour-long tour through the maze of temples surrounding the old *durbar* (palace). This final doorway was the part we'd been most looking forward to. It was the reason we'd really taken his tour: a chance to glimpse the living goddess in one of the exquisite carved bay windows overhead.

Behind the dark-wood lattice we could hear children playing and a TV blaring. It was a surprise to learn the goddess had access to Hindi soap operas.

'Unfortunately,' Rama continued, 'because you came too

late in the afternoon, it is not now possible to see the Kumari. You will have to come back another day.'

We were disappointed, finding it enchanting that somewhere inside lived a young girl worshipped as a deity. That the king of Nepal was chief among her worshippers made it all the more so.

The Kumari and the king go way back. No one can agree exactly when their relationship began, nor quite how it happened, but one of the more popular tales is this: in the early eighteenth century, the goddess Taleju and the then King of Kathmandu, Jaya Prakash Malla, would regularly meet at the palace to play dice. When the king began to lust after the goddess, however, she got angry. She informed him she would no longer meet with him directly, but would appear in the form of a virgin girl whom he could worship.

Whether or not Jaya Prakash Malla thus instituted the royal worship of the Kumari, or whether it was another Malla king a century or so earlier, didn't much matter. As protective deity of the Kathmandu Valley, she has always been an important goddess for any king to have on side. Which could be why, when he found his kingdom under increasing threat through the 1750s, King Jaya Prakash offered the royal Kumari a most extravagant gift. He initiated an annual chariot festival in her honour and built her the house we were now standing outside. Perhaps it wasn't enough.

By the autumn of 1768, the people of the Kathmandu Valley had been under siege for the better part of twenty years. Their harassers were hill men from the tiny state of Gorkha – poor, hard peasants whose military fame would later spread across the world as the British Army's favourite mercenaries, the Gurkhas. The Gorkha leader, the upstart king Prithwi Narayan Shah, had another factor working for him. Moving through the crowded, narrow streets of Kathmandu was a secret army of his Brahmin spies, spreading a feeling of inevitability about the Shah king's ultimate victory.

The Brahmins whispered the story of how the saint Goraknath had promised the valley to the Shah king; and that years earlier, when Prithwi Narayan Shah had taken *tika* (a red mark placed on the forehead) from the child goddess Kumari, she had handed him a lotus flower, the valley's symbol. The goddess had thus already promised Kathmandu to the Shah dynasty.

That autumn, as the Shah king's army came ever closer to the walls of the kingdom, the spies informed Prithwi Narayan Shah that the festival of Indra Jatra was to be celebrated as usual. *Rakshi*, the local rice spirit, would be flowing freely.

What happened next remains a blur of history. With the people of Kathmandu dragging the Kumari's chariot through the streets amid much merrymaking, the Shah king's troops entered the city with little resistance. After some twenty-five years of continuous warfare, Kathmandu suddenly had a new king. With a ceremonial throne already set up in Durbar Square, Prithwi Narayan Shah's first act as monarch was to sit in it and have the Kumari put her reddened finger to the centre of his forehead, conferring on him the right to rule the city.

Ever since, Prithwi Narayan Shah's descendants have ruled Nepal (as the Kathmandu Valley was then known), and have maintained a little girl as the Kumari. And every year, the king bows before her to take *tika* as she confirms his right to rule. Or not to rule, as we later learned from an historian, Professor Tulsi Ram Vaidya.

The professor told us of a strange performance his father had witnessed between the Kumari and King Tribhuvan, grand-father of the slain King Birendra. It was the autumn of 1954 and King Tribhuvan had gone to take *tika* from the goddess.

'But goddess Kumari did not give it,' explained Professor Vaidya. 'So her assistants said to her: "The king has come. Please, give him *tika*." Goddess Kumari just folded her arms.

'So then King Tribhuvan told his son Mahendra, the crown prince, to go forward. Goddess Kumari smiled, ready to give the *tika*. At that, Mahendra moved aside and asked his father to take it. But when King Tribhuvan went forward, goddess Kumari again folded her arms. She would not give him the *tika*. This happened two or three times.

'At last, goddess Kumari started weeping, looking at the face of the king. King Tribhuvan also felt uneasy. He withdrew, offered his golden coin, and bowed down to the feet of goddess Kumari. He told his son to take the *tika*. About six months later, Tribhuvan died, and Mahendra became king.'

The Kumari caretaker, Jujubai Shakya, told us he had seen signs before King Mahendra died, too. Every day, for seven days before his death, a dead snake appeared in the doorway of the Kumari's bedroom, blood oozing from its mouth.

It was also Jujubai who saw the strange circle of pimples on the face of the Kumari before the royal family massacre. 'It means our queen did not have her own face when she died,' he explained. Indeed, Queen Aishwarya had suffered some of the most horrific injuries in the massacre. At her funeral she wore the haunting, open-eyed mask of a china doll to hide where half her face had been blown off.

We later returned to the Kumari Ghar (house) with our guide Rama, to get a glimpse of the child goddess. Through the narrow doorway, we stepped into a sun-drenched court-yard, in the centre of which, spindly trees shaded a stone idol and *mandala* (circular design symbolising the universe). Around it was built the Kumari's three-storey house.

Rama called up in Nepali to the empty windows. We could just make out an old woman in the shadows. A minute passed. We followed Rama's instructions to drop a few rupees in the donation box, and another minute went by.

Then, up in the window, a little girl in red appeared. She looked about five years old. Her tiny face wore a streak of heavy black eyeliner that stretched out to her temples. We pressed our palms together and bowed our heads in *namaste* (a traditional Hindu greeting). The child smiled, flicked us a shy wave, and bounced away.

And that was it.

It left us wanting more. Knowing how goddesses were impossible to pin down for a meeting, however, we decided to try the next best thing. We would find an ex-goddess.

Our friend Pankaj rang to say he had found a former royal Kumari. We were invited, he said, to visit Rashmila Shakya at her family home in the heart of old Kathmandu. Before hanging up, Pankaj offered two pieces of advice: we should bring Rashmila a gift (having been a goddess for eight years, she was apparently not used to visitors turning up empty-handed), and we weren't to mention the subject of marriage.

We already knew the M word was a sore point with Kumaris. There was a strong belief that marrying an ex-goddess would lead to a man's early death. One explanation we'd read was that, during sex, snakes would emerge from her vagina to devour the man. Of course, it could be more that a former goddess was such high maintenance she sent the husband to an early pyre.

Rashmila sat in an old-style window, a glassless frame of dark, carved wood. The noise of children playing echoed up from the narrow street. She wore a simple black *kurta suruwal* (long tunic and matching loose trousers) and just a touch of eyeliner. To her side rested a large portrait of her when she had been a goddess – regal and unsmiling under elaborate gold headdress and heavy red brocade, her forehead painted red around a golden third eye.

Rashmila was just an ordinary four-year-old girl when, in 1984, the presiding royal Kumari showed signs that her reign was coming to an end. The caretaker alerted the royal priest, who in turn informed King Birendra. The royal astrologer was called on to decide an auspicious day for the selection of a new Kumari, and the search began.

While the Kumari is a Hindu goddess, only girls from the

Newar Buddhist caste of Shakya are eligible for the role. And, for the goddess's spirit to enter her, the girl must be pure. She can have no blemishes, no serious illness in her past, and she must have suffered no loss of blood.

Rashmila's mother was approached by the caretaker, Jujubai, and asked to present her daughter as a candidate. Rashmila didn't remember much of what happened next. Or if she did, she wasn't telling. The selection process is mysterious and guarded.

According to Dr Michael Allen, an anthropologist who studied Kumaris, a committee that included the royal priest and royal astrologer would then have examined Rashmila and the other candidates at the old palace. They were looking for thirty-two perfections found in goddesses.

It's an improbable list of features. On their own, some of the simpler attributes seem logical – well-proportioned feet and nails, broad shoulders, long arms, white teeth with no gaps, and a pure and robust body – but some of the rarer qualities create a rather odd picture. She must have the feet and hands of a duck, a chest like a lion, the thighs of a deer, a neck like a conch shell and the eyelashes of a cow. Her body should be shaped like a banyan tree, her head round with a cone-shaped top. Her complexion should be golden, her cheeks like a lion's, her tongue small, moist and sensitive, and her voice 'clear and soft like a duck's'.

None of this matters, however, if the little girl's horoscope is not compatible with that of the king. Once Rashmila was found to have all thirty-two perfections, the royal astrologer compared her chart with King Birendra's. It was favourable.

She still had to pass one final test, the darkest and most secret stage of the process. On the evening of the eighth day of the Dashain festival, the four-year-old was taken to a small courtyard at the old royal palace, Hanuman Dhoka. Throughout the country, goats, buffaloes and chickens were being sacrificed to various bloodthirsty goddesses, in keeping with the traditions of Dashain. In the Hanuman Dhoka courtyard, 108 buffaloes had been killed and their blood offered to Taleju, the goddess whom the Kumari is said to personify.

It's not clear what happened next. The courtyard would have been dark and bloody, with the freshly severed buffalo heads illuminated only by lighted wicks. It was a scene designed to terrify an ordinary child, but not the earthly representative of a bloodthirsty goddess. Rashmila must have greeted the carnage with regal composure. That night, the spirit of the goddess entered her body. She had become a deity.

A huge Minnie Mouse doll sat in the corner at the far end of the tidy room. Tacked to the walls were shiny serenity posters and Buddhist platitudes. Rashmila accepted the boomerang we had brought her and set it on the lacy white tablecloth. Now twenty-two, she had a pretty, open face and smiled often, particularly when she recalled her days as a goddess.

'From the age of four I understood that I was a Kumari and that I had some sort of power. I felt special because everyone, even the elderly people, came to pay respect. They would bow at me, so I knew I was different from other kids – even other adults. Because the king used to come, I felt especially powerful.

'My daily life wasn't structured. Every morning at six o'clock I had to do *puja*. From nine till ten I took a class with the local teacher – Nepali, basic English, general maths. The class wasn't very strict. If I had visitors coming, I could break class. That's changed these days. The present Kumari has to take classes for three hours a day and sit formal exams.

'Besides that, I would go to the window when there were visitors and give audience to the local people or tourists. Parents with children who had speech problems would bring them to me for private blessings. There is a belief that the parents should fast before bringing their child to me. Then some water purified by my feet would be given to the child and the child would start speaking. In a few cases there was good success.

'I can recall one incident where a child had some problems with his eyes. They wouldn't open fully. The water from my feet was put on his eyes, and drunk by the child. He got better. Not in one go. They came many days, but gradually he was good. I was very happy to see that . . . I felt like a goddess.'

Rashmila's mother, wrapped in a black shawl, popped her head into the room. She pressed her palms together and nodded in *namaste*. We asked her what it had been like the first time she worshipped her child. 'I didn't take her as a daughter,' she replied. 'I just felt she was the Kumari. She was a goddess.'

It was only then that we realised another young woman had crept in and was sitting in silence by the oversized Minnie Mouse. It was Rashmila's elder sister, Pramila. We asked if she could remember the day her baby sister became a deity.

'She was dressed in red, her hairstyle had changed, and all the people were telling me: "Now she is the Kumari, bow in front of her." In the morning she was my sister, but I came home from school and had to treat her like that. Of course, I just bowed in front of her. Even my parents were worshipping her, so why wouldn't I?'

Pramila sat back and Rashmila continued.

'Indra Jatra, the chariot festival, was the best time of the year. My attendant would do my make-up and dress me up. That would take almost an hour. Then, before I sat on my chariot, a goat – a black goat – would be sacrificed, and the blood smeared over it. And they would also have a *puja*; that means we would get things like flowers, fruits and red powder brought from the royal palace. I normally wasn't allowed to leave the Kumari Ghar, but during the festival I would come out for four days and the king would come to take a blessing and *tika* from me.

'If something was going to go wrong for the king, symbolic symptoms are shown by the Kumari. That's why, for the king, it's very important for the Kumari to be pure and flawless.

'I remember back in 1989 when we still had a king's monopoly . . . I was not feeling very happy, I used to cry without any reason. I used to feel irritated and stressed. That time was definitely not good for the king. That was when there was political change going on in the country. The power of the king was coming to the people.' Rashmila was referring to the period of India's trade embargo on the country that led to violent protests and King Birendra eventually introducing a constitutional monarchy to Nepal in February 1990.

'What I felt was symbolic. The crying, not feeling good, the stress, all meant there was some problem coming to the king. A sort of warning.'

Rashmila retired in October 1992. She was twelve and had just got her first period. Once a goddess shows signs of impurity, she has to go, and loss of blood is the most sure sign.

'I had mixed feelings,' she admitted. 'I felt bad because I had to leave the Kumari Ghar where I had spent almost eight years. I knew I had my own parents, but I wasn't very close to them. They were allowed to come and meet me any time, but they couldn't stay overnight. Those feelings which we have for our parents, I had for the caretaker.

'The new Kumari was brought to the Kumari Ghar, and we sat together. We were worshipped together. Then the new Kumari was put in my place and I was taken home.'

Her sister, Pramila, still sitting at the other end of the room, suddenly spoke up: 'I think it took her a long time to adjust . . . When she was Kumari, she was not supposed to put both feet on the ground, right? Whenever she had to go out, she was either carried or on a chariot. And so when she retired, she didn't even know how to walk on the road. She just walked on the road like a horse. She didn't know how to speak with strangers. She just kept quiet. She wanted to go outside, but she didn't know the way.'

During that time, Rashmila yearned to go back to the Kumari Ghar. She was four grades behind other children her age, and struggled to accept her mortal status. 'When she was upset I felt that maybe I made a mistake sending her there,' her mother later told us. 'She just wanted to go back. She didn't want to be here.'

We'd read of other ex-Kumaris left bitter by the experience, but now she was at college with dreams of studying engineering in Calcutta, Rashmila didn't regret it at all. 'Everyone does not get the opportunity to be a Kumari,' she told us, 'and I was selected because I was special. It makes me feel good.'

chapter 2
the most powerful woman in the country

Ɗ uring one of our visits to the Kumari Ghar, we were talking to the caretaker, Jujubai Shakya, about the Kumari's
ominous acne before the royal massacre, when there was a loud
bang upstairs. Jujubai gave a start. His wife leaned out of
the upstairs window and shouted for her son. Jujubai looked
worried.

'Did you hear that sound?' he asked. 'For six years that
sound has been happening. Just one week before the Maoists
announced their war, that bang started. The Kumari's bedroom
is up there. The noise comes from somewhere in her room. It
usually happens four, five times a day. Sometimes eight or ten
times.'

Jujubai had told the royal priest about the sounds. 'He
said it was just mice. We have a special government office that
looks after this sort of thing. They sent two people to investigate. They stayed the whole day, noted how many times it
happened, proved it was happening. And nobody cares! They
haven't done anything about it.'

What we had just heard was no mouse. But it was Jujubai's tense reaction that was most unnerving.

'These problems we have now with the Maoists, we can solve them by ourselves. We have Tantrics, astrologers, Brahmin priests. If we sit together and discuss these things, we will find a solution.'

Since our arrival in Kathmandu, everyone we'd met was talking about solutions to the Maoist insurgency. The royal massacre may have grabbed all the international headlines, but it was the guerilla war in the hills, slowly encircling the city, that was shaping up as a bigger disaster for the little nation. And with the country under a state of emergency brought on by this People's War, we felt compelled to find out more. We wanted to meet a guerilla.

On 4 February 1996, the Communist Party of Nepal (Maoist) delivered to the government a list of forty demands and an ultimatum to respond by 17 February. The government paid them no heed. On 13 February – four days early – the Maoists launched a series of attacks across the country and declared a People's War.

Back then Kapil Adhikari was a bright young idealist from a remote village in eastern Nepal. Born into the 'superior' Brahmin caste, his life up to that point had been dictated by tradition. At the age of five, he had started learning Sanskrit; at eight, he was given a secret mantra and sacred thread in a ceremony reserved for high-caste men. By his late teens, his parents would arrange his marriage to a Brahmin girl of their choice, and the newlyweds would have children and raise them the same way.

But all around him, Kapil saw inequality and stagnation. His village had no electricity and the nearest road was a two-day walk away. The first time Kapil had travelled on a bus he was fifteen years old. He thought it was an aluminium house until the landscape started to move. His older sister had seen aeroplanes overhead but as the twenty-first century dawned, she had still never been to the road. She had been married off when she was twelve and moved to her husband's home. Kapil knew she wasn't happy, but she'd been taught from birth that fulfilling her duties would mean good karma for the next life.

After King Birendra introduced multi-party democracy to Nepal in 1990, Kapil joined one of the communist parties. But democracy had seen few improvements in the village. Indeed, it centralised power even more, exposed more flaws, opened up more avenues for corruption and abuse.

There were men in Kapil's district who beat and raped their wives and got away with it. Women disappeared, and no one was accountable. He knew families who, unable to pay for their children's weddings, had enslaved themselves by borrowing from big landowners. The peasants couldn't read or write. The landowner would add a zero and, bingo, a 500-rupee loan had catapulted to 5000 rupees, and the family would be repaying the debt for generations.

After six years of participating in the new political system, the Maoists decided that this way would never lead to a true class revolution. Among the forty-point list of demands they presented to the government in February 1996, the Maoists called for the drafting of a new constitution; the abolition of royal privileges; land reform; an end to the exploitation of women, ethnic minorities and untouchables; the elimination of corruption; and water, roads and electricity for all. When they launched the People's War nine days later, Kapil put up his hand.

'At first, three police outposts in the country were attacked,' he told us over lemon tea in a hotel bar in Patan, just across the Bagmati River from Kathmandu. Kapil had a dimpled smile and a sparkle in his eyes.

He had left the Maoists in dramatic circumstances and was living a somewhat risky existence in Kathmandu. We couldn't decide, though, whether he felt more in danger from the Royal Nepalese Army or from his former comrades. The war had escalated in the last few months, which was why the government had declared a state of emergency.

Kapil told us about his role early in the war.

'There were attacks on big land-holders, where we would distribute the rice, corn and millet to the villagers. My first action was an attack on a land-holder in Kavre. An ex-army officer. He was a big feudal of the district. Many people said that 500 families had migrated from his village to Kathmandu and the Terai because of his corruption. He had 150 kilograms of gold in his home and five guns.

'When we were planning the attack we used his servants. We asked them: "What is his routine? What is his style? How many bedrooms in his house? Where is the gold?"

'His family was feuding at the time, so his sister and brother-in-law were also involved in the attack. The Maoists use contradiction against the enemy,' Kapil explained. 'It's a major strategy of the war.'

Kapil also had to convince the local peasants to support the rebels.

'Mao says the people are the barracks of the guerilla. We asked the young men and women, "What is the cause of your poverty?" They listened to our philosophy and our politics, and it was very attractive to them. This is what gave birth to the People's War. So at first there were 500 peasants in the attack. We all attacked the food and the wells. But we respected the feudal's wife and daughter and sister. When I *namasted* them, I told them, "This war is also your war." They realised we weren't terrorists or thieves.

'We didn't hurt the feudal. We just threatened him: "We are taking your wealth. You have to move away. Go to Kathmandu. Your field will be distributed among peasants." And he left.'

But when he got to the city, said Kapil, the landowner

became a police informer. 'So we attacked him in Kathmandu, and now he can't leave the house because his legs are cracked.'

The waiter came over to top up our tea.

'In that period, the Maoists were a little bit like social workers. The bureaucrats at the district level were corrupt and weren't looking after the people. They gave them all sorts of grief. The police raped people. The Maoists attacked them first, so the villagers realised we were their friends. We were saving them. I know many mothers, many grandmothers who wept to meet me because we had attacked their enemy.'

Kapil said one man was known to have raped fifty-five women.

'He used to be my friend. His family are mostly business-men. Black market. At first I just told him: "I'd help you, but your past is too bad. You have to leave and go to the city."

'He didn't take my warning. He went to the police and they arrested me. I was in jail for six months. When I returned from jail I told him again to leave. He threatened my life and told me: "You'll have to kill me to make me leave. This is my home."

'His house became like a police outpost. He was like an adopted relative of the police. They investigated us for six months . . . I had a bomb and a gun. This guy lived on the banks of the river. We planned an ambush. He had left home early to go to the market. It was 4 am. We were wet. It was the monsoon season and there'd been a big rainfall that morning.

'He and his two porters came by. I was commander. I shone the torch on his chest. He jumped like a monkey when I fired at him. He fell in the river. The monsoon river is huge. He was never found.

'The two porters are in prison now. They are innocent.' Kapil had a grin on his face. 'They will live in jail for twenty years.'

We sat in silence. It was hard to know what to say; diffi-cult to reconcile the gentle intelligence and social passion of the man we'd been listening to for the past hour with his apparent disregard for the porters. Kapil didn't seem to sense our discomfort. After a few moments he continued.

'When I started in the People's War, I was the commander of just two people. I had a small homemade pistol and a small *khukuri* [Nepalese knife]. Easy to hide on the body. We had no uniforms, no communication. All we had was the ideology of the Maoists and commitment for the people. I was surprised by how many rallied around us. But the Nepalese people very much wanted change.

'In the last 200 years we've had three major political changes in Nepal, but nothing has changed at grassroots level. My father worked in the field, my grandfather worked in the field, and my grandfather's father worked in the field. The villages are 200 years behind Kathmandu. The women are so unhealthy, the children are unhealthy. They don't know about balanced diets. They don't know that boiling water is better than not boiling water. This is what fuels the Maoists.'

By the first anniversary of the People's War, Kapil had a platoon of twenty-seven under his command. His team carried out regular attacks, held weapons demonstrations, dispensed propaganda in the villages and recruited from all castes and ethnic groups. 'In my team,' Kapil said, 'untouchable and touchable are the same.'

Many women joined the rebel army, too.

'I think 55 per cent of the guerillas are women. In the army and police, very few women are included. In the bureaucracy, only two women. In political parties, only a handful of women. So all our women are joining the Maoists because there's no other way they can change this situation. "Get married, get pregnant" – they feel that's not life. They want to be brave, they want to have guns, they want to fight.'

It was only then that Kapil told us his wife Devi had been a guerilla in his platoon. We asked if we could meet her.

A week later we were woken by the phone at 7.20 am. It was Kapil. He was inviting us over for breakfast.

An hour later, we met in the lobby of our hotel and followed him out into the cobbled lanes of Patan. As we passed through the square, old bent-backed women were feeding the pigeons. Others held trays of flowers and vermilion, finishing their morning *pujas*. Kapil, his black cap pulled down over his eyes, guided us towards the Bagmati River.

We passed a soldier in fatigues, a semi-automatic slung over his shoulder. Kapil seemed less nervous passing him than we did. We wondered whether he might have alliances on one or other side these days. It seemed strange that he could walk away from the war and expect no repercussions. 'The only security I've got is myself,' Kapil declared once we were out of earshot. 'I live in a secret place. I move rarely and most carefully. Kathmandu has people following everywhere.' Before we reached the river, he turned off the road.

Kapil and Devi lived in an apartment in one of the city's small modern concrete blocks swallowing up the fields and paddies encircling the exquisite Newari architecture of the old cities. They had one room and a kitchen.

We removed our shoes and stepped inside. The room was neat and sparse, with little more than a double bed, a TV and a low coffee table. We sat on a thick rug on the floor and a shy young woman appeared. It was Devi. She wore a red cotton *kurta suruwal* and had a plump, bare-bottomed baby on her hip.

Devi was twenty-two with fair skin and a delicate sprinkling of freckles across her nose. She smiled hello, handed the baby to Kapil and returned to the kitchen to cook breakfast. Kapil cradled his daughter. She made happy baby noises and flapped her feet.

'I fell in love with Devi six months after she joined the Maoists,' Kapil laughed. 'I wanted to marry her. I knew she had a really nice heart. She'd only finished seventh class, but she had big hopes and I loved her.

'There was no big age difference. No difference in ideology. But the party wouldn't give us permission to marry. They brought her to Kathmandu for five months. I think my friend wanted to marry her too. He told her: "You could marry me. I'm a big, powerful commander. Kapil is nonsense. Don't worry about him."'

Kapil spooned some dahl into his daughter's mouth.

'They couldn't keep us apart. I was so determined, I went to Kathmandu. They couldn't win. Our love is too strong. In the end our leaders married us in a communist ceremony. We were in hiding in Kathmandu. It was a simple tea party. Devi gave me a *malla* [floral garland] and then I gave her a *malla*.'

Even then, Kapil still had to convince his family to accept the union. 'At first my father wouldn't eat the food my wife prepared,' he explained. 'Because she is a Chhetri, from the warrior caste, and we are Brahmins – "superior caste". But he was here seven days ago and he ate.'

Kapil smiled and laid his now sleepy baby on her blanket. She started to whimper. 'It's okay,' he soothed her. 'It's your duty to cry.' And he slipped out to help Devi.

The couple returned bearing a breakfast banquet. Steaming bowls of rice, dahl, spinach and vegetable curry filled the room with deliciously warm, spicy smells. The four of us sat cross-legged around the low table. As we feasted, we asked Devi to tell us about her life. A tiny smile came across her lips. She lowered her eyes and whispered to Kapil in Nepali.

'She is shy,' he laughed. But she kept talking and Kapil translated. 'She grew up in a very poor family. They had no land so she had to do another man's work. Labouring for the feudal and looking after the babies. She earned about thirty rupees [less than one Australian dollar] a day.

'Her mother and father couldn't give her an education. She didn't start school until sixteen, in sixth class. Then when she was in seventh class she joined the Maoists. The Maoists had impressed her elder brother and her teacher. We were neighbours, so I used to go to her home every day. I would gather many children and tell them: "Our nation is in trouble and we have a duty to do something. This is our plan. This is our ideology."

'She was impressed, so in 1998 she left her studies and

joined the war. She was the first female guerilla in my district.'
Kapil flashed her a dimpled smile.

'Being the first, there were many people watching her.
It was her job to convince other women to join. She'd tell
them how we had to change male domination in society. Some
people saw her positively – she was working for the nation, for
women's rights – but others looked at her like she was a prosti-
tute. That was difficult, but she knew this wasn't just about her.
And over time she became more and more convinced she was
doing the right thing. She was able to convince other women.
Now there are more than 150 female guerillas in the district and
it all started with her.'

The baby had woken and was now nestled in Devi's lap.
With her free hand, Devi mashed a mixture of dahl, rice and curd
for the child. We asked, through Kapil, how she felt the first time
she held a gun. Devi smiled at the memory. 'That was the first
time I had ever felt power in my life. I held the gun in my hand
and thought, I am the most powerful woman in the country.

'I took part in many actions. Not on police outposts, but
on rapists, feudals, other enemies of the people. At first it was
tough, because man-killing is not good in our culture. I was
thinking, Why do we need to kill this person? But later I found
he had raped some girls, or drunk too much *rakshi* and hit his
wife. Murderer husbands, rapist husbands. And when I killed
them, I felt happy.'

'The action,' Kapil clarified, 'would depend on his
wrongdoing. If he was a little corrupt, she would just hit him.
But if he had killed or raped a young girl, we'd have to try to
kill him.'

Devi wrapped a shawl around her shoulders to breastfeed
and we asked how many people they had killed.

'Ten, eleven people, I think. Not me,' Kapil noted. 'My
guerillas killed them. I was the commander so I just gave the
order to kill.'

It was a lot of power.

'Yes,' he smiled.

But there came a point when it wasn't enough.

'I had fought for two years,' Kapil recalled. 'Towards the end, one of my friends was killed by the party. He was a district member. I asked my politburo member why he was killed. He told me that he had been receiving money from the mafia. They killed my friend in August, but didn't tell us until December. Why would we just believe he was a criminal? I wanted to find out the truth so I started an investigation.'

Kapil began to look at his party with a more critical eye. 'One of my commanders in eastern Nepal was not a good ideologist. His army plan and reaction plan were completely wrong. I wanted to criticise the policy, the leader, but nobody would listen. Maoists have no democracy. It doesn't work. If you do the wrong thing, then I want the right to criticise you. We all have different opinions. I might like rice, you like bread, and you like potato. We have to find unity in diversity. In communism, though, we all have to like bread.

'One day we were at a training camp. We had 150 guerillas there. On the last day, we were finishing up, and I got this huge shock. Devi and I were arrested by the party. "Why do you arrest me?" I asked. They answered: "You are having an illegal relationship and you're going to destroy the party. We're going to kill you."

'I had criticised the commander so he charged me with all these different things. Illegal intercourse with a girl, illegal relationship, backstabbing the leader. The major charge was that I was a government informer. I had worked in the party for eight years. I was a real cadre. My life, my blood, was for the people. And then they charged me as an informer!

'They interrogated me: "Why don't you support your leader?" I told them: "Because he is wrong." They also interrogated Devi. They would hit me with a stick if we didn't answer. Legally, there is a justice system in the Maoists, but not in practice.'

Kapil and Devi knew what they were in for. They had watched it happen to five or six comrades. Kapil would be shot and his body thrown in the Sunkoshi River. Devi would be forced to watch.

'Devi was really scared. Really sad. We'd worked for the party for a long time, but they wouldn't believe us. It was all games. The leaders were so clean on the surface, but inside they were dirty. They took us to a jail in the jungle. I was tied up by my feet and hands. I slept on the ground.

'In the evenings I would tell them I had to piss. After three days [of being let loose to urinate], they believed me. "He's not going to run away if we let him go to the toilet." '

Devi was being kept in an outbuilding. On his way out to the toilet, Kapil managed to tap her awake. 'She was smart. She knew what I was doing. While I was going to the toilet I jumped down onto the terrace below, looked both ways, and in about five minutes I was two kilometres away. Ten minutes later they came searching, but there was no light.

'I was hiding and I heard my name being called. When I stood up and saw Devi I was so happy. We walked five, six hours. We stayed in the jungle all night. We were so hungry and so tired. We were in Kathmandu a day later, but I had a huge problem. I had no relationship with the government and no relationship with the Maoists. Our family was also afraid of us because the government was looking for me. One time before, when I'd been in jail, the police had arrested my father and elder brother. The police had hit them, destroyed our land. My dad was sixty-five. He hit back and they put him in custody for thirty days. He was so sick. He'd never seen anything like it. He told them, "My son's a Maoist but I'm not." They didn't believe him.'

Kapil couldn't put his family in any more danger. He contemplated moving to India, but couldn't bring himself to leave. He decided to contact the media. 'I wrote an article. All this propaganda about me leaving the Maoists.'

A journalist made contact with the government on Kapil's behalf. He was reluctant to trust anyone, but eventually met with a minister. 'He told the police and army not to arrest me and I was released after fifteen days.'

It took a lot longer to deal with the rebels, however. 'A year later the party took action against my old commander – the one who had tried to kill me. At first they hadn't believed my criticisms of him but once they investigated, they found he had forty-eight criminal charges to answer. There were twenty-two *lakhs* [2.2 million rupees, or 55,000 Australian dollars] missing. He was charged with corruption. He also took weapons and commissions from the mafia. He was put in a labour camp. Now he just works and eats. The party realised I was a good man. I was struggling against him for a reason.'

After all the time we'd spent talking with Kapil, it was still difficult to gauge where his allegiances had fallen. He claimed he wasn't working for either side, but admitted he maintained contact with his friends in the Maoists. We gathered he also had some high-up army contacts. He seemed to be managing a delicate balancing act. 'The army says I'm under suspicion. The Maoists still follow me around. But their leader tells me they won't kill me.'

To us, at least, Kapil's heart still seemed tied to communism, although he could see its flaws. Particularly following the horrific violence in the recent months since the declaration of a state of emergency. In that time, the very people the Maoists claimed to be helping were suffering most. The rebels were torturing civilians, destroying electricity and water pipes, sending the country's development hurtling back decades.

'Their behaviour has changed,' Kapil agreed. 'They feel big and proud, and they are betraying people in many ways. They are cheating the innocents. But the Maoists are not only violent towards innocent people. They are also killing bad people. And that's good. It's right.'

We felt compelled to point out the discrepancy between his approval of killing people without trial, and his denunciation of the treatment meted out to him. But Kapil didn't see there was any choice.

'Six years of People's War has achieved something. They have totally damaged the touchable/untouchable culture in the village, totally damaged the male-dominated culture, totally damaged the feudal culture.

'They don't like war, they don't like killing people, they

don't like the day-to-day fighting. But the government isn't doing anything for them. People are trapped. The king and the army and the feudals are living 200 years in the past. The government is democratic but mostly corrupt. The politicians' sons are in the US, they have houses in Switzerland, Mercedes in Kathmandu – but we knew them five years ago, and they had barely sandals on their feet.

'Then again, the Maoists kill teachers and innocents. One is terrorist, one is fascist. Given a choice, the poor people will mostly choose the Maoists. The rich will choose the government. We have a problem. There is no third way.'

We were curious whether they'd tell their daughter about their roles in the People's War when she grew up. Kapil thought for a moment. 'Maybe,' he shrugged. 'Some of it.'

We had been there three-and-a-half hours. 'I think you were happy in my house?' Kapil enquired as he walked us out to the street. 'Please forgive me if I have done anything to offend you.'

On the walk home, we struggled to reconcile the morning we'd enjoyed in the company of such a warm, interested, bright young couple with their complete lack of remorse for their victims. We knew Kapil was also struggling for answers. For himself and for his country.

Given his background and revolutionary tendencies, we'd been struck by one of the last things he'd said to us before we'd left: 'If the army doesn't win,' he'd remarked, 'Nepal is going down.'

chapter 3
EMERGENCY

*A*ll the ambassador's secretary had said was, 'I'm not sure it's going to be on tonight.' But it was the way she said it.

We were due at a function at the Australian Embassy that evening and had rung to check the details. Now it seemed the soirée was off and, judging from the woman's tone, there was more to the story than she was letting on.

We decided to eat in and resigned ourselves to hoping for an explanation in the morning newspapers. There was no guarantee of that, of course. It seemed that Kathmanduites gathered much of their news – certainly the most noteworthy stuff – from the grapevine.

Bemoaning our inability to become fully ensconced in this social loop, we tucked ourselves into bed with orange cordial and chocolate to watch the much-hyped premiere of the Indian version of *Popstars*. Then the phone rang. It was Dinesh.

We had been introduced to Dinesh, via email, by a Sydney friend after she learned we were planning a trip to Nepal. After months of corresponding across the globe, we finally met him when we stepped off the plane in Kathmandu. Dinesh had been at the airport to welcome us, a handsome young man, stylish in a black leather jacket, with his pretty girl-friend, Shanti, by his side.

In the Hindu tradition, Shanti had slipped garlands of marigolds over our heads, and, in the Buddhist tradition, cream silk scarves around our necks. Much later we would come to realise just how much this cross-cultural act symbolised their relationship. In the meantime, the four of us quickly became friends.

Dinesh was ringing now to tell us that the Maoists had called a *bandh* (a general strike) for the following two days, to mark the sixth anniversary of the People's War. 'A Maoist was shot today in Patan,' he added. 'Down by the Ring Road.' That was a fifteen-minute walk from where we were.

This all explained the sudden cancellation of the embassy bash. 'Don't go too far tomorrow, okay?' Dinesh advised.

The following morning we slept in. It was eight before we even looked at the clock. It felt much earlier. Then we realised why: the silence.

No angry horns outside, no bus boys shrieking for business, no hooning motorbikes. It was so quiet that when we opened the curtains, it was a surprise to see anyone out there at all. But a light stream of pedestrians and bicycles passed below our window, along with an occasional army truck, UN vehicle or media van.

When, hours later, we ventured out for a walk, we found it like this everywhere. Apart from pharmacies – which the Maoists cleared to open without fear of reprisals – and hordes of soldiers, the town had pretty much shut down. The main road leading down to the Bagmati River was a corridor of rusty roller-doors. But it was peaceful, and the sky was blue. The salty smell of roasting peanuts and popcorn drifted from wooden, roadside carts. Men leaned their elbows on the green guardrail skirting the road, as if waiting for something to happen. Among the few to brave the strike were the street-sweepers, at work on the unusually spotless streets. It felt like dawn rather than midday.

Reaching the bridge, we paused for a view down the black waters of the Bagmati. Apparently, dyes from new carpet factories have turned it this colour only in the last decade. There seemed to be more plastic flowing in it than water. At the river's edge, a couple of little girls were washing clothes amid piles of garbage.

We walked for an hour to the commercial centre, New Road, where we found an open newspaper stand. We bought the *Kathmandu Post* and stopped beneath a pipal tree to scan the front page.

The big news was that parliament had extended the state of emergency for another three months. A lower story – 'Sporadic violence on eve of two-day general strike' – detailed yesterday's assortment of bombs and attacks. That wasn't unusual. Every day we had become less shocked by the death count, which usually ranged from five to fifteen. Mostly, though, the violence kept its distance from the capital. We gathered it was a ploy by the Maoists to keep the smell of war away from the powerbrokers. It was, after all, the rich whose lives would be most affected by a revolution.

But yesterday, violence had come to town. Among the valley's catalogue of bombs and injuries, we found a couple of lines on the Patan shooting that Dinesh had mentioned. It turned out that a rebel had been killed by plain-clothes soldiers when they found him hanging a bomb alongside an anti-monarchy banner.

Since the start of the People's War, the Maoists had made clear their wish to get rid of the monarchy, but their chief target had been the elected government. And King Birendra, although he had come close a couple of times, had never deployed the army to fight them. The Maoists had applauded his inertia and claimed it as tacit support, while they toyed with the hapless police.

The royal massacre changed everything. In the week

following the slayings in June 2001, the Maoist mouthpiece, Dr Baburam Bhattarai, wrote an article in the opinion pages of a mainstream Nepali newspaper, *Kantipur*, in which he expressed what so many Nepalis were already thinking: 'A future king, love crazed, may relinquish claim to the throne, but he will not bring physical end to his entire extended family and to himself just for that reason.'

Making use of the nation's grief, Dr Bhattarai went so far as to praise the late King Birendra's 'patriotic spirit and liberal political character'. Indeed it was these traits, he contended, that had irked the 'imperialists and expansionists' so much that they had decided to do away with him. And so it was, he concluded neatly, that Indian intelligence, with the help of the CIA, had used the king's brother, the present King Gyanendra, to take control of Nepal from within the palace.

Dr Bhattarai finished by calling on patriotic Nepalis – the army included – to rise against the monarchy and uncover the truth. The new king was enemy number one. (For publishing all this, the newspaper's editor and two senior directors were promptly arrested on charges of sedition.)

For many Nepalis, the conspiracy theories were easier to swallow than the official line. The Maoists, already estimated to control around a third of the country, had been handed an opportunity to crank the rebellion up a notch. Large numbers of insurgents gathered in the capital, ready to pounce. Over the next month and a half, the violence intensified.

Then, one week in late July 2001, events suddenly changed tack. Prime Minister G.P. Koirala quit. His successor, Sher Bahadur Deuba, heading Nepal's eleventh government in as many years, immediately appealed to the Maoists for a cease-fire. The rebels agreed, and on 23 July a truce was declared.

The two sides sat down at the negotiating table the following month. Through round after round of talks, however, there was a sticking point. The Maoists argued that the monarchy had ended with the massacre of King Birendra and his sons. They demanded its abolition and elections for an assembly to draft a new constitution. The government refused to bargain over the royals. By late November that year, the Maoists announced that peace talks had failed and Nepal braced for the fallout.

The rebels launched a four-day killing spree which reportedly left more than 150 people dead, including many of their comrades. For the first time, the rebels didn't just attack the police. They went for the Royal Nepalese Army.

Prime Minister Deuba and King Gyanendra responded on 26 November by declaring a state of emergency. The Maoists were proclaimed 'terrorists', and the army was sent in to crush them.

Within one month, a non–government organisation report estimated that at least 698 people had been killed. Of those, the report went on, 80 per cent had been killed by the state. Despite reports that innocent bystanders were among the casualties, the army was winning.

It was a bright winter's morning when, out of the blue, our phone rang. The stranger on the end of the line introduced himself as an army captain. He had heard, he said, that we were interested in the People's War. He was keen to talk but said he had to return to his barracks at lunchtime. Would we like him to come over now?

Fifteen minutes later, we were sitting down for tea with the anonymous captain. He was thin and precise, his dark hair immaculate. He could have passed for an accountant.

Before we began, he told us he would only speak provided that we didn't identify him. He didn't want to put his wife and daughter's lives at risk. He was away from home for long stretches and felt unable to protect them. We agreed. 'Just call me Ram,' he smiled. 'It's the Nepalese equivalent of John.'

'Ram' had been in the army for more than fourteen years, and knew he'd be there till he retired. He had trained overseas at the prestigious military academies of Sandhurst and Fort

Bragg, and specialised in areas like civil affairs, special warfare and fighting guerillas. He remembered thinking how the possibility of using his training on home soil had seemed remote.

More recently, Ram had specialised in peacekeeping. On overseas missions, he'd always felt so sorry for the people who had to live through war. 'Now I look here, and it's much worse.'

Since the army had been brought in to fight the Maoists three months ago, he had led eight short-term missions into affected areas. His first mission had been an eye-opener.

'We had information that some militant leaders were gathering in a village about nineteen kilometres from where we were posted. They were preparing to attack Dhulikhel [a district headquarters thirty-two kilometres east of Kathmandu] . . .

'The place was about 800 metres below the road. It was a moonlit night. We moved with about fifty troops in a disguised vehicle. The last three kilometres we switched off the engine and the lights, and rolled down the hill.'

A police officer had guided them to the vicinity where the rebels were gathered, but didn't know which house they were in. So, leaving an element of his squad up on the road, Ram and another officer crept down the hill and entered the village from below.

'And there we noticed a person in civilian attire. No weapons sighted, but very suspicious. I mean, no villager would be out at eleven at night looking up to the road like this. We managed to crawl up very close and grab him from behind. He had no idea. He was watching the road, as he should. But we came from behind . . .

'We didn't kill him, of course. At that point we weren't even sure if he was innocent or not. So we dragged him downhill and questioned him. He was so shocked he didn't even think about trying to hide something. It was too easy, in fact. He said, "Okay, if you promise not to kill me, I will tell you everything." And we said: "Of course! There's no question of killing you. You surrendered." We played it that way.

'So he said: "Okay, in this house, there's thirteen Maoists

and in that house there's two." I said, "Any family members?" He said, "There's eight of them." Those eight were not Maoists, this was a house that the rebels had just overtaken. That changed the picture, because you couldn't go in there guns blazing. Then we asked him, "Any weapons?" And he said, "385 bombs." Whoa!' They had stumbled across the cache for the upcoming attack at Dhulikhel.

'Anyway, we decided we'd cordon off the two houses and take it from there. We didn't want to cause any unnecessary casualties.

'So we surrounded the house and next thing, they got wind of it somehow. And out come the family members. There were two daughters-in-law and the mother of the house, and children, crying and wailing, "Don't kill us!" I said: "Of course we're not going to kill you. Quiet down, quiet down." For a minute we almost lost control. We knew that in this house five metres away there were thirteen Maoists with 385 bombs. And here's the family coming out.

'So I decided, we'll just grab them, pull them onto the field – luckily there was a small dip in the field there, a hole – and we'll search them. Then, when we knew they weren't armed, we put them in the hole. It was a cold winter's night. One of the ladies had brought out a blanket and we covered them up. "Just keep quiet and sleep here. We're not going to harm you."

'Apparently, the Maoists had been telling people over the last six years: "The military has not come out yet, but when they do they are going to rape and pillage." That's why the family was so afraid . . .

'While this was going on, the Maoist leader came out behind three human shields: a senile eighty-four-year-old man, a nine-year-old boy, and a newborn baby carried by the nine-year-old. This guy was hiding behind them.

'My friend [the other officer] immediately gave the order: "Don't shoot! Let him escape." So this guy dragged those three people right up to the edge of the cordon, and this being a hilly area, the jungle started after that. And then he left them and he jumped [into the jungle below]. When he jumped, a couple of my soldiers fired. We thought he was hit, but we didn't know. It was too thick . . . We asked the family members, "Anyone left in the house?" They said, "No, that was the last guy." They said the other house was the one to watch . . .

'I started announcing: "The army has surrounded your house. You'd better come out peacefully and surrender. I'll give you five minutes." And would you believe it, a lady inside the house, a Maoist, was naive enough – I mean, they're in peanut heaven, they're not in touch with reality – she started giving me a political speech! "Brothers and sisters of the army, throw down your weapons and join us. Let's open up a new revolutionary people's Nepal." I was like: "What are you talking about? Wake up. This is no longer a joke. If you don't come out immediately we are going to shoot you." Of course it was a threat. We probably wouldn't do that. We'd probably just wait and starve them out.

'At that point, one person came out shooting. And he had a bomb in his left hand. So we fired. He went down, but he was only injured. There was chaos, of course. It took some time to get my soldiers to stop shooting because, you know, that was the first time we'd been in combat.

'I got my medic to look after him, tried to save him . . . He didn't make it. After that, we again offered to let them surrender, which today – to be honest, I don't know what I'd do today. After eight missions and seeing the way they torture people, seeing the way they've slit the throats of policemen who've surrendered. Chopped their heads off and put them on the windowsill. I hope I can still pull out the moral courage.

'I started a countdown. When I got to three minutes and thirty seconds, they shouted from inside, "Okay, we'll surrender."

'In the morning we brought in the technical people, explosives experts . . . and we went after the guy that had got away. We were re-entering a small stream way down deep, and as we got there, we heard some noise. My friend indicated "possible enemy". We started crawling and then we noticed him. He had been hit in the hip but he'd bandaged himself. He wasn't bleeding any more. He couldn't run away, but he had two grenades and a pistol lying next to him . . .

'He'd heard noises as well but he was looking the wrong way. As we crawled forward, he suddenly saw us. He went to throw one of the grenades and I yelled: "Throw it down! Throw it down!" He didn't throw it down, and we shot him. It wasn't nice, killing your own country-people. It was nasty, because it was close range.

'Anyway, that mission was wrapped up. It was considered a grand success because no one got away. There was minimal collateral damage, only one window of the house was damaged. None of the oxen were damaged. We were really thanked by the family in the morning. That was the rewarding part. To be honest, I think they were involved up to here, but what else would they do? Armed Maoists come to your door with all these weapons – the government's never been – and they say, "We want to stay in your house." Who's going to say no?'

Ram looked up and drew a long breath. 'When this war started,' he confessed, 'there was a part of me that believed, because they're holding genuine grievances, that some of what they [the Maoists] were doing was correct. To be honest, the police did plunder, the government has been bad, misrule is rampant, rule of law nowhere. There's exploitation, social causes. I'm not denying that. But with every passing day I realise, okay, maybe they have identified the correct factors, but they are not the answer.

'I went on one mission where we had a report that twenty-one Maoists were holed up in this town. I landed by helicopter, and these two women came running towards me. It's so hard, I mean, did they have socket bombs in their hands? Were they attacking us? What's going on? But something didn't look right and I called to my soldiers, "Don't shoot, don't shoot." They came in, we threw them on the ground and searched them . . .

'They actually wanted to offer information. They were being oppressed by the Maoists. These were ladies from the Brahmin caste, the priestly class. Very staunch Hindus. They'd been forced to eat cows, forced to pee in the temple. Okay, Mao said you shouldn't follow religion, but come on, that was for feudal China. Try applying that to Nepal where there are more temples than houses. Forcing Hindus to eat cows? This is the level of people you're dealing with.

'The other thing is, we've faced a lot of child soldiers. Do you shoot them? Do you not shoot them when they're shooting at you? It's so difficult. Once you disarm them, they look like your younger brother or sister.

'I have captured a fourteen-year-old girl. Apparently she was used as a personal wife for some of the leaders. She admitted she'd taken part in attacks. How did it start? Her father couldn't pay a certain amount of money to the Maoists so they said, "Right, we'll take your daughter." It's not like she volunteered.

'The success has gone to their heads. I mean, they hadn't had one reverse until the army came into play. I'm sure there is a hard core that are true believers. But they grew so fast, their ranks are filled with criminals now. They're guerillas only insofar as the tactics they use. The way I see it now, they're just rabid terrorists.

'I met this old woman – very recently, my last mission – she was about sixty-five. Her son was a policeman. That was her crime. Her son had been shot in the head. He was long gone. Her husband had been beaten close to death and, fearing for his life, was staying with a relative in Kathmandu. She had stayed in the village.

'The moment she saw me – apparently I look like her son, that's what she said – she put her arms around me and she cried for half an hour. There I am in the middle of an operation and my heart told me, Don't leave this poor old lady.'

The captain looked at his watch. It was time to go back to work.

'I never expected to have to shoot my own countrymen.

Right now, yes, we'll win the war. I actually believe that. But our main job, as our chief told us, is to bring them to the negotiating table. Not to decimate everyone.

'We are the final straw. We have no choice but to win.'

We picked up the newspapers from the rack at the Bakery Café. 'Bathed in blood', 'Maoists strike big', 'heavy losses' – our eyes raced across the page too quickly to absorb the events. At least 138 people had been killed, the *Kathmandu Post* reported, mostly soldiers and police.

Where had it happened? How close was it? We flew through the copy, trying to make sense of it. Our thoughts went to Ram.

The action had taken place a long way west, at a place called Achham. According to the Defence Ministry, forty-nine police officers, five civilians, and all but one of the fifty-eight soldiers at a single barracks were confirmed dead.

In a stomach-churning twist, locals had reported finding around forty heads 'of unidentified people' scattered across the fields. We later learned that the Maoists often cut off the heads of their fallen comrades to hamper identification.

It was, said the *Post*, 'the deadliest ever attack by Maoist rebels on Government security forces'. While the Defence Ministry also claimed heavy Maoist losses, only three rebels had been confirmed dead. Achham came as a terrible shock. It was the army's first routing.

At the gates of the military hospital in Kathmandu, a small crowd huddled around the guard. A second guard stood slightly back, consulting a list in his hand. Across the top were the words 'Death list of Achham.'

He looked up and pointed to a woman in the crowd. She was cocooned in a heavy, dark shawl. She stepped forward and he let her through the gate.

Another woman spoke to him. Again he consulted the piece of paper. He looked at the woman and shook his head.

She turned and left. Supported by two relatives, she began to sob. It wasn't clear which woman was the lucky one.

A week later, on the other side of town, we met a man called Bishnu. He was lying sick and forlorn in an old metal hospital bed. Outside, a violent storm blackened the morning, unseasonal thunder growling down from the Himalayas.

From the colour of the little hole in his chin and the thick split in his lip, it was clear that whatever had happened to him had happened recently. The room was still. Bishnu turned his head away from the door. His hair was neat and his moustache trimmed but the look on his face was pure hopelessness. Two steel rods were clamped down his plastered right arm, the antiquated contraption hooked to a stand over his bed.

Tribhuvan University Teaching Hospital was the country's top public hospital. It had been swamped with casualties since the start of the emergency. We'd decided to come and see how bad it was. Our friend Dinesh offered to translate, and the hospital staff had directed us to Bishnu.

His expression didn't change as we entered the room. Standing by his bed was an old gent who looked up to greet us – Bishnu's uncle. He had a fine-featured face and wore an apricot scarf around his neck.

In a hushed voice the old man told us Bishnu was a policeman. His family came from Dadeldhura in the far west. 'The home town of our prime minister,' Dinesh translated. 'Bishnu was born there. Before joining the police he used to work in a factory. Five years he worked there. Then the prime minister, who was home minister at the time, helped him get into the police. That was eleven years ago. Bishnu was twenty.'

Bishnu looked up with his lost eyes and, in a weak voice, spoke: 'My family didn't want me to join the police.'

'His parents are very old,' explained the uncle. 'They didn't want him to move away. They needed him to look after them. Since he joined the police, he's been away from his village the whole time. Sometimes it takes six or seven months to see his family. Sometimes it takes a year.' But there was never much choice. His family were subsistence farmers and needed his income.

'He is married and has three children,' the uncle expanded. 'The eldest is seven. And he's got three brothers, two sisters. One of his brothers has been disabled since birth. There are fifteen, sixteen people in his home and he's the only breadwinner.'

So is there any money coming in now?

'No,' whispered Bishnu.

Fragility filled the room. Dinesh gently asked him where he'd been working when he was attacked.

'Achham.' The name now elicited horror.

His voice frail, his face expressionless, Bishnu began to tell us what had happened in the early hours of 17 February. 'I was on guard duty in the trench when we heard the shooting start. It was 12.30 am.'

There were close to 100 police officers stationed at the hillside headquarters, but many were asleep. Out of the darkness a series of loud explosions slammed into their dreams and sent them racing to join Bishnu in the trench. The men slid into position. Some lay on their stomachs, others were standing. The policemen trained their weapons through gaps in the sandbags. There was no one to shoot at.

But they could hear fighting. The staccato of automatic gunfire told them that Maoists were attacking the army barracks on the ridge overlooking town. The police chief tried to contact the army barracks, but no one would answer. Eventually the line went dead.

While the guerillas continued their explosive assault on

the ridge above, a handful of their comrades entered the town to keep the police pinned down. The attack on the army lasted less than half an hour. Then, the pitch-black night was silent. Up on the ridge, fifty-seven soldiers lay dead.

Suddenly, from over the hill, thousands of Maoists charged into the town. Bishnu guessed there were 4000 of them. Men and women, screaming and shouting slogans.

From behind their trench, the policemen listened as the Maoist leader announced through a loudspeaker: 'We have captured the army. You have no automatic weapons. We have plenty. We have all the army's automatic weapons. You cannot fight us. You should surrender.'

Bishnu was armed with just an old .303 rifle, a World War I relic. He had 200 bullets and four hand grenades. Bishnu wasn't even a member of the armed police. He was civil police. He had never received any battle training, unlike the army guys who had just been slaughtered.

The Maoists sprayed bullets and launched grenades. The explosions made it difficult to shoot back.

'Don't be afraid,' the police chief told his men. 'They're just trying to scare us. Don't worry. Keep firing.'

'Look over there!' Bishnu yelled to his friend. 'Go! Go!'

'Over here!' another cop cried out.

The Maoists were running at them from every direction. It was so dark and so confusing all Bishnu could see was individual guerillas lunging towards the trench and shooting. The screaming, the blasts, the gunfire filled the night with terror. All the while, the loudspeaker continued to attack their resolve.

Bishnu knew they had to hold the guerillas back. If the Maoists captured the trench they would capture the headquarters. And if they captured the headquarters they would massacre everybody. Maoists didn't let policemen go. He had to make it till morning. Till the sun came up. Then the army would send helicopters.

Hour after hour, the battle never let up. Bishnu shot two Maoists, both men. They were wearing white jackets. Maybe he shot more, but it was hard to tell.

Just before dawn, the policeman fighting beside Bishnu took a hit. 'Brother,' he uttered, 'I have a bullet in my chest.'

'Just sit back there,' Bishnu instructed, before calling for help to move him inside. It was too late. His friend died.

At last the sun came up. They had made it. Bishnu listened for the helicopters. His face was cut up and bruised from shrapnel, but he was alive. He even had some ammunition left.

But the helicopters didn't come. The fighting continued into daylight.

Just before seven o'clock, Bishnu felt a burning pain rip through his arm. A bullet had pierced a gap in the trench. His arm suddenly wouldn't work.

He left the trench and returned to the headquarters, but there wasn't much he could do about his arm. There were no medical facilities and no doctor at Achham. They didn't even have painkillers. There was a police hospital more than 100 kilometres away at Nepalgunj, but the only viable way of reaching it was by helicopter. Bishnu could only sit and wait.

Finally, at 8.30 am he heard the whump-whump-whump of a chopper. It was coming in to land at the army barracks. The rebels turned their attack on the aircraft. Bishnu heard it fly away. They had been abandoned.

It wasn't until 10 am that the first army helicopter landed. Twenty-one of Bishnu's colleagues were dead.

'Nine hours,' Bishnu recalled. 'Nine whole hours of war.'

His eyes were dead. His expression had never changed as he narrated the story. It seemed to take all the energy he had just to speak.

'They flew me to hospital at Nepalgunj at midday, then brought me here later that night. I had an operation on my arm. They put a steel pin in it. The doctor says I'll be all right.

'If I'd have died, the government would have given my family 800,000 rupees [20,000 Australian dollars]. It would be enough to support them. But for this, no compensation. I might have to go back to the police. Go back and fight the Maoists.'

How does your wife feel about that? we asked.

'I haven't spoken to her. My uncle called and told her what happened. I didn't want her to come to Kathmandu. It's too expensive here . . . My uncle's here to look after me. There's no need for her to come.'

Bishnu dropped his eyes to his pillow. The room was enveloped in an aching silence. 'I think we should go,' whispered Dinesh.

Out in the run-down corridor, none of us spoke. Dinesh looked shattered. He pressed his fingers into his temples. We were all numbed by what the policeman had been through.

We'd been getting this war in little Orwellian dispatches from the front: *X number of Maoists killed and captured; so many weapons seized and bombs defused.* The sterile Defence Ministry press releases were designed to prevent demoralisation of the security forces and glorification of the Maoists. They also removed all trace of the noise and smell of war.

The social worker showing us through the hospital guided us along dark, crowded corridors. 'The situation has been much worse since the emergency,' he said as we walked to the orthopaedic ward. 'More innocents are being attacked.'

He left us outside another door, with no further explanation. We knocked before entering the small room.

Ashok, a thirty-two-year-old farmer from the far west, was working himself into a sitting position in his bed by the window. He was matchstick-thin and trembling. Behind him, the paint on the windowsill was peeling. Through the grimy window, the day had turned still and grey.

Sticking out from Ashok's olive-coloured blanket, his right leg ended in a freshly bandaged stump below the knee. He spoke in a soft voice. Dinesh leaned in to hear him.

'For the last two or three years the Maoists have been very active in my district,' Ashok began. 'They ask for donations and give us worries, you know.'

Ashok looked up at the door. A little boy of about two had just been brought in.

'He's my youngest,' Ashok nodded weakly towards the child. 'My other two are at home in the village. My wife is here in Kathmandu. She stays with me in the hospital.

'My parents are looking after the kids, but I'm really worried about them. How can I relax? There are so many attacks these days. They didn't even threaten me before my attack. Just suddenly, about two weeks after the emergency started, they came and attacked me.'

It was eleven o'clock at night. The young family was sleeping when Ashok woke to people calling his name. Outside, he was confronted by a group of young men and women. The women were all in their late teens or early twenties. They were dressed in white and wore their hair short.

Ashok locked his wife and children in the house and before he even had a chance to speak, the women jumped on him. They began kicking him in the chest.

Still on his front verandah, a couple of the men tied Ashok's hands behind his back and roped his ankles. They placed a large stone beneath his knees while a dozen women held him down. A young woman pulled out an axe and started swinging. Ashok watched it all happen but his mind was blank. He couldn't comprehend it.

The frenzied attack went on and on. The women took turns pounding him with the blunt side of the axe. He looked up at their faces and they seemed like witches. Demons.

Ashok knew he was going to die. He remembered them chanting. 'Long live the Maoists! Long live the Maoists!' They pumped their fists into the air in jubilation.

Then everything went black.

When Ashok's wife ventured outside, she found her husband close to death. Their verandah was drenched in blood. Bits of bone and flesh splattered the walls. She brought him inside and asked a neighbour for help.

At 4 am, they loaded his limp body into an ox cart and started the bumpy three-hour trek to the nearest road. Ashok regained consciousness but he had lost a lot of blood. Each jerk of the cart on the gravel track was a shot of hell. While their neighbour whipped the ox to go faster, Ashok's wife, sobbing, tried to stop the bleeding.

Even after they reached the road, they still had to travel another four hours by bus. Ashok finally got to hospital at 11 am.

'I have had three or four operations on this,' Ashok whispered, patting his half-leg. 'There is a steel pin in the other one. I have to stay in hospital maybe one or two more months. Then I'll get an artificial leg.'

'Will you be able to go back and work the farm?' Dinesh asked him.

'I don't think so,' Ashok murmured with an ache in his voice. 'I'm so scared. I have no idea what I'm going to do. I can't see any future. I'm the backbone of my family. I'm the one who looks after them. If I am gone, my children and my family are gone too.' He looked as though he'd given up.

Dinesh gently rested his hand on Ashok's arm. 'Don't get frustrated,' Dinesh soothed. 'Lots of people lead good lives with an artificial leg. Please don't suspend your life.'

Ashok's chin started to tremble and he turned his head away. A single tear rolled down his cheek. He lifted his hand up to his face. Dinesh was crying too.

Ashok's little boy was asleep by the door under a dirty yellow towel, as we silently left the room.

chapter 4
birthplace of a dynasty

'Good luck,' said the man at the hotel reception as we dragged ourselves out to a waiting car. It was an offensively early hour, and only when we'd sunk into the back seat did we wonder: why did he say 'Good luck'?

We were going to Gorkha. A little town 141 winding kilometres west of Kathmandu, regarded by the city dwellers as a no-go zone. The district was the birthplace of Maoist mouthpiece Baburam Bhattarai and had been a fertile breeding ground for the insurrection.

The reason we wanted to go there, however, was because it was 'the birthplace of modern Nepal', where the royal family's great ancestor Prithwi Narayan Shah was born. What better place to begin our journey into the world of the Shahs? We had also heard that, just as the dynasty began with supernatural forebodings, so too did it almost end, with some mysterious, prophetic rain that fell on a clear Gorkha evening prior to last year's massacre.

We picked up Dinesh and were out of town before the

sun rose behind us – a huge tangerine unveiling the hills in a buttery glow. We wound out of the valley then hooked into the river gorges which, if we fell off the road into the brown torrent, would carry us down to the Ganges.

Dozens of bedraggled *saddhus* were walking to Kathmandu on pilgrimages from India and Nepal's semi-tropical plains, known as the Terai, for the upcoming Shiva Ratri festival. Some had bare feet and none carried any warmer clothing than the robes on their backs. One meditated cross-legged just off the bitumen, oblivious to the thundering trucks in front and the abyss just behind.

We coiled through the spectacularly terraced mountains that Nepalis insist on calling hills. Everywhere, women bent over tubs and taps, their bright saris taut over the curves of shining thighs. A beautiful young girl slowly brushed her long black hair as the twenty-first century rumbled by. A woman picking watermelons piled them into her satellite dish. Men peed and squatted without discretion.

We were descending into a more tropical zone, but the trees, which should have had a broad-leafed exuberance, had been stripped down to leafy poles, giving the countryside a look to match the mangy dogs roaming about. The cause was clear enough: dozens of women were carting great chunks of forest on their backs for goat fodder.

A couple of right turns on, and after a breakfast stop of masala omelettes and milky Nepalese tea, *chia*, we were on the small road to Gorkha. There were two security checkpoints to pass through. First, a once-over from the police, then the army checkpoint a few metres beyond.

Dinesh explained to them that we had an introduction from a colonel in Kathmandu, and, after some confusion, a soldier in civvies appeared and got into our car. We never learned who our new companion was, but he stayed with us for the rest of the day.

We'd gone to the colonel for advice on the safety of Gorkha. He said we could go, provided that it was just a day trip. 'No military personnel will travel with you because you will be targets,' he'd told us. So the soldier's presence wasn't entirely reassuring, even if he was in plain clothes.

The most obvious thing to fear were the homemade land-mines, which regularly claimed the lives of military personnel. You couldn't talk your way out of those. There was also the responsibility we felt for the three men in the car – the soldier, Dinesh and Rakesh the driver – because it wouldn't be the two of us the Maoists would target. And these men were only here to help us.

We felt especially responsible for Dinesh because we knew his fiancée, Shanti, hadn't wanted him to come. She seemed to slip into a quiet panic when we first mentioned the trip.

We continued through the mangy-dog landscape, past armed soldiers atop ridges and behind sandbags. Through a gateway decorated with a portrait of the great Gorkhali king, Prithwi Narayan Shah, as usual portrayed gesturing 'number one' with his index finger.

More sandbags and barbed wire led us into the bustling Gorkha bazaar. Directed by our personal soldier, we stopped at an army barracks, where we were told to leave the car and start walking up the hill to the palace, Gorkha Durbar. Our entourage grew again, joined by another soldier in civvies. His T-shirt, with an M16 assault rifle drawn on it, wasn't quite our idea of discretion.

The cobblestoned lane with its narrow pink and yellow houses had a distinctly European feel. The grey stone path curved into a steep staircase zigzagging up the hill to a palace way out of sight. The two soldiers set off at a cracking pace and left us behind gasping and sweating, concentrating on putting one foot in front of the other. The sun was frying our scalps, the workout burning our chests. It felt better when we saw a few locals pausing for breath. They were twice our age, how-ever, with basketloads of sand and logs hanging down their backs.

About halfway up, we caught our first glimpse of the palace and began to find our rhythm. The higher we went, the larger and leafier the trees became, and the cooler it got.

Splatters of blood led us up the final staircase around the side of the fort-like palace. We were greeted by yet another soldier, this time in combat gear with green sandshoes. Being a temple as well as a palace, it was a no-leather zone. We took off our shoes and belts.

A crowd of soldiers and other hangers-on joined our gang. One of the soldiers pointed to the peak just above us, where a tower emerged from the forest. 'The only telecommunications tower left in the west,' he said. It was guarded against the Maoists by some eighty soldiers, and testified to the defensive strength of the hill where the Shah dynasty got its start.

The most striking thing about the handsome orange-brick palace with dark lattice windows was its size. It was no bigger than a large Australian home. But this was where it all began for Nepal.

Poking our heads down a narrow set of stairs, we could see a near-naked priest waving incense around a dark room – a Kali temple. Kali is the most bloodthirsty of the Hindu gods, hence the splatters we'd seen coming up the stairs. She is portrayed half naked, with a garland of skulls and a belt of hacked limbs. She dances on the body of a male figure – Lord Shiva – who gazes up at her in rapture. Her tongue lashes out to suck up blood and any negativity that passes through the minds of her devotees. For, more than just the goddess of destruction, she can be construed as the goddess of positive thinking and bold endeavours. Of no fear.

Lawyers like her. Bureaucrats who want to shaft a rival might sacrifice a goat to her. And she has an important temple here in the tiny royal complex of Gorkha, because 250 years ago, the Shahs needed everything she had to offer in their thrust for a hill empire.

A little boy appeared from down in the temple carrying a knife and holding a rooster by the neck. He laid the bird on a log sticky with downy goo. Within seconds, its headless body was flopping like a drunk in a mess of blood and feathers. The boy took the head to the priest, ignoring the bird's pathetic dance.

We were introduced to Ganesh Bhattarai who, as a

Gorkha Durbar guide, wasn't doing much business these days. He led us around to peer into a shadowy, low-ceilinged room. It looked like a tiny stable. 'This is where Prithwi Narayan Shah was born,' Ganesh announced with reverence.

Then he told a story about a famous holy man named Goraknath who, having been ignored and humiliated by the people of Kathmandu, came here to Gorkha, where he was welcomed by King Prithwi's ancestor, King Ram. Ram wanted to conquer Nepal, which was then the name of the three kingdoms of the Kathmandu Valley – Patan, Bhaktapur and Kathmandu. But Goraknath told him he could not. In ten generations' time, however, the sage said Ram's descendants would rule over the valley. The Shah family awaited its destiny.

'Ten generations later,' Ganesh continued, 'Prithwi Narayan Shah was born here. Then, when he was six years old, he was walking around here when the guru Goraknath appeared again. He told Prithwi Narayan Shah, "If you take what I give to you, then your wish will come true." And Prithwi Narayan Shah said, "Okay."

'Then the guru asked the young prince, "Please give me some curd." So he went inside and asked his mother. His mother gave him a litre of curd, which he brought back outside. The man drank all the curd and vomited some back up again. He said: "Please drink it." But the prince dropped it and tramped on it like this.' Ganesh stomped his feet. 'The guru said to the prince: "If you'd have eaten it, then wherever you spoke of, you would win every battle. But since you didn't, only where your foot touches will you win the battle."'

'That fact was proven,' interrupted the army captain heading our entourage. 'It is true. Wherever he went, he won the battle.'

King Prithwi Narayan Shah became the tenth Shah king of Gorkha when he ascended the throne at the age of twenty. His kingdom was one of forty-six tin-pot monarchies that occupied the area now known as Nepal.

The three kingdoms of the Kathmandu Valley were ruled by different branches of the Malla family, which centuries earlier had been the last family to rule large slabs of the Himalayan foothills before their empire had split and crumbled, and the Mallas retreated to the richest, most fertile pocket of the land. While the Malla dynasty's greatness had waned, all three Malla kings were still individually more powerful than the Shahs of Gorkha.

The Mallas were Newars, the ethnic group still prevalent in Kathmandu today. The Shahs, however, styled themselves as Rajputs, the heroic defenders of the Hindu faith who stood firm when the Muslim Moguls invaded Rajasthan, in modern-day India, in the fifteenth century. They can't have stood too firm, however, because with all the people claiming descent from them in what is now Nepal, they must have fled en masse to the hills.

Many historians contend that the Shahs are in fact Magars, the tribal ethnic group that makes up a large percentage of the modern-day Gurkhas and were prevalent around Gorkha. Whatever their origins, the Shahs also claimed to be descended from the god Vishnu. This didn't give them a great advantage over their rivals in any sort of supernatural arms race because all the kings claimed similarly divine heritage.

The Shahs kept their heads above water in their poor little hill kingdom of Gorkha, which had no agricultural surplus and no trade to speak of. Then Prithwi Narayan Shah ascended the throne in 1742 with a clear sense of destiny.

Returning from his wedding in another kingdom, he was brooding over having been ill treated by his new in-laws. He'd demanded the jewellery worn by his bride, plus a one-horned elephant, as dowry. But the in-laws were unforthcoming to the poor hill raja. So he'd left without his bride. On the way home, he and his entourage had climbed a hill overlooking the Kathmandu Valley and he stared in awe at the huge pagoda temples, the giant Buddhist stupas and the two-crops-a-year marvel of it all.

He would later write: 'At this time . . . two astrologers said to me: "O King, your heart is melting with desire." I was struck with wonder. How did they know my inmost thoughts and so speak to me? "At the moment your gaze rested on Nepal you stroked your moustache and in your heart you longed to be king of Nepal, as it seemed to us." '

On his return to Gorkha, he summoned his nobles.

'I have come to Nepal and I have seen it,' he told them. 'And I have decided it must be mine. What say you?'

'Attack, O King,' they said, assuring him that his was 'the voice to frighten elephants', and that if other princes attacked Gorkha while he was off waging war, 'a river of blood will flow'.

In 1743 he visited India and arranged the finance to buy a small arsenal of the most advanced weapon in the world, the musket. One imagines that he didn't buy too many, though, because his little subsistence economy did not have much to trade. He also had to buy steel for the manufacture of *khukuris*, the curved knives used by most of his soldiers and carried by Gurkhas to this day.

Prithwi Narayan returned to the hills and raised an army of about 8000 men, all of whom had to be convinced it was a good idea to take on three separate armies, each far larger than their own. The Gorkhalis were tough, independent peasants, and not likely to follow the quixotic dream of a foolish young monarch. But he promised them a share of the conquered land, thus feeding 'the land-hunger that ground at the belly of every hill man', and follow they did.

After twenty-four years of continuous warfare, as the Gorkha men closed in on Patan, the Malla kings called on the British East India Company to help lift the siege. The colonial trading company promptly dispatched an expeditionary force.

But the British column hit the jungles of the Terai and was ravaged by malaria. The troops were already in tatters by the time the Gorkhalis routed the force. Only 800 of the 2400 who'd set out made it back to India alive. This was the first meeting between the British Empire and the 'Gurkha', and it would not be forgotten by either side.

Having seen off that distraction, Prithwi Narayan Shah again turned to the valley. On 29 September 1768, with the city distracted by its observance of the annual Indra Jatra chariot festival, he marched into Kathmandu and took *tika* from the Kumari.

One of his first acts as King of Nepal was to ban outsiders. It was an isolation from the rest of the world that would last almost 200 years. His attitude to missionaries was summarised thus: 'First the Bible; then the trading stations; then the cannon.' Such was his xenophobia, he banned musicians and artists merely influenced by the style of neighbouring northern India.

By the time of his death from fever in 1775, aged fifty-two, Prithwi's 'little painfully acquired kingdom', as he called it, had expanded to include much of what is now eastern Nepal. But the military juggernaut he created would, over the next forty years, go on to conquer a vast tract of the Himalayan foothills – far larger than present-day Nepal – right up to the border of Kashmir.

We stepped over the fresh chicken blood and peered through one of the ground-floor lattice windows of the palace. As our eyes adjusted to the dark, we made out a piece of glittering furniture. Prithwi's throne, our guide Ganesh told us.

We turned his attention to the omens here that were supposed to have forecast the royal massacre. 'Sometimes our goddess Kali and god Goraknath give us information,' Ganesh explained, 'that something is going to go wrong in our country. Sometimes Hanuman also gives us information.' The guide was referring to Hanuman the monkey god, whose vermilion-smeared idol stood just outside the palace walls.

'When World War II was going to start,' he continued, 'Hanuman started sweating. Many people rubbed cloths over his body but it wouldn't dry. That was giving us information that there was going to be a world war. When the war finished, the sweating stopped. It sweated for the whole of World War II.'

So what about the omen last year?

'It was a day just like this, no clouds at all, and the sun was shining.' Ganesh led us down some steps to the far end of the temple. 'In the evening, there was nobody here. Just the security man.'

The soldier cut in: 'He was thirsty, but there wasn't any water. And he was on duty so he couldn't go down to the tap to get some. Then after some time . . .'

'Right from the upstairs window,' Ganesh took over, pointing up, 'water fell down. But there was no rain anywhere! Then after fifteen days, same day [in the lunar calendar], same time, four bricks fell down from that same roof. Those bricks were sent to the royal palace.'

What did they do about it? we asked. Did the king send a sacrifice?

'No, the priest just gave some worship. At that time the priest goes to Kali and says, "Sorry, if we have done anything to offend you, please forgive us."'

We'd heard about another widely held belief among the people of Nepal: that when Goraknath offered the Kathmandu Valley to Prithwi Narayan Shah, he also told him his family would only rule it for eleven generations. We'd wondered, though, whether it might be one of those stories that arose in the wake of a tragedy, to explain it in the cosmic scheme of things. The crowd around us insisted that the story was well known long before the massacre. But, Ganesh clarified, it was only a rumour. 'There is no specific story or evidence of it.'

Nevertheless, it's the story that holds the most currency now. The gun-wielding Crown Prince Dipendra was the twelfth generation.

chapter 5

star-crossed lovers

n a grey stone courtyard in downtown Kathmandu, the feast was in full swing.

Rows of men, women and children sat cross-legged on bamboo mats stretching from one end of the courtyard to the other. We spotted Dinesh making his way along the middle row with an enormous saucepan under his arm. He joked with the guests and ignored protests of 'Too much!' as he dished another curry onto their plates.

At the front of the party area, below the narrow house where Dinesh grew up, a garland of flowers hung from a large portrait of his grandmother. This was the one-year anniversary of her death.

The first dinner sitting rose and disappeared as one. Plates were cleared, the courtyard swept, and water sprinkled over the ground for purification.

Then, removing our shoes, we took our positions on the bamboo mat beside Dinesh and his brother-in-law, Pankaj, for the second shift. The leaf plates in front of us began to pile with food. The trick now was to get the sloppy dahl and curries from the plates to our mouths without cutlery and without embarrassing our hosts or ourselves. The catch was, we had to do it using only our right hands, and – raising the degree of difficulty somewhat – remain in a cross-legged position for the duration of the attempt.

While Dinesh and Pankaj pinched neat portions from their plates and deftly swept them to their mouths, we dripped goop across our laps and acquired a mat of beaten rice on our chins.

Meanwhile, the food on our plates continued to grow. We knew we were being watched. The only way to handle this was to fake aptitude: ignore the sauce running down our arms, the pins and needles in our feet, and tuck in. After a while, we even managed conversation between mouthfuls.

'Shanti's not here tonight, Dinesh?'

'No,' he replied with a shy grin.

He took a sip of warm *rakshi*, the Nepalese rice spirit, as we explained how we'd been trying to meet the royal astrologer. We were keen to see what the stars had held for Crown Prince Dipendra and his forbidden lover, Devyani.

'Yes,' said Dinesh, 'in Nepal we go to the astrologer when we are getting married. He looks at both charts and picks when would be a good day for the wedding.'

'Will you and Shanti go to one before you get married?'

'No, not us.'

'Why not?'

'Because Shanti and I are from very different castes. She is Lama, like the Dalai Lama. They are the Buddhist priests. And I am a Hindu Newar guy. They are totally different. If I take our charts to the astrologer, he will say we should not get married.'

Since becoming secretly engaged at a Buddhist temple on New Year's Eve 1999, Dinesh and Shanti had known it was going to be tough. They weren't just from different castes, they were from different religions. For them to marry, Dinesh risked isolation from his family; Shanti, an only daughter, feared breaking her mother's heart. But the couple couldn't bear the thought of a life apart, so they stayed together and kept it secret. That's why she wasn't here.

'It's not just our crown prince who has these problems getting married.' Dinesh grinned again but it was clearly weighing on his mind. 'After my grandmother passed away we weren't allowed to get married for one year. That period is up now.' He sighed. 'I will tell my parents next year.

'They will not approve, but I will convince them. Shanti and I are strong.' He paused and smiled. 'We will stay together.'

'On the face of it, his birth chart looked really good,' said Dipak Gyawali, referring to the late Crown Prince Dipendra.

Dipak spoke fast and loud. His hair was styled in a smooth wave; he wore a sports shirt and boating shoes. He was a member of Kathmandu's social elite, and he knew an astrologer, he said, who had seen Dipendra's birth chart. Apparently, the analysis showed that the crown prince had what is known as *raj bhanga yoga*.

'You have in birth charts certain astrological combinations which give what are known as *raj yoga*,' he explained. '*Raj* means rulership, so *raj yoga* means he becomes a king. Not necessarily a king, but a captain, a leader . . .

'In any normal horoscope you start looking for *raj yoga* to see if the person's going to be great at all. You have all kinds of combinations which will give the person a very exalted status in life. Most people who become king have one of these traits . . .

'Now, *raj bhanga yoga* means "royalty destruction yoga". So you can have a very good horoscope, it looks like you have all the signs of an exalted life . . . but there is a certain combination which means the *raj yoga* destructs. And Dipendra is supposed to have had that.'

Middle-class Kathmandu had long been concerned with

Dipendra's horoscope. It was common wisdom that he might never be king. At one dinner party we heard speculation that, because of the crown prince's birth chart, the king and queen may have neglected their son. Not because he wouldn't be king, the chatter went, but because his chart also revealed he would not be good to his parents.

On the marriage front, astrologers were supposed to have warned King Birendra that he would die if his son wed before turning thirty-five. The other story was that Dipendra's chart and Devyani's chart were not cosmically synchronised and a union would result in tragedy.

We knew the royal astrologer had a house somewhere near the Golden Temple in Patan. So one afternoon, we walked up there to ask around. It had rained all day and the lane was covered in a thin film of mud.

At the Golden Temple, some men directed us to a 'medical hall' around the corner. From there, we were pointed down an alley and came to a square walled with doors – but no obvious sign as to which one might be the astrologer's. Then, from a green door, a young man appeared.

'Dr Joshi's not in,' he said, without us asking. 'Try later.'

Since then, we had tried numerous times. Dr Mangal Raj Joshi was a busy man. Finally, we'd managed to impart our times and dates of birth so he could prepare our horoscopes, and, some weeks later, we were on our way to meet him.

By now, the unseasonal rain had turned the laneway to mush. A woman thrust a stick down a blocked sewer and three onlookers pulled their saris to their scrunched-up noses.

Above the same green door, we noticed a head in the first-floor window. 'Dr Joshi?' The head slowly nodded.

We stepped inside and climbed a ladder to a poky office. 'He's out,' a man in a Nike tracksuit informed us. 'At the royal palace. You can wait in here.'

A young man with thick glasses sat on the floor preparing a chart. He worked from a calculator, a bottle of ink by his side. Royal portraits and dreamy pastel images of Hindu gods covered the walls. As we waited, we pondered what Dr Joshi might be doing at the palace. The royal family planned nothing without astrological advice.

He appeared twenty-five minutes later, wearing the Nepalese dress required for an audience with the king: *daura suruwal* – a cross-over shirt and tight pyjama pants – with a tweed coat. Dr Joshi's brown face was small and lined. He reached into a cupboard, removed two scrolls, and led us up another ladder. He apologised that it had taken so long to meet – 'I am eighty-two and working twenty hours a day.' He had been particularly busy, he said, preparing the almanac for the new year, 2059 by their calendar.

Dr Joshi's family were said to have been royal astrologers for more than twenty generations. 'My father taught me astrology predictions from the age of six. He was a gifted astrologer. He received a boon from the goddess.'

We looked at him, confused.

'Every night from nine o'clock until three o'clock in the morning he would meditate. Six hours every day for ten years. And so he got very good at this. One day, a goddess appeared to him in human form. And the goddess gave him the power of prediction, for seven generations. Whatever he said, it should come true.

'I am the second generation,' he smiled. 'But, to become a good astrologer also takes sixteen years of study. I had to study geology and geography, geophysics, astronomy.'

Dr Joshi was now sitting on the bed in his dingy bedroom. The only light came from an open window. A large photograph of Crown Prince Dipendra hung behind him.

We asked what the future held for the new king, Birendra's brother Gyanendra.

'I did a reading for His Majesty one-and-a-half months ago,' he replied. 'But I cannot talk about the royal family. I am not allowed to talk about that.'

He was happy to recall past glories, though. He claimed that, in 1942, he predicted the end of World War II. 'I was about twenty years old. The prime minister at that time asked my father how long the war would continue. On the basis of Hitler's horoscope we gave the prediction.'

More recently, he said, he accurately predicted the start of the 1991 Gulf War by calculating Saddam Hussein's chart. (Given that it started on the day of the deadline set by President Bush, that didn't seem so impressive.) He did not, however, predict the duration of the war. Astrology was not an exact science, he explained.

We wondered whether this last remark was a lesson he'd learned from one of his predecessors. There was a well-known story in Nepal about an astrologer who'd predicted that on 14 January 1934 a huge disaster would befall the kingdom. The sun, the moon and five planets were lined up in a most inauspicious conjunction.

But the date passed with no disaster. The astrologer was reprimanded by the royal priest for putting fear into the people, and he duly committed suicide. Then, at 4 pm the following day, the ground started shaking and did so for just over two minutes. The earthquake registered 8.3 on the Richter scale and killed 8519 people, including two infant princesses. Some 15,000 people were badly injured and 200,000 homes destroyed.

'Planets give off rays,' Dr Joshi elaborated. 'We can't see them, but they are bent by the stratosphere, the ionosphere, troposphere. So many spheres. They bend the light the same way as when you put a rod in water it looks bent. Therefore, you can't say exactly where and on what day something will happen.'

As he spoke, his voice rose and fell in a gentle rhythm.

'God proposes, man disposes,' he said. 'You know the remote control of the television? The planets are like that to people and life on the earth. They are our remote controls determining everything that we do.'

Right now the remotes were tuning in to a pretty bleak news channel.

'This is not a good time for the world,' he confirmed. 'The Middle East is suffering the most, like Afghanistan, Iran, Iraq, Israel. This will continue to 1 April 2003 . . . In that time there will be some, well, might be some big rains, might be big droughts, the spread of some new disease. This is not a good year.'

And what of 2001? Was there any indication that the royal family would be killed?

'We cannot pass that on,' he said firmly. 'It's professional ethics.' His knees jiggled back and forth. Again, the subject of the Shahs was closed.

Instead, Dr Joshi unfurled the scrolls he'd brought along – our birth charts. He began to read: 'Amy, 28 October 1975. Born in the Scorpio. The moon was in Leo. Taurus was ascendant . . .'

He continued the reading through each of the planets, but we were really just waiting for the predictions. When they came, it was clear that Dr Joshi knew how to please a crowd. Decades of travelling the world, he promised, healthy babies, intellectual enterprise, happiness in the heart. After all, you couldn't keep a court position in the family for twenty generations by predicting doom and gloom.

Dipak Gyawali laughed when we told him about our meeting with Dr Joshi. 'He's a character,' he chuckled. 'His nephew Dipendra is a better astrologer now. Go and see him.'

Some months later, Dipendra Joshi ushered us into the back of his ayurvedic shop in Patan. Snapshots of the ubiquitous Indian guru Sai Baba adorned his walls.

The junior Joshi was young and serious. As he seated us around his small desk, we asked how the coming year looked for the king.

'I cannot talk about our king,' he answered, echoing his uncle's words, 'but as far as our nation is concerned, after July, the situation will definitely improve. Just a week before our king's assassination last year, Saturn moved from one constellation into another. It takes about twenty-seven years for Saturn to move into that constellation, and it has always been disturbing. We knew well before that as soon as Saturn moved into that constellation, it would disturb the whole world. It's still got a few months to go.'

We handed him our charts and got down to business. Could he tell us, we asked, whether we were compatible. We'd decided we wanted to know how it felt for people like Dinesh and Shanti – or even the late Crown Prince Dipendra and Devyani – when love was left up to someone else to decide.

The young astrologer studied our charts solemnly. We waited for the reassuring smile, but there was none. He hesitated before speaking.

'Compatibility is pretty low, so you will have to be very careful.'

A long pause. He flicked through a thin-papered book.

'Compatibility is not good,' he said shaking his head. 'Amy's moon sign falls in eight, and Mark's moon sign falls in six. These two signs we always avoid for marital compatibility. We also take some other factors into account. If you two get married you may have to face some other problem, especially in children.'

No matter how much we dismissed astrology as mere superstition, it felt like he'd diagnosed a terminal illness. His English was clipped and functional. His words delivered with such certainty, such gravity, it felt like he was reading an x-ray.

'Physical compatibility is there,' he continued. 'No doubt. But you may have some problem. You may have some trouble conceiving. Even after giving birth there may be some problem with the children.'

Long pause.

He continued examining the chart, as if to reassure himself he hadn't made some terrible mistake.

'Still,' he said after another long pause, 'I told you there is no compatibility, but if you want to carry on, do not argue a lot because there may be some differences of opinions between you, especially if there is a problem with children. If you are planning to get married anyway, do it before the second of July, or postpone it for fifteen months. Keep on fasting every Tuesday . . . and Mark, you wear a yellow sapphire. Amy, wear a white pearl and a ruby.'

We had entered the world of the cosmically unsynchronised. Thank God we were already married.

chapter 6
a wedding
season

The winter chill had eased and we could no longer see the Himalayan peaks from our window. Now, on all but the crispest of days, the dusty spring air clogged the view.

Overnight, curtains of party lights appeared, fringing entire buildings. Candy-striped marquees were suddenly propped against houses, and raucous brass bands were marching the streets. It was some days before it dawned on us what this new festival was. We were in the heart of the wedding season, and it felt as if the whole city was celebrating.

The following Sunday morning, we read a striking story in the *Himalayan Times* under the headline, 'A childhood tied up in knots'. The piece began: 'Child marriage is banned in Nepal . . .' Law enforcement agencies, however, apparently 'turned a blind eye to this social evil'.

Fifty children aged between six and nine were going to tie the knot today in a village just fifteen kilometres from Kathmandu. It was Saraswati Day, which to most Hindus honours the goddess of learning. But every year, the small, largely illiterate Balami community uses the auspicious day to marry off its children en masse. So, while Nepalese children elsewhere are being taught to write their first words on temple walls, Balami girls become child wives.

We were keen to explore the Nepalese attitude towards marriage, particularly as it was at the heart of Crown Prince Dipendra's murderous rampage. While the details of the Balami nuptials may have differed from a royal wedding, the beliefs were much the same. So we threw on some clothes and hopped on a bus.

A thin young man – wedged between our knees and the 300 squeaking chicks across the aisle – passed the hour-long journey eavesdropping on us. As the groaning bus wound its way into the north-west hills, he spoke up: 'If you get off here with me, I'll take you to that wedding.'

It was only when the bus pulled away that we realised how lucky we were to have met the young man, for there was no town here, just a sandy strip of road skirting the hillside, with goat tracks carved through the terraces below. He introduced himself as Kumar. He had wide eyes and floppy black hair. Kumar announced we had an hour's walk ahead and took off down one of the slippery tracks. We scrambled behind.

At the bottom of a lush green terrace of wheat, a new road was being cut into the slope. A grader rumbled by, heralding a shift in the Balamis' isolated lives.

We coiled our way down the valley dotted with thatched-roof homes and Kumar chatted about his life. 'I am Brahmin,' he said. 'I am spiritual-minded person and pure of heart.'

He pulled his wallet from his pocket and flipped it open. Inside was a photo of a man with long, glossy black hair and a beaming smile. 'That is my *baba*,' Kumar smiled. 'He is my spiritual guide, like a teacher. Guru, we say. Every night I go to his house and we meditate.'

When he wasn't meditating, Kumar was studying computer science in Kathmandu and had a part-time job as a milk boy. Every day before college he would collect the milk from his village and deliver it to the city by bus.

As we walked, Kumar pointed out his family's land. He knew many of the ethnic Balamis only because his father hired them to work the family fields, for 100 rupees (about $2.50) a day. 'Most of them are too poor to send their children to school,' he said.

Just then we met a Balami woman along the trail. She was barefoot and had a beautiful, angular face with three small, dark tattoos across her chin. She wore a cropped green bodice and red sarong.

Kumar stopped her to ask about the wedding. Only then did we learn something was wrong. The woman said the mass nuptials were off. She provided no explanation, just pointed us to the next village. There, she said, a single union was going ahead regardless.

It seemed strange, and as we continued down the slope we wondered if she was mistaken. Then we came across a middle-aged man who repeated the news. Again, we were unable to obtain more details but he was happy to recall his own wedding at the age of seven.

'I'd never met my wife before our wedding,' he said. 'I didn't understand what was going on. I didn't even know what marriage was.' They didn't sleep together at first, he said. Only once they'd reached puberty did his wife move in with him.

'Why did you marry so young?' we asked.

'My parents only had one child. They needed someone to help with the work.'

Parents also gain religious merit for marrying their children young. This isn't unique to the Balamis. It's also true among orthodox Hindus, who place enormous value on the purity of their children – particularly daughters – at marriage. A girl is considered polluted once she starts her period or loses her virginity, so ideally she should marry before puberty. Parents who achieve this receive a substantial boost to their karma. Underage marriages being illegal in Nepal, however, many parents, particularly urban, high-caste Hindus, are now happy to wait for their children to finish their education.

The Newars take a more novel approach to avoiding child

marriages – their prepubescent daughters ritually marry a bel fruit, a sub-Himalayan quince. This satisfies the religious demands on her parents, while allowing the daughter to wait until much later to become a real wife. It also solves the potential problem of widowhood: her first and true husband, the fruit, never dies. Nevertheless, across Nepal, anyone who approaches the age of thirty still single is regarded with a degree of suspicion – as was the case for Crown Prince Dipendra and his lover Devyani.

We pushed on and reached the village that the Balami woman had mentioned. Word of our arrival spread through the cluster of mud-brick houses crammed against the hillside. Soon we were being dragged through ochre alleyways – not to the wedding, but to 'engagement' parties. These were more a coming-of-age, Kumar explained, than a commitment of marriage. The children involved were now ready to wed.

Huge copper pots of buffalo simmered over an open fire as a snotty-nosed boy and a taller girl were ushered towards us. The boy, wearing a tinsel lei, couldn't have been more than four years old. The girl, a little older, stood tall and stiff. She wore matrimonial red.

We were shuffled on through the steamy, crowded darkness of several more houses to admire a string of nervous child couples, before Kumar dragged us out, sweating, to the wedding. A tangle of kids sprinted up a steep track to the festivities, to warn of our arrival. We found the haphazard crowd sitting in the dirt, hunched over leaf plates piled with beaten rice and sticky buffalo curry. A man was scooping yellow dahl from a bucket with his right hand as a chicken ruffled the dust. But there was no sign of the bride.

A boy of perhaps twelve, neat in blue shirt, grey scarf and *topi* (Nepalese hat) was pushed towards us. Kumar introduced him as the groom. A couple of old tattooed women watched us with broad smiles, pulling on fat cigarettes like joints, their loose, wrinkly bellies exposed below their bodices.

And then we spotted her – a slight young girl, chewing on the corner of her beautiful red bridal shawl. She was leaning against a verandah pole, crying. Her forehead was smeared with vermilion rice, her eyes swollen and red. She wouldn't come near us.

Another girl was brought over instead. She was exquisitely pretty, with dark almond eyes, flushed cheeks and swollen lips. Splashes of gold were woven into her crimson shawl. A slash of vermilion stained the part in her hair.

Her name was Gita. She was thirteen and had been married for a year. We asked her what she thought of it.

'I don't like it,' she whispered. 'It's hard work. I have to cook, I have to cut rice, cut firewood, wash clothes.'

We asked if she'd ever been to school. She lowered her eyes and shook her head, flirting coyly with our camera.

Quietly, the reluctant bride, whose name we learned was Radhika, appeared by Gita's side. The groom, who had disappeared inside, was called back to pose for a photo with his new wife. His mother straightened his scarf while an old woman barked instructions at the two girls to tidy their hair. Radhika finally allowed herself a giggle.

It was standing room only on the bus home. As dusk approached, we passed faded temple walls with the names 'Ram', 'Sita' and 'Ganesh' written in large, spidery scrawl – reminders of today's celebration of learning.

It was some days before we discovered the mystery behind this year's cancelled wedding ceremonies.

Fifth-grader Sabitri Balami and her husband-to-be Akhabari Shrestha were among the couples due to marry. They were also among the few Balamis lucky enough to go to school, and were keen to continue their education. The bright, wilful pair wrote a letter to the government asking it to stop their wedding. The request was granted, and their wedding postponed for five years. The boy's mother, however, threatened to kill herself if it did not go ahead as planned. Her son said he'd commit suicide if it did.

It was contagious. The threats and counter-threats soon echoed across the valley as Sabitri and Akhabari's classmates also opted out. By Saraswati Day, all but two of the marriages had been postponed.

A small revolution had taken place. The new generation had threatened to shed its own blood as a rebellion against their tradition-bound parents. We were struck by an echo of the royal massacre.

chapter 7

the bodyguard

We left the taxi a kilometre before the Pashupatinath temple. The road was jammed with trucks, buses and worshippers on foot, all edging forward like a football crowd on grand-final day. Twenty-odd pilgrims jumped off one of the open-backed trucks. It had been a long ride, judging by the way they all lined up against a nearby wall to pee. Clusters of young men danced towards the temple, faces glowing with electric-pink powder and blissful smiles. A rainbow of saris illuminated the mob.

The event was Shiva Ratri, the most important festival at Nepal's most important Shiva temple, Pashupatinath – the only one of Hinduism's five holy sites in this tiny kingdom. In February/March every year, devotees from across the sub-continent converge here in their hundreds of thousands. Their manic energy wavered between lifting us to rapturous heights and crunching us in the throng.

Down by the Bagmati River, the air was thick with incense and the smoke of six funeral pyres. Reedy music snaked from speakers, accompanied by the drone of a conch shell echoing up from one of the funerals. From here we could watch the queue that inched along the opposite bank, behind the cremation ghats, into the temple. The same ghats where King Birendra and his family had been cremated nine months earlier.

We were on the side of the river where the *saddhus* had set up their camps. The ascetic holy men flocked here each year to worship Shiva. The dreadlocked god's penchant for marijuana made smoking ganja a holy pastime for these followers. So when King Birendra banned pot just before his coronation in 1975, this day was exempted on religious grounds. But still, the prohibition for the remaining 364 days of the year enraged the *saddhus*. When the palatial parliament building, Singh Durbar, burned down the day after the ban, many said it was no coincidence.

Freak-show displays of devotion by the *saddhus* during Shiva Ratri – lifting bricks with their penises, piercing their tongues and cutting off body parts – are legendary. But as we wandered through the camps, the most action we could find was a very stoned man applying a layer of ash to his near-naked (and intact) body.

We had also hoped to catch a glimpse of the elusive King Gyanendra, who was due here this afternoon. The royal family has had a close and continuous connection to Pashupatinath. It was a visit to this temple by one of the king's ancestors that, some 200 years before Crown Prince Dipendra's affair with Devyani, saw the start of the family's first conflict between love and succession.

Rana Bahadur Shah, grandson of the first Shah king of Kathmandu, the great Prithwi Narayan, had ascended to the throne when he was just two-and-a-half years old. His pampered upbringing left him without the skills to run either his own life or the country. Shortly after he reached adulthood and took control of the state from the regent, Rana Bahadur visited Pashupatinath, where he laid eyes on a bewitching beauty. Besotted, he had her forcibly brought to the palace, intending to make her his wife. But there were several obstacles.

She was a Brahmin, and despite the fact this was a higher caste than his own (Thakuri), it meant marriage was strictly forbidden. She was also a widow, and in the world of high-caste Hindus, the widow is a lowly creature, forbidden to remarry. All this could have been overcome by the fact that Rana Bahadur was king and could therefore do as he damn well pleased. But the Brahmin widow, Kantawati, refused to marry him.

It took six months for her to relent. In that time, she extracted a promise that any son born to her would become king. Despite already having two legal wives and two sons, King Rana Bahadur agreed.

Kantawati duly gave birth to a son, Girvan Yuddha Shah, shortly after which she learned she was dying of tuberculosis. In a desperate attempt to buy off the gods and cure his queen, Rana Bahadur consulted doctors and lavished donations on Brahmin priests and temples.

Meanwhile, Kantawati reminded him that his horoscope foretold that he, too, would die young – that he would not live beyond his twenty-fourth year. Their son would thus be at the mercy of all those courtiers contemptuous of their love. She urged the king to abdicate and put their son on the throne while the succession could not be contested. Believing he hadn't long to live, and impelled by his love for Kantawati, he agreed. Thus, Girvan Yuddha Shah, the son of a Brahmin widow, became king of Nepal while his father donned the saffron robes of a *saddhu*, but remained in power as regent.

When Kantawati died, Rana Bahadur's grief was unleashed in what has been described as a mad orgy of violence against the doctors, priests and temples that had failed to cure his beloved. In one case, he commanded three companies of soldiers to destroy the temple of Bhuwanee in Kathmandu; when they declined, he had boiling oil poured over them. The temple, one of the most revered in the city, was eventually demolished and as one observer put it, the regent 'put many of the Brahmins belonging to it to death, branded others, and deprived of their caste all he could seize, by the most offensive means'.

This was pertinent to our research because it struck at the heart of the problems faced more recently by Crown Prince Dipendra and his lover: it was the need to protect the royal bloodline from a perceived impurity of caste that led to the palace's objections to Devyani. In truth, not only had Rana Bahadur already compromised the royal line when he married his Brahmin widow, but the subsequent suspicious events surrounding his death sparked a trail of compromise that ultimately makes the Shahs' twenty-first-century demand for purity a sham.

In 1806, Rana Bahadur, aged thirty-one (in defiance of his horoscope), summoned his half-brother Sher Bahadur Shah to court, to answer charges regarding the misappropriation of 18,000 rupees. In his defence, the brother drew his sword. The first blow struck the ceiling. The second cut the regent in half. Rana Bahadur's bodyguard, a man by the name of Bal Narsingh Kunwar, then drew his *khukuri* and cut Sher Bahadur in two. At least, that was the version of events given by the bodyguard – who only wrote it down more than thirty years later, when Rana Bahadur's grandson started kicking up a fuss.

However, immediately after the two royal brothers died, guards surrounded the palace and, acting under the command of Rana Bahadur's right-hand man, Bhimsen Thapa and in cahoots with the bodyguard, massacred just about everyone inside, on the pretext that they had been involved in the murder plot. The senior queen, Rana Bahadur's first wife, and her fourteen maids were forced to burn alive in the ritual *sati* – the unfortunate maids on mere suspicion of having had sex with the late regent. In all, ninety-three members of the royal family and the nobility were killed.

The twelve-year-old fourth wife of Rana Bahadur was declared regent. With a child ostensibly in charge, the former adviser, Bhimsen Thapa, was then in a position to take control of the country and rule without interference from the royal family. It was a pattern that would be repeated many times in Nepalese history. For all but a few of the next 145 years, 'King of Nepal' would be little more than a title.

In all but name, Bhimsen Thapa ruled Nepal for thirty-one years. It is curious to note that, through bloody palace intrigues, intermarriages and more royal compromises, the man whose genes would spiral most through the players in the drama of June 2001 was not the former king Rana Bahadur, nor even the dictator Bhimsen Thapa, but the lowly bodyguard who slew the regent's brother – Bal Narsingh Kunwar.

King Birendra was descended from him through both his mother and father. Queen Aishwarya was a direct descendant, as were both of Devyani Rana's parents. In fact, just about anybody who is anybody in Kathmandu society claims to have inherited his genes. And it was his very suspicious actions on the day the regent and his brother were sliced in two that began his progeny's rise from soldiers to gods.

chapter 8

delinquent princes

The royal palace is not in the Yellow Pages. We couldn't even find a White Pages, and the number we thought might have been directory assistance was permanently engaged. It had, therefore, taken us much longer than expected to find the king's press secretary to seek an audience with the monarch. Now, six weeks into our stay, we had pinned him down for an appointment.

Neither of us had ever been to a real-life working palace before, so we spent a good part of the day wondering what to wear. Our choices were somewhat limited (the sandals or the hiking boots?). Unfortunately, we knew such things were important because when Nepalis go to the palace, full traditional dress is required. We checked ourselves in the mirror – he in synthetic tie, she in pink pashmina – and headed out the door.

The palace gates were topped by theme-park snowy peaks, below which khaki-clad guards turned as one to observe our approach. Stepping inside the gates was an underwhelming experience. We were led across the rubble of an incomplete pathway to the nearest building, an orange-brick box which could pass for a block of flats by a suburban railway station. We later learned that it housed all palace business, including the king's office.

Our guide took us past a mounted deer's head and into a bare concrete cell. In quick time, the principal press secretary, Mohan Bahadur Pandey, arrived.

'The king is in mourning for one year,' he said, without us asking directly. 'He will not give interviews to anyone until after 1 June. After that time you can write and ask to talk to him. If it pleases him, he may talk to you.' That was more than three months away.

Mr Pandey also pointed out that, of the twenty-one members of the royal family, ten had been killed in 'the incident'. And Queen Komal, Crown Prince Paras, his wife Crown Princess Himani and the queen mother would also not be talking.

He gave us the names of retired prime ministers, priests and judges we should meet. It was hard to tell if he was being helpful or just loading us up with old coots who'd bore us into submission.

We asked if King Gyanendra was attending any public functions in the near future, and Pandey suggested Ghode Jatra, the upcoming annual horse festival at the parade ground in Tundikhel. A day at the races.

The street sweepers wore heavy make-up. In pale green saris, these most glamorous of untouchables marched down the street ridding the paths of dust and rubbish in preparation for the king's passage. It seemed ridiculous that the authorities went to so much trouble to tidy the streets and tuck away the rabble, when King Gyanendra had spent his adult life free to observe as many beggars and smell as much shit as the rest of his subjects.

The traffic police made a farcical display of trying to stop cars driving on the road beside the parade ground. They had a tough opponent: the rugged individualism of the Nepalese driver is hard to tame. The result was a draw.

The child goddess Kumari was there down the far end of the parade ground because, in a sense, she began this festival back in the mists of time. The area that is now Tundikhel was once fertile farmland, but it is said that peasants began to disappear and the people became afraid to come here. Then Taleju, the goddess who lives in the Kumari, came to the king in a dream and told him that a demon called Tundi was knocking off the farmers; she advised that the thunder of hooves would scare him away. So, every year since, the horse festival has been held on Tundikhel (literally, 'demon field'), to keep him at bay.

Shiny cars with flags flapping out front started to appear. Pakistan, Australia, China and Israel arrived before our flag knowledge failed us and all sorts of strange banners paraded by. Policemen moved us along a few times before we pressed our way into the ten-deep crowd lining the footpath across the road from the park. More people climbed trees, fences, bus roofs and houses hundreds of metres back. The air was hot and thick with the stench of sweat. As the minutes passed, the traffic dwindled and the car horns stopped.

A hush came over the mob as the convoy arrived. In the middle was a Mercedes limousine bearing the new monarch who so many thought was a mass murderer. Unable to believe their adored Crown Prince Dipendra was responsible for the massacre, many blamed his uncle, King Gyanendra. Yet here they all were, pushing in the stinking heat to catch a peek. Silent.

The limo's windows were clear. We glimpsed Queen Komal – a big woman, big hair, all in pink. The man in her shadow must have been the king. Their wayward and wildly unpopular son, Crown Prince Paras, was somewhere in the convoy too. The soldiers at the gate held their salute as the cars pulled up to the royal grandstand.

It was quite staggering how undemocratic it all was. Tundikhel is the only patch of greenery in downtown Kathmandu and when we'd first arrived, in the middle of the northern winter, it was a dustbowl infested with people sitting, talking and playing. But as soon as a bit of rain fell and the grass started to grow, policemen patrolled it to keep everybody off. Now the nearest the public could get to it was on the far side of the wide roads that circled it. If you weren't a VVIP (a very, *very* important person) you were nowhere.

Deep in the crowd as we were, we were well and truly nowhere. We couldn't see a thing. Still, at least we'd glimpsed the royals, so we jumped on the bus back to the hotel.

We asked a man with a pleasant smile sitting next to us if the people were here to see the horses or the king.

'This is a yearly festival we have with horses,' he answered. We thought he'd misunderstood the loaded question. We asked him again: the horses or the king?

A flash of concern crossed his face. 'We have problems here in Nepal,' he replied. 'We don't talk about these things.'

Nobody seemed to like talking about King Gyanendra. His image problem went a lot further back than 'the incident' at the palace, but the things that people said about him when he was just a prince didn't seem to be spoken so freely now.

In newspaper shorthand, Gyanendra was styled as a businessman and conservationist. But as his cousin, Prabhakar Rana, explained to us, he was nothing like a businessman. He did not run any businesses or have anything to do with day-to-day hiring and firing. He merely acted as the conduit between the royal family and those who ran its considerable interests in the Soaltee Hotel, the Surya Tobacco Company and the Himalaya Tea Garden. The late King Birendra naturally could not dirty his hands in the tawdry humdrum of commerce, even though he was a shareholder.

As a conservationist, the then Prince Gyanendra was the active patron of the King Mahendra Trust for Nature Conservation. Aside from that, little was published about him. Rumours, however, had abounded about 'the Dark Prince'.

It was said that he and his younger brother, Prince Dhirendra, used their positions to smuggle drugs and gold, and to loot the country of its art treasures with impunity. But those stories have died away with the passage of time, and with the rise of an even worse public-relations nightmare: King Gyanendra's son Prince Paras.

We were waiting at the Chhang House in Patan Durbar Square to meet a guy who had encountered Prince Paras on some of his wildest nights. Sunil was running late so we squeezed into a table with some locals and got stuck into the *chhang*, the roughly brewed rice beer that sold for about a dollar per large plastic jug.

The dingy little restaurant was wonderfully dark. The only natural light entered via a hole in the low ceiling, which served as a chimney to the cooking stove. Strips of buffalo meat hung from the beams, drying in the smoke. Two women sat at the round hot plates in the middle of the crowd, the folds of their bellies oozing out of their saris as they prepared the traditional Newari foods.

Sunil arrived about an hour later, slick and street chic. He'd gained an insight into the younger generation of royals, he told us, after he met Crown Prince Dipendra's younger brother, Prince Nirajan, through a common friend. This could be good, we thought, and ordered another jug of *chhang*.

'I went to the palace once. Man, we had to go through the back gates. He had our names there. We got searched with the metal detectors, you know, all over. He showed us [his great-grandfather] King Tribhuvan's bed. It was all made of glass. Everything in the room was glass, even the pen on the desk. There were tigers there ready to pounce on their kill. It was so amazing. All sorts of deer, rhino heads. I was really jealous . . . [Prince Nirajan] was really talented, like his father.'

In what way?

'He just talked like his father. He knew about things. He said how his father told him, "Never pull a gun unless you're going to use it".'

Sunil and Nirajan used to hang out at the same night-spots as Prince Paras. In light of the rumours that King Gyanendra and his son were behind the royal massacre, we were keen to find out where their unpopularity began.

Sunil remembered one night when Paras was dancing exuberantly. His arms flayed about and hit another dancer in the mouth. There was a little blood, and the other dancer was enraged. He grabbed Paras around the neck and told him he didn't care what happened, but the prince should take more care when dancing.

Some weeks later, Paras spotted the guy at another club. Sunil watched as the prince drew out a samurai sword and, raising it above his head, slammed the blade down on the guy's table. 'Those things are meant to be able to chop seven people's heads off in one go,' Sunil explained. A few weeks after that incident, Paras took out a pistol at a disco and fired blanks into the ceiling.

It all gelled with stories we would later hear from one of Paras's relatives, who said he started brawls in bars: 'If he didn't like something, he'd go berserk, whereas Crown Prince Dipendra was great at PR, a different person in public. Paras didn't care.' The *New Yorker* reported that, after one violent incident, Crown Prince Dipendra used his position to rescue his wayward cousin from a police station.

Sunil got onto the road most travelled by Paras's detractors. He maintained that one night at the Yak and Yeti hotel, Paras argued with a well-known musician, Praveen Gurung, over a woman. Paras waited for Gurung to come out of the hotel at the end of the night. As the musician rode his motor-bike home, Paras ran him down in cold blood near the southern gate of the palace. The whole thing was cleaned up, according to Sunil, leaving no trace. The widow was paid to keep quiet.

Sunil did not witness those events, but the story held

currency among a great number of the local population. What was not disputed was that Paras was in the blue Pajero that killed the musician on 6 August 2000. The vehicle, which belonged to the King Mahendra Trust for Nature Conservation (the organisation patronised by his father Gyanendra) left the scene. According to reports in the local press, the young prince masked his face when he went to a near-by police post and threatened the policemen on duty 'not to leak' the matter.

Reports vary, but Prince Paras is said to have killed some-where between two and four people in road accidents. Kathmanduites will tell you about the reckless abandon with which he used to throw his car into the chaotic local traffic. For while few rules appear to apply to any drivers in Kathmandu, it is rare for anybody to go much faster than forty kilometres an hour. The system works as long as everybody honks their horns incessantly and drives slowly enough to stop the instant a cow or an old lady strays in front of them. Paras only cared for the horn honking.

During the previous elections he had made the news-papers for driving when all vehicular traffic was banned. A policeman foolish enough to challenge him was threatened with a revolver at Pulchowk, in Patan. Three weeks before the death of Praveen Gurung, he had smashed into a three-wheeler near the palace and manhandled its driver.

The people had had enough. After Praveen Gurung's death, hundreds of demonstrators from a cross-section of polit-ical allegiances protested outside Nirmal Niwas, the modern mansion where Paras and Gyanendra lived. They demanded Paras be stripped of his royal status and punished for Gurung's death.

The day after the incident, members of parliament demanded action be taken against him. MP Ramesh Lekhak of the ruling Nepali Congress said Gurung died because of the prince's 'excess'.

The king was the only person in a position to take action against Paras, because the constitution apparently made him immune from normal prosecution. A petition was presented, demanding action. King Birendra did nothing, however.

Then a soldier came forward claiming to be the driver of the car, and Gurung's widow came out and said it was an accident. The issue died away from the front pages, but Kathmanduites were never going to believe the explanations.

Many people have said it would be the end of the monarchy if King Gyanendra suddenly died, leaving the much-despised Paras to take the throne. In which case Goraknath's popular prediction of the Shah dynasty lasting only eleven generations may still come true.

Certainly Paras's unpopularity is not without precedent. The last time there was a crown prince to match him, it almost led to the end of the line.

Crown Prince Surendra, grandson of Girvan Yuddha Shah, was a diligent and tireless delinquent. Once, when his mother, the senior queen, returned from Pashupatinath, the twelve-year-old Surendra closed the palace doors on her, forcing her to sleep in the garden house for days. King Rajendra – described by the British resident, Brian Hodgson, as a 'hopeless little recluse' – never disciplined his son and nobody else dared.

In 1841, still aged twelve, Surendra was married off to two nine-year-olds, giving him two new objects of derision. Soon after the weddings, he drove his wives out of the palace naked. When the king tried to intervene, Surendra drew his sword.

Five months later, the powerful senior queen died. Rumours spread that she had been poisoned and a Calcutta newspaper picked up the story. The article was brought to the attention of King Rajendra, who became so furious that he stormed off to see Hodgson at the British Residency, with the crown prince in tow. India being under British rule, the king demanded that Hodgson hand over the journalist who wrote the story. 'I will have him and flay him alive and rub him with salt and lemon till he die,' Rajendra vowed. 'If the infamous culminator is not delivered there shall be war between us.'

During the tirade, Surendra became annoyed with his father and started abusing him. They were soon exchanging blows in front of the bemused diplomat.

Stories of Surendra's capriciousness abounded. He had people thrown before elephants and trampled to death. Innocents walking on the streets were beaten.

On 2 May 1842, Surendra put three army captains into separate wells up to their necks in water for an unspecified time. Two weeks later, the thirteen-year-old had one of his wives put in a water tank. The princess was let out at 9 pm the following day. She fled the palace and hid in the house of a Brahmin, but she had been ill before she was put in the tank and she died a few days later. The Brahmin was imprisoned for hiding her.

King Rajendra's younger wife, Rajya Laxmi, the junior queen, also suffered much at the hands of her stepson Surendra, and had fled the palace months before the senior queen died. In the same month that Crown Prince Surendra killed his young wife, the junior queen returned to the palace at the behest of officials and dignitaries who wanted her to lead the push against the crown prince. She became a rallying point for the belittled and aggrieved gentry.

The army, alienated by two years of Surendra's excesses, was openly defying King Rajendra and in late 1842 a mass movement pushed the king to the brink. It was Nepal's first people's movement. Rajendra was forced to hand over power to the junior queen. She was given the prerogative to appoint public servants, to wage war, to imprison, to mutilate and to execute all but the royal family.

She became more assertive with the crown prince. She caught him trying to set fire to the curtains of the palace and threatened to have him whipped. But the king continued to refuse to control his son, and the junior queen was often seen having to rescue her husband from the boy's attacks.

Her resolve that Crown Prince Surendra would never be king hardened. She had become hugely popular in court circles by curtailing his excesses, so felt she had a mandate to put her own son on the throne. This created opportunities for ambitious young courtiers to climb on board her bandwagon.

One such person was Jang Bahadur Kunwar, a young man with heavy gambling debts and no means of support beyond his wife's dowry. He was the elder son of Bal Narsingh Kunwar, the bodyguard who almost four decades earlier slew the king's brother and may have assassinated King Rana Bahadur himself.

Jang Bahadur had married well and worked his way into court circles. He was a daredevil, completely unscrupulous and a consummate opportunist. He would become the most important figure in Nepalese history.

Once, on a royal elephant hunt, a wild bull was causing all sorts of trouble. Jang Bahadur leapt off his elephant and got a rope around the animal's hind leg. This act of insanity in front of the monarch saw him become an officer in the king's artillery, on the spot.

On another occasion, a rogue leopard was causing panic on the outskirts of Kathmandu and had occupied a house from which it could not be dislodged. Jang Bahadur went into the house with a wicker basket and chased it from room to room. He caught it alive and presented it to Crown Prince Surendra. Soon, Jang Bahadur became a royal bodyguard like his father.

In a written account passed down through his family (recently published as *Jang Bahadur Rana: The Story of His Rise and Glory*), there is a story about the time he was walking with the crown prince beside the Trisuli River. 'In his eccentricity, [the crown prince] asked Jang Bahadur to jump into the river on horseback. Had Captain Jang Bahadur not obeyed the Prince, he would have been beheaded for sure.'

Jang took his legs from the stirrups, and jumped from the horse into the brown-and-white torrent. 'Everyone was sure he would not come out of it alive. Even Prince Surendra began to regret the order he had given and asked his guards to search for Jang Bahadur.' They found him way downstream, alive and well.

Having inveigled his way into the royal circle, Jang Bahadur planted the suggestion in the minds of the king and junior queen that the new prime minister, Mathbar Singh Thapa, was scheming to take full control of the state. When they heard that the prime minister had raised three regiments under his own command, it was time to get rid of him.

They chose their daredevil young officer Jang Bahadur Kunwar to do the dirty work. (The small detail of Jang Bahadur being the prime minister's nephew would not get in the way of his ambition.)

The assassination should be carried out that very day, Jang insisted, to avoid the possibility of the plan being leaked. So that night, 17 May 1845, the prime minister – whose portrait shows him with elegant muttonchops and festooned in jewellery – was told that the junior queen was suffering from colic. He should hurry to her at the palace.

Inside the palace, Jang Bahadur was hiding behind a screen at the top of a staircase. As the prime minister was led up, Jang shot him in the head at close range. The body was rolled in a cloth and taken to Pashupatinath to be cremated without ceremony in the middle of the night.

Jang Bahadur's performance bonus was the command of three regiments. He appointed his brothers to important posts, all the while taking every opportunity to flatter the junior queen and assure her that he would work relentlessly to make her son king.

While he cultivated the junior queen, there was another person whose goodwill was equally essential. The junior queen had taken a lover, Gagan Singh. Some historians have described him as a former royal tutor. Others have said he was a palace slave, a chamber boy who would make love to the junior queen while cleaning her room. Whatever the truth, it was thanks to her patronage that he was now in charge of seven regiments and was the most powerful non-royal in the country. Jang Bahadur knew that Gagan Singh was pulling all the strings so he made sure to win his friendship, while showing no signs of personal ambition.

It seems it was something of a sport for ambitious young nobles to cultivate palace maids as spies. Scores of servant girls acted as a de facto harem to the king, but unlike the harems of the Middle East, the women were expected to leave the palace, on religious grounds, during their periods. Jang Bahadur had found one such maid, Putali, the junior queen's chambermaid. She told him secrets in bed and passed on messages through one of the minor palace priests, Bijay Raj Pandey. Jang Bahadur was in a good position therefore to judge the way the wind was blowing when the king found out about the affair between Gagan Singh and the junior queen.

King Rajendra gathered his sons in a private chamber and asked them to save the family's honour. Gagan Singh had to die. According to *Jang Bahadur Rana*, the king and his sons wanted Jang Bahadur to do the job. Within days, an assassin had climbed onto the roof of Gagan Singh's house and shot him as he knelt in prayer in his private chapel. It was 10 pm, 14 September 1846.

The identity of Gagan Singh's assassin remains a hot topic among Nepalese historians. Certainly, Singh was getting too big for his upstart-slave sandals, and just about everybody but the junior queen wanted him dead. The same account says that Jang's younger brother did the job.

Regardless, Jang Bahadur was certainly the only person ready for what followed – the infamous Kot Massacre, perhaps the single most important episode in modern Nepalese history. A massacre that would ultimately graft the lowly genes of the bodyguard Bal Narsingh Kunwar into the Shahs' lofty family tree.

chapter 9

the rise of
the ranas

for the last century and a half, Kathmandu has been dominated by two dynasties: the royal Shahs and the Ranas. The
Ranas are the descendants of Bal Narsingh Kunwar, King Rana
Bahadur's bodyguard. Thanks to the vaulting ambition of his
eldest son Jang Bahadur, their surname would soon be changed
to the higher-caste 'Rana'. Crown Prince Dipendra had more
Rana blood than Shah – three of his four grandparents were
Ranas – but, owing to the patriarchal hierarchy, was identified
as a Shah. His lover, Devyani, was pure Rana.

The two families' histories are interwoven in a tapestry of
love and deathly ambition. When they weren't marrying each
other, they interacted in a state of polite hostility, delicately
wrestling for control of the state. For most of the past 150
years, the Ranas have come out on top. And it all began with
the events that followed the assassination of Gagan Singh in
September 1846.

Two hundred metres from Singh's house was the large, vermilion-stained monkey idol Hanuman, which guards the front gate to the old royal palace, Hanuman Dhoka. Inside the palace, the junior queen was given the news that her lover had been killed. Equipped with a sword and accompanied by four armed maids, she ran from Hanuman Dhoka to Singh's residence.

As she stood seething over the corpse, she placed herbs and gold on her lover's lips and vowed revenge. She immediately allocated 100,000 rupees – a huge fortune – for the funeral rites, and forbade her lover's three wives from committing *sati*. Then she returned to the palace and, although it was nearing midnight, ordered buglers to blow the signal for a grand meeting. Senior courtiers and army officers knew to get to the palace immediately.

Jang Bahadur was among the first to arrive. With him were his six brothers and his three regiments. The junior queen was shocked to see so many men, but Jang put her at ease: the soldiers were needed to protect her from whomever had killed Gagan Singh.

By 1 am, the nation's elite had assembled in the courtyard of the palace armoury, the Kot. The crowd shuffled as the queen delivered an emotional tirade. She would not eat nor drink until the culprit was delivered, she promised.

But in her mind, she had already convicted one poor soul, an innocent whom she demanded the military commander behead on the spot. He refused, looking to King Rajendra for support. The king, who almost certainly knew the identity of the real killer, told the military commander not to do it, then quietly left the scene.

There are many versions of what followed. One has it that as the various factions nervously awaited some sort of confrontation, the furious junior queen ran down with her sword to do away with the accused herself. She was placated and dragged back upstairs.

Jang Bahadur took the opportunity to warn the junior queen of an imminent coup. The prime minister's troops were on their way to the Kot, he insisted, and she should act quickly lest her supporters be annihilated. She paid heed and ordered the prime minister's arrest. When he tried to leave, Jang's troops shot him, but as the prime minister fell, he shouted that the real murderer of Gagan Singh was Jang Bahadur Kunwar.

Fighting broke out all around. Swords and knives flashed in the flickering light. Jang Bahadur's troops flayed the crowd with musket shot.

The junior queen watched the carnage from above. By its end, a stream of blood filled the gutters. The pathetic cries of the wounded continued for hours, with no one prepared to help. By morning, vultures filled the sky. About thirty nobles had been killed, plus an unknown number of their retainers. Jang Bahadur and his six brothers emerged unscathed while their rival clans were obliterated.

Early that morning of 15 September, the junior queen appointed Jang Bahadur prime minister and commander-in-chief of the army. The odds were stacked against him: none of his five predecessors had died a natural death. He knew that if he were to survive he had to straddle the power structure completely. Jang immediately launched a purge that killed many of his surviving competitors and drove 6000 people into exile in India. He appropriated the property of the dead and banished, and doled it out to his six brothers, whom he promoted to the senior-most positions in the military and the government. The new aristocracy had arrived.

After just a fortnight, the junior queen better understood the source of real power in Nepal. Realising she had been out-witted, the junior queen conspired to murder Jang Bahadur and invited him to a gathering in a garden next to the palace. There, he would be killed. But again Jang got wind of the junior queen's plans via his spies, the chambermaid and palace priest.

He mounted an elephant and led his army to the garden.

They rounded up the conspirators and executed twenty-three of them on the spot. The junior queen was stripped of her powers and banished to Varanasi in northern India. King Rajendra followed her there voluntarily rather than take his chances with Jang.

After a time, the king began plotting his own coup from Varanasi. It failed, and in May 1847 Jang Bahadur announced that, owing to his treasonous activity, the king was henceforth dethroned and the delinquent crown prince, Surendra, was king of Nepal. Jang had emerged on top, and kept the new king a prisoner in his own palace, surrounded by spies. Surendra could not leave, nor receive visitors, without Jang's permission – a state of impotence the Shahs would endure under the Ranas for over a century.

Two years after the massacre, in 1848, Jang Bahadur began his ascent up the caste ladder by commissioning an apocryphal genealogy of the Kunwar family. The Brahmins appointed to the job duly came up with the story that Jang was descended from the house of Rana, the fourteenth-century rulers of Chittor in Rajasthan, whose heroic defence of the faith against the Muslim Mogul invaders was the stuff of legend across the Hindu world.

But according to historian Adrian Sever in his *Nepal Under the Ranas*, until Jang Bahadur's rise, the Kunwar family was part of that section of the Gorkhali elite that 'had distinguished itself in the middle echelons of the administration and the army', not in mainstream politics. Therefore, it was not of a caste status higher than that of the other families belonging to the traditional Gorkhali nobility.

Nevertheless, King Surendra soon issued an edict that recognised this new family history and put Jang Bahadur's caste on an equal footing with his own (which may also have been dummied up a dozen generations or so earlier). Despite the fact that the king's edict expressly forbade these upstart 'Ranas' from marrying any of the Shah family, within six years, Jang Bahadur had married a royal relative. He then had the temerity to ask King Surendra to give his eldest daughter to Jang's eldest son, Jagat Jang.

According to the Rana family history, the king was furious. 'As a man who is not born in a respectable caste, how dare you ask that my daughter be married to your son?' he thundered.

'Your Majesty,' answered Jang, 'your own caste is not a superior one. Your grandfather Girvan Yuddha Shah was born of a Jha Brahmin . . . that too a widow. You know that only too well, so why do you consider yourself to be of a superior caste?'

At this, King Surendra quietened down and insisted they both remain silent on the matter. Over a century and a half later, it remains a subject on which the Shahs like to stay silent.

In 1856, Jang Bahadur still had a mountain of social climbing left to do. He forced the king to formally surrender all power to him and his heirs, in perpetuity, and to declare him the maharaja of the small hill states of Lamjung and Kaski. This let Jang wear a bird-of-paradise crown, like the Shahs', and would allow his family for the ninety-five years of their hereditary dictatorship to pretend they were of royal birth.

Jang Bahadur set up a system of succession whereby the prime ministership would pass to his brothers until they had all died off. Then it would revert to his eldest son, passing down through Jang's younger sons and their paternal first cousins in order of age. This system was designed to eliminate any possibility of future Rana prime ministers encountering the difficulties of succession that the royal family had encountered. Jang was keen to avoid the Shahs' constant problem of having infants ascend the throne, thereby diverting power to often manipulative regents.

What he hadn't foreseen was that siblings, uncles and cousins could be just as power-crazed as any regent. Added to that was the Rana men's passion for multiple wives and concubines, the result of which was a family tree that started to look very bushy. Jang Bahadur had twenty-two official wives and more than 200 women and girls in his harem. He fathered ten legitimate sons, and as many as 100 in total.

The final, and biggest, hurdle of the Rana ascendancy was surmounted in 1857 when the ten-year-old Crown Prince Trailokya, Surendra's son, married two daughters of Jang Bahadur. All the kings of Nepal would henceforth be descended from Jang Bahadur Rana. From then on, it became the practice of the Rana prime minister to arrange the marriages of all the Shahs, preferably with his own immediate family. Thus the two families became inextricably linked.

So persistent were the Ranas at joining the royal family that modern royals would be more Rana than Shah. It made a further mockery of the Shahs' dubious claims to a pure Thakuri Rajput bloodline. These matters of fact, however, were lost on the Rana women who dominated the palace in the early twenty-first century, when they decried Crown Prince Dipendra's chosen one, Devyani Rana, as their inferior.

chapter 10
the battle of the bedchambers

~~A~~s we delved further into the history of the Ranas and the Shahs, it became clear just how powerful bloodline and caste were to their story. We were told by people in a position to know, that family background was the only reason Queen Aishwarya objected to her son marrying Devyani Rana.

As foreigners, though, it was difficult for us to understand quite how significant and emotive this issue was; how it could be used as an entry card, a weapon and a political tool. And the more history we learned, the more astounded we were at the hypocrisy that seemed to accompany the rules. So we sought out someone who could help us understand.

Pramode Shamsher Rana was living in a wing of an old family palace, Seto Durbar, opposite the Narayanhiti Royal Palace. It was once the most magnificent of the Rana residences, and had dominated the royal pile over the road. Now, the one small wing that remained was crumbling and neglected.

Inside the thick stone walls, Pramode wore a scarf around his neck, despite the warmth of the day. He had a shiny bronze

97

pate and a cheery round face. Everything about him suggested culture and leisure, and diminishing means. Even within the Ranas, there were degrees of superiority. And Pramode was not in the 'A class'.

When Pramode was born, the family astrologer predicted he would bring great misfortune to his family. So his parents abandoned him to an elderly aunt and he grew up alone, rarely leaving these cold walls, which even then were past their glory days. His position, however, has enabled him to dig up much of the family dirt, resulting in his book, *Rana Intrigues*.

In the book, Pramode tells the story of his great-grand-father, Bir Shamsher Rana, who was similarly discarded by his family due to an astrologer's prophecy but went on to be the fourth Rana prime minister (in 1885) and marry a princess. The princess had a particularly beautiful maid, and before her wedding her father warned her not to take the maid to her married home. The princess ignored the advice, however. The servant girl was only a Newar, after all, and therefore was looked down on by such noble Rajputs.

When the princess later discovered her husband Bir was having his way with the beautiful servant, she attempted to blind the girl by throwing acid in her face while she slept. The girl's eyes were unharmed, but her face was scarred for life.

Bir reacted by freezing the princess out. Her further punishment was to see his two daughters by the maid married off in 1889 to their third cousin, King Prithwi Bir. It was a mark of extraordinary arrogance that Bir would give the daughters of his Newar concubine to the thirteen-year-old king. There was considerable resistance to the marriages within the palace, and some extraordinary bedroom games ensued as two powerful blocs battled to control the royal bloodline.

The queen mother was among the most horrified at the impurity of Bir's daughters – despite the fact she was Jang Bahadur's daughter and hence of a questionable pedigree herself. It is said that on the nights when it was the turn of the young brides to sleep with the king, the queen mother would send beautiful maids to his chamber, in the hope he would be spent before he got to his wives.

Pramode's version of events, however, is that Bir enlisted trained dancing girls to lure the teenage King Prithwi Bir away from his first two wives (princesses from India) and towards the two Newar Rana girls. Perhaps all these maids and dancing girls did their jobs too well, because many years went by and no heir was forthcoming.

Bir Shamsher Rana died in 1901 – only the third Nepalese prime minister to die of natural causes – never knowing that he lost this battle of the bedchambers. It was in 1906, twenty years after King Prithwi Bir's first marriage, that one of the Indian princesses gave birth to the future king, Tribhuvan.

While the royal bloodline had been saved from that contamination, more dubious pedigrees were still to be thrust upon it. Perhaps the most intriguing question mark hung over the provenance of Prime Minister Juddha Shamsher Rana, who assumed the leadership in 1932. This was because Juddha's future descendants would include both King Birendra and his wife Queen Aishwarya.

How Juddha Shamsher made it onto the roll of succession in the first place was something of a mystery. His older brother, Chandra Shamsher Rana (an ancestor of Devyani's), had declared during his rule that only Ranas born from legally married wives of the right caste, so-called 'A-class' Ranas, could become prime minister. This wiped off the many sons of concubines and lower-caste wives who had previously been in line for the top job. But, while Juddha's patriarchal line was beyond reproach – his father was Dhir Shamsher Rana, younger brother of Jang Bahadur – nobody seemed to know quite where his mother came from.

'Some people say she was the daughter of Muslims,' said Purushottam Shamsher Jang Bahadur Rana, a family historian, who, on the afternoon we met, still had orange petals scattered across his silver hair from his morning's *puja*. 'Other people claim Dhir went to Pashupatinath and saw a lady with nothing on . . . and took her to his *durbar*, and from that match, Juddha was born . . .' According to Purushottam, the problem was Dhir's penchant for the ladies, and the sheer number of wives he had.

But still, how could Juddha get into power if he was so low caste?

'Well, when Dhir Shamsher was dying, they took him to Pashupatinath. Before he died he called his eldest son, Bir. He told him: "You should take care of Juddha's mother, because I am dying. Be careful with her. She served me very nicely so take care of her. Not only you, but all my sons." '

Then, when Bir became prime minister by coup d'etat in 1885, he legitimised Juddha's mother by taking rice from her in a formal ceremony, and honoured his half-brother Juddha by putting him on the roll of succession. In 1940, as prime minister, Juddha ensured his genes would continue in future kings when he arranged the marriage of his granddaughter, Indra, to the heir apparent, Crown Prince Mahendra. Like many Ranas before him, Juddha continued to use his power to force further marriages on the Shahs.

The year after Indra was married off to Crown Prince Mahendra, Juddha's son, Rabi Shamsher Rana, was betrothed to King Tribhuvan's daughter, Tika.

We found Rabi Shamsher living in a grand, modern house across the Bishnumati River from old Kathmandu. Like so many Ranas, Rabi's modern red-brick home was next door to his old palace, Rabi Bhawan, which was big enough to warrant a mark on our map of Kathmandu. Rabi had sold the palace some years ago to an American school. Our hope was that he could tell us who Juddha's mother was.

Brigadier-General (retired) Rabi Shamsher J.B. Rana shuffled along the parquet floor of his elegant living room and onto a red velvet lounge. He was old, his hair and moustache white. His wife had passed away some years ago. 'She was very beautiful and very docile,' he told us. This was high praise indeed. Still, Rabi was full of spark. The sleeves of his grey business shirt were rolled up to his elbows, revealing large tattoos on both forearms.

He remembered his father as a strong man, and although not well-read, 'he had a lot of experience.' Juddha wore a fearsome expression and an elaborate handlebar moustache, and in the evenings would take his elephant for a ride around the city. Or, if he was just doing the rounds of his palace, he'd mount a saddle on the back of one of his servants and be piggy-backed.

To the adoring younger son, Juddha may have appeared a great family man, but he certainly wasn't one in the usual sense. To boost his sex drive, he took aphrodisiacs prepared by his traditional doctors, and, according to Pramode, he ate dozens of fried sparrows to supplement his masculine hormones.

The British envoy to Nepal, Sir Geoffrey Betham, was obviously less than impressed with the prime minister when he wrote to his superiors in London in 1939:

> Sir Juddha Shamsher is a naughty old man and his way of life has left much to be desired . . . His illegitimate children are said to have been a legion. A conservative estimate is one hundred sons and daughters spread all over the length and breadth of Nepal. Officially he claims nineteen illegitimate sons. It has been and still is as far as I am aware his practice to pick up any damsel that takes his wayward fancy and then to return her, with a few rupees clutched in her hand, to her parents or her husband. Naturally this kind of behaviour does not earn him the respect or affection of the masses in Nepal. Like his predecessors, he has since his accession pocketed the whole of the surplus revenue of Nepal and he is now reputed to be an extremely wealthy man though his large family must cost him a pretty penny to support.

When we got to the point of our visit to Rabi – the identity of his grandmother – the old brigadier-general didn't seem at all put out that we were implying she was of dubious background. 'She was not a Muslim,' he laughed. 'That much I can tell you.'

As one of Juddha's last surviving offspring, we'd hoped Rabi may have actually known his grandmother, but he never met her. He leaned back into the sofa, a mischievous smile on his face. 'My grandfather [Dhir Shamsher] married her on his way back from the mutiny,' he explained.

Rabi was referring to an incident in 1857, when Jang Bahadur went to the aid of the British East India Company, which was copping a hiding from the widespread mutiny of its Indian soldiers, the Sepoys. The Nepalis cut a swath through the rebels and won the eternal gratitude of Britain.

But if the brigadier-general's family history is correct, we'd have to believe that his grandmother was with Dhir Shamsher for eighteen years before their only son, Juddha, was born in 1875.

So, the identity of Juddha's mother remained a mystery. But that alone tended to indicate her roots were far from distinguished.

chapter 11
the toppling of the ranas

$\mathcal{T}$he Rana regime was doomed by a changing world it did its best to ignore.

Nepal had been isolated well before the Ranas took over in the mid nineteenth century, but the dynasty ensured that the country remained closed to the world. Within that insular little realm, they sealed the kings in a gilded cage for 100 years, wheeling them out of the gaudy splendour of the palace only for occasional public events, or to meet a visiting ambassador. The monarch's only job was procreation.

Still, the king remained the *Maharajadhiraja* (the supreme king), in the eyes of the people and the gods. And throughout the 1930s, enough information had filtered through the palace walls for the then king, Tribhuvan, to offer tacit moral support to an emerging underground opposition. And somehow, behind his foppish wad of hair, Tribhuvan developed a certain shrewdness.

To the north of Nepal, Mao's People's Liberation Army took China in 1949 and the following year, on 7 October, invaded Tibet. Across the southern border, Mahatma Gandhi took India to independence in 1947 and created a democratic government hostile to the Ranas. The Gandhi-inspired Nepali Congress Party soon abandoned its creed of non-violence and voted to take up arms against the Rana regime.

Dipendra's and Devyani's ancestors were set for another stoush.

Princess Ketaki, the product of one of Prime Minister Juddha's arranged marriages, was eleven months old when her parents, Prince Basundhara and Princess Helen, departed Kathmandu for a trip to Calcutta in the late '40s. The baby girl was left in the care of her grandfather, King Tribhuvan.

Even after her parents returned, however, the little princess remained with the king. She was his excuse to leave the palace. With the Ranas' permission, the king would regularly load her into his favourite car – a big, cream convertible limousine – and take her to visit her parents at their mansion just west of the city. She wasn't allowed to stand up in the car but, nestled against the leather upholstery, she watched the buildings scroll by overhead.

Once inside her father's compound, Ketaki would see her grandfather the king lean a ladder against the wall, then disappear over the top. Next door, he would hold clandestine meetings with Nepali Congress members to plot the Ranas' downfall.

King Tribhuvan, like his great-grandfather Jang Bahadur Rana, picked his time to step out of the shadows. He asked the new prime minister, Mohan Shamsher Rana (Devyani's great-grandfather), for permission to go hunting on 6 November 1950. Permission was granted.

The king packed several steel boxes with his most valuable possessions, then loaded them into his limousine and four other vehicles as if for a picnic. With his two wives, three sons, their Rana wives and his oldest grandson, Birendra, the convoy headed off.

As it drove through the outskirts of the city, the king's limousine suddenly swung in towards the gate of the Indian Embassy. A Sikh sentry leapt to open it and the royal convoy pulled in. The gates closed and King Tribhuvan and his sons went to the ambassador to seek asylum.

Back at the palace, young Princess Ketaki watched the maids boiling oil on the roof ready to pour on the Ranas should they come.

The Rana government had always needed a docile monarch, so the next day, the prime minister called a meeting of his newly formed rubber-stamp parliament where he made each member sign an order stripping King Tribhuvan of his sovereignty.

The king had left behind his second grandson, three-year-old Prince Gyanendra, partly so the hunting trip wouldn't look too conspicuous and partly for insurance. If the plan went horribly wrong, the Shah line could continue through him.

With King Tribhuvan out of the way, the Ranas wheeled Gyanendra out and installed the little boy on the throne – a farcical yet historically consistent attempt to garner some legitimacy for the regime. Deputy royal priest Hem Raj Pandey duly put the crown on the bewildered child's head.

Meanwhile, four days after entering the embassy, a deal was done to get King Tribhuvan out of the country on an Indian Air Force aeroplane. The very next day, 300 members of the Nepali Congress Party launched a guerilla war in the Terai from bases in India. There were demonstrations in the towns, culminating in 50,000 people turning out in Kathmandu to demand the return of the king. Fighting spread up from the Terai into the hills and rebels took the central town of Pokhara for a day in January and briefly occupied the country's spiritual home, Gorkha. Troops began to surrender. The Rana regime was crumbling.

On 15 February 1951, three months after leaving, Tribhuvan received a pop star's welcome when he flew into the little airstrip at Kathmandu that now bears his name. He wore dark sunglasses, two-tone brogues and a heavy garland of flowers. Prime Minister Mohan Shamsher Rana was there to meet him and hand power to the king after 104 years of Rana dictatorship. The Shahs were back.

Little King Gyanendra resumed his position as third in line to the throne, although his time would come again.

chapter 12
devyani's father

The Maoists had called another *bandh*. This time, the general strike was for five days, the longest ever attempted. We had busied ourselves stockpiling bottled water, biscuits, cheese and honey. We hired bicycles.

It was now 7 pm on the eve of the strike. The one thing we hadn't yet hoarded was fruit. We were just about to go down to the orange and banana sellers when there was a huge explosion outside.

We grabbed the camera bag and were rushing down the stairs when there was a series of smaller explosions. Gunfire just outside. We scurried back to our room, turned the lights off and pressed our noses to the window. All we could see in the twilight was the fruit sellers running their bicycles down the hill towards Kathmandu. There would be no fresh fruit for five days.

The gunfire didn't last long. After a few minutes' peace we ventured out. Already, truckloads of armed policemen and an armoured personnel carrier swamped the little intersection fifty metres from the hotel door. A man urgently waved us back as we approached the petrol pumps next to the police station. We crossed over to the military crowd, but could see no bomb damage.

The sound of roller-doors being dragged shut rang along the street. Fast Food Tandoori was emptying as we walked in the door. Even as they served us, they were bringing the tandoori skewers down from the window, turning the lights off and half-closing their roller-door. It was about 7.30 pm. The streets were deserted.

The strike had started early. There'd been a government campaign encouraging the people to defy this *bandh*, but now it looked like another failure.

As we walked back past the police post where the bomb went off, we noticed the soldiers had all left. It was business as usual, with a policeman peering over the sandbagged wall.

There were a lot of men milling about in Pashupati Shamsher Rana's courtyard when we dragged our bicycles in there the next morning. Even people of modest means had one man whose job was to staff their gate, but here, there was a platoon. They conferred on what to do with us and our rental bikes. A uniformed guard directed us down the side of the sprawling brick bungalow.

For months now, we'd been curious about what lay beyond these walls, for this was the family home of Crown Prince Dipendra's thwarted love, Devyani Rana.

Her father's manicured garden was a world away from Kathmandu's polluted streets. Birds sang and butterflies danced in the flowerbeds. Straight eucalypts towered over the fence. We waited at a marble table on the verandah until a Doberman jumped on the double swing next to us, announcing Pashupati's arrival.

Devyani had clearly inherited her striking looks and

sensuous lips from her father. He had just a flash of grey in his immaculate hair and didn't look anything near his sixty years. As we exchanged pleasantries, his impeccable manners were almost intimidating.

Pashupati had made it clear that he would not talk about Devyani. We were equally interested in his story, however – the Ranas' lavish lifestyle and mercurial relationship with the Shahs.

Pashupati's branch of the Ranas (descended from Juddha's brother, Chandra Shamsher) were said to be better educated and richer than all their Rana cousins. This was largely because Chandra was prime minister for twenty-eight years; his descendants thus had time to accumulate more wealth and learning.

Pashupati's grandfather, Mohan Shamsher, became the last Rana prime minister when he handed the country back to King Tribhuvan in February 1951. Four decades on, Pashupati would maintain the family tradition by negotiating with King Birendra over Nepal's next major political change.

We asked Pashupati about life as a Rana.

'In fact, I was born in that house over there,' he began, gesturing with a relaxed elegance towards the huge white palace next door, now converted to an army barracks. He flashed a diamond so big it should have had a name. 'As a child I myself had five maidservants, including my wet nurse. And I would have five servants outside. I was put on a mountain pony with a ring saddle at the age of three because we Ranas all had to learn to ride. You were taught to ride. You were taught to shoot. All these things that Rana men were meant to do. And we also had quite a good education system, because we had the best teachers.'

Pashupati was sent to boarding school in India at the age of seven-and-a-half, and it was during a visit home that King Tribhuvan fled to India, leaving Prince Gyanendra behind. When Pashupati's grandfather decided to crown Gyanendra, Pashupati was brought along to offer support to the bewildered little boy, who then came to live at their palace. He was given the job of entertaining the infant king while their grandfathers fought out the end of the Rana regime. 'I was eight and a half and he must have been four, so it's not a memorable relationship . . . Of course with the king's family there's always a certain distance.'

Shortly after the fall of the Ranas, Pashupati was sent to England to be educated – 'Public [i.e. private] school, Oxford and all that.' While at Oxford University, he got to know the future King Birendra, who was studying at Eton College. 'His guardian, Lord Camoys, was a good friend of mine so we used to see each other occasionally.'

Were you friends? we asked.

'No, no, we weren't friends. I knew him, but you couldn't be a friend of the king. You called him "His Majesty" and you were deferential. Even when he was a boy of fourteen and I used to take him out to lunch, I had to call him "Your Royal Highness".'

Pashupati returned home when he was twenty-two. 'We were still living in the palace then. We had far fewer servants and we had closed most parts of the building. We had to. If we had a major dinner or something then we'd open up the state rooms, but otherwise my uncle lived on the northern wing and I lived on the southern wing.'

Soon after, King Mahendra nationalised all the largest Rana palaces. Partitioned into public-service buildings, they provided one of the few lasting legacies of the Rana regime.

After Birendra became king in January 1972, Pashupati went into the family business, politics. Nepal was then ruled according to a *panchayat* system, whereby local concerns could be aired through a series of village-level elected forums, which then elected members to the National Panchayat. It was little more than a rubber-stamp parliament for the king since political parties were banned.

Pashupati became education minister in 1976 and held the post until students rose up in riots against the government in 1979. 'Some shooting occurred and several students were killed. I resigned, saying that since I couldn't manage the student unrest, it was not ethical for me to stay on.'

Sixteen days later, King Birendra bowed to the protesters

and put the question of a new system to a referendum. There followed a year of open campaigning by the banned political parties. 'This was a period of great liberation,' Pashupati explained, 'and as a result the country got used to a situation in which everybody voted.'

Despite this, in May 1980 the *panchayat* system won the referendum – 54.7 per cent to 45.3 per cent – and the status quo remained. The country settled down, but discontent with the absolute monarchy festered.

Then in 1989, India slapped a trade embargo on Nepal after trade talks collapsed. This was a disaster for the landlocked country, which required all its imports to come through India. Resenting India is a national pastime, so at first the people rallied behind the government. But as the embargo began to bite and critical shortages of fuel and food dragged on for months, the leaders of the banned political parties capitalised on the ill will to launch a united democracy campaign.

The protests began in February 1990. There were riots, curfews, strikes. Several police officers and protesters were killed. Thousands of people were arrested, many of whom were tortured. The protests simmered and flared.

Protesters dug trenches around Patan and held the police and army at bay for four days. Patan's protest leaders sent saris and bangles to Kathmandu's protest leaders to say they were timid women who should come out and fight. The Kathmandu leaders took heed and turned up the heat.

Min Bajracharya is a photojournalist who was just getting started in the business in 1990. On the morning of 6 April, he was listening to the police walkie-talkies and heard orders given to allow the people to protest, but to surround and defend the palace. Hundreds of thousands of people had roamed the streets from 6 am in a series of peaceful rallies, smiling and uplifted by the spirit of change.

That afternoon, an estimated 200,000 protesters were at Ratna Park, in the centre of Kathmandu, when the mood shifted. A militant mob headed up Durbar Marg, the classy shopping avenue leading to the palace gates. They chanted slogans and ripped down monarchist signs. A police booth was torn from the ground and rolled towards the army line guarding the palace.

A young boy climbed the statue of King Mahendra on Durbar Marg. An American photographer, Alison Wright, swung around to snap him. Wright later wrote that the boy seized the sceptre from the statue's fist and waved it triumphantly, just before the police shot him.

The police then weighed in with batons and tear gas. Then more bullets. Min was one of those forced off the street by tear gas. He reached the top of a nearby clock tower and looked down to see bodies lying all over the ground as the crowd scattered.

Wright followed the army as it advanced on the retreating mob, with the soldiers firing bullets into the crowds, which were fenced in by barricades. In dumpsters fires burned, filling the air with black smoke. The numerous dead lay in the street, the wounded frantically being carried to hospital, many having been shot right outside. 'A battlefield of bodies' lay on the floor of the lobby. Wright's boots 'tracked bloody imprints on the floor' as she went from person to person.

A doctor asked Wright to photograph as many of the bodies as possible. 'Police trucks are gathering the dead bodies from here and in the streets,' he told her. 'We don't know where they're taking them. We hear they may be dumping them in a mass grave near Gokarna. We'll never know how many people have really been killed today. Bastards.'

Just as the shooting began, a new prime minister was driving into the palace to be sworn in by King Birendra. The king wanted an interim government set up to negotiate with the protesters, and he wanted Pashupati Shamsher Rana to join the interim ministry. Pashupati wasn't keen.

'The chances of resolution were not that obvious,' he told us. 'And the consequences to my career personally could have been quite dire – as they proved to be for a year. But this was a crisis and since the king and the country needed me, it would have been wrong not to take whatever risks were involved. My whole family was against it because of the risk to our lives.

'There were riots every day. One of the centres of unrest was this hospital,' he gestured to the hospital opposite his house. 'Because it was the professionals leading the show. There were demonstrations outside our gates every day. Not against us, but it was one of the points at which the demonstrations would start . . . On the day that I joined the interim government, the crowd must have been over 100,000 . . .

'So, we got sworn in, and the first cabinet meeting that evening decided two things. One, we would impose a curfew – because, you know, things were boiling, so a lid had to be put on it. The second decision we made was that we would start negotiating with all the party leaders.'

Many of the Nepal Congress Party leaders were under house arrest so they were easy to find, but the communists were deep underground.

'We didn't know how to get at them. Some of the parties, we didn't even know who the leaders were . . . That left us really groping in the dark.'

With the city locked down, Rana did the rounds of the opposition leaders' houses and the army was sent to find others. 'We finally got hold of all eight phalanges of the left . . . We got them all in one place, and I talked to them individually. Over the forty-eight hours I slept two hours, I think.

'The Congress Party was convinced at the end that if partylessness was removed from the constitution, then it would withdraw the movement. I think the Congress felt that things were out of hand. They were all under house arrest, isolated, not clear about the things that were going on. By then nobody knew who was in charge of the movement. It had become autonomous, almost.'

And what was King Birendra doing during all this?

'He didn't negotiate directly at all. He was very aware what was going on . . . If you wanted to talk to the king at an odd hour, you had to talk to the ADC [aide-de-camp] on duty. And the ADC at the time was a brother-in-law of mine, so it was getting through quite clear.

'The king knew every move we made. We didn't make moves without the king's say-so. The point came where everybody agreed, and the king had agreed, that partylessness would no longer exist from that night on . . . I'm sorry, this has gone cold.' He pressed a buzzer to summon a servant and ordered more tea.

The announcement was made on the television news at eleven o'clock that night: the king was to meet the democracy leaders and the curfew was lifted.

Television was still a rarity in 1990, but a cheer went up from the few people who had sets. They called to their neighbours across narrow alleys. People who had been locked down in tiny houses for two days spilled onto the streets banging drums and tin plates. Unfortunately, the message had not filtered down to the nervous soldiers and police officers on street corners, who had been on a knife edge for days. When they saw these raucous throngs pouring out of Kathmandu's maze of old streets, a fresh slaughter began.

Nevertheless, the negotiations went ahead. For days on end, Pashupati Shamsher Rana and the *panchayat* negotiators made small concessions and thrashed out minor agreements with the democracy leaders – only to have the movement's leaders refuse to sign at the last minute. It became clear that the movement was not going to accept anything but total capitulation. After twelve days of deadlock, they were gearing up to hit the streets again.

'We hadn't eaten from about noon till three in the morning. So we were having breakfast. I told the prime minister that we should now announce that all the structures of the *panchayat* would be dissolved and that our cabinet would resign, allowing the king to form a new cabinet from the movement. Because if we didn't do that, the movement would start again. And if the movement started again and we had to fire on people, then there was no point to the whole exercise. So instead of waiting for the movement to start, then making concessions afterwards, it would be much more graceful to make the concessions there and then.

'I rang up the king at six o'clock in the morning, and we went to him, and we said this was how we felt. And the king agreed, and we tendered our resignation.'

Suddenly, Nepal was a democracy.

As he had suspected, Pashupati Rana did become a focus of the anti-monarchy forces during the following year's elections. He survived eight attempts on his life, but was elected, nevertheless.

And what of King Birendra in the new democracy?

'Ah well, I think – at first they gave him a very bad time. What happened to the queen and all. There was great opprobrium against him. Particularly against the queen.'

chapter 13

CRACKS in the
VENEER

A cartoon was once tacked to the wall at Tribhuvan University showing King Birendra with a padlock on his mouth. Behind him, Queen Aishwarya held the key.

She was said to have hurled a teapot at the king when he caved in to the popular will and granted democracy in April 1990. Despite the perception that she was all-powerful, the *Times* of London reported that, for this indiscretion, she was locked in her room for a week.

The public portrayal of Queen Aishwarya had long been tarred with malevolence. She was seen as the strong woman behind the intellectual but indecisive man; the one who resisted democracy against the better judgment of her husband; the one who was in it for all she could get. Perhaps she was just a scapegoat for a nation that could not bring itself to hate its king, the living incarnation of Vishnu. When, a decade later, her eldest son swaggered into a family dinner armed to the teeth and massacred half his relatives, no one came straight out and blamed Aishwarya, but . . .

So much speculation surrounded Crown Prince Dipendra's relationship with his parents in the wake of the massacre on 1 June 2001 that we were keen to learn more about King Birendra and Queen Aishwarya. As soon as we started asking questions, we were struck by the absolute adoration that those around King Birendra had for him. He was godlike, a Buddha, exalted, we were told.

'I think the principal thing about King Birendra,' Pashupati Shamsher Rana had told us over tea, 'was that he was a good man.'

Born on 28 December 1945, Birendra Shah was a shy and quiet boy. His father, Mahendra, packed him off to the Indian hill town of Darjeeling with his two younger brothers to be educated by the Jesuits. Then in 1959, aged thirteen, he was separated from Princes Gyanendra and Dhirendra and sent to England, to attend the prestigious boarding school Eton.

Following his arrival into this strange world of morning suits and fagging, Birendra's housemaster was faced with a dilemma regarding the Hindu boy's religious education. He telephoned the Nepalese Embassy.

'Should Birendra go to chapel?' he asked.

'No, not chapel,' the ambassador replied.

'Well, what about God?' asked the master.

'But he *is* God.'

To his boarding-school contemporaries, however, the quiet teen was known simply as 'Nipple', a corruption of Nepal. They would remember him as a nice bloke who was embarrassed when his title was read out at school assembly.

He did his bit, dabbling in football and rowing. He showed a talent for oil painting, and generally stayed out of trouble. He struggled academically, though. As if English wasn't tough enough, he also had to wrestle with Latin and French.

Fortunately, in 1963, a young master named Tom

Holden took over as his tutor. He lobbied to strip Birendra's subjects back to intensive English, geography and a little history. People at the school presumed he was thick because he couldn't do Latin, but Holden would always maintain that Birendra had genuine wisdom. 'He was so worldly in a sort of Oriental way, which was far, far beyond his peers at that time.'

Holden also noted that Birendra always seemed on edge: 'When you walked into his room he suddenly jumped around as though someone was coming to get him. We really thought that his reign would be very short . . . [The Nepalis] were very scared of China at that time.'

In 1964 Birendra left Eton as a lance corporal in the cadet corps and returned home as a general in the Royal Nepalese Army. Yet he was a stranger in his own country, with only a basic grasp of his native language. In order to acquaint him with his subjects, his father, King Mahendra, sent the then crown prince trekking. He and a lightly equipped group of soldiers went off on a series of two-week hikes into the hills west of Kathmandu.

Travelling incognito and without porters, they told people they were just on a training exercise. They ate local food and took every opportunity to listen to people's concerns, and find out what they thought the government should be doing. It was only after they'd left that word tended to seep out: the attentive young soldier in sunglasses was the future king.

'In those days,' recalled Tara Bahadur Thapa, one of the soldiers who accompanied Birendra, 'the housewife had to walk two or three hours to get a jug of water, down the hill and back up again. King Birendra used to try to ask them: "What do you want? What is your priority?" They used to say "Schools." So that's what he did when he became king. He announced free primary education and said: "No child is to walk one-and-a-half hours to school." Enrolments shot up 93 per cent.'

In 1968, Birendra was sent for brief spells at Harvard University and the University of Tokyo, before returning to be engaged to his third cousin, Aishwarya Rana, in 1969.

Aishwarya was born on 7 November 1949, in her family's palace, barely a stone's throw from that of her future husband.

Like him, she was the great-grandchild of Prime Minister Juddha Shamsher Rana. They were also eighth cousins through their common descent from the bodyguard Bal Narsingh Kunwer. And Aishwarya's mother was from the Shah clan, a very distant relative of the royal family.

Aishwarya was educated at Catholic schools in Kathmandu and went on to do arts at Tribhuvan University. Aside from details of the numerous international charity medals awarded to her during the *panchayat* years, however, there wasn't a great deal on the record. She wrote poetry under the name of 'Chandani Shah' and many of her verses had been turned into popular songs. Other than that, the Queen of Nepal appeared to be a regal, reserved and distant character.

The Kathmandu grapevine, however, had produced more colourful tales over the years. It was 'well known' that Aishwarya was emotionally distant from Crown Prince Dipendra and closer to her younger son Nirajan. According to one story-teller, when Dipendra was suffering from typhoid while at boarding school, the queen was alerted to the seriousness of his condition with the expectation that she would come and get him. Instead, she instructed the school warden: 'Take him to the school infirmary.'

We'd heard that in more recent years, Aishwarya spent hours every day obsessively doing *puja* to ensure that Dipendra did not marry Devyani. According to the story, an astrologer had told her that if Dipendra married before he was thirty-five, it would bring great disaster. 'She was, like, crazy, praying to those stones all day,' said our informant.

We asked the royal priest, Ramesh Prasad Pandey, if he knew anything about that. He said she had never come to him for advice on how to do such a *puja*, so the story was highly unlikely. However, she did pray for two hours every day, far more than the average Hindu wife, and for the last sixteen years of her life, had fasted for five days every year to ensure she would never become a widow.

For those five days she had to avoid talking to people, he said. On the first day, she could eat only a lunch of fruit and vegetables, nothing more. The next day she ate nothing at all. On the third day, she could not prepare any food for herself, but could eat something brought to her by others (presumably not so difficult for a queen to arrange). On the fourth day she could neither eat nor drink, nor sleep in a bed. After waking on the floor on the last day, she would do a lengthy *puja* and finally be able to eat a good meal. All this to make sure she died before her husband.

Queen Aishwarya finished her most recent fast a month before she was killed, and she told the royal priest that it would be her last. It was getting too difficult.

One of her ADCs told us she was 'a very brilliant, very clever person'. He elaborated: 'If you started to tell her something, after a few words she knew exactly what you meant. She was very fast. She had a temper. She used to get angry quickly. And she used to cool down very fast also . . .

'She used to talk in a very stern voice. Not shouting, but you would know from the tone of her voice when she was angry. But on the whole, she was a very nice person. The only thing was, there was a tension between the crown prince and the queen, because they both had the same characteristics.'

So was the queen dominant over the king?

'Yeah. Actually in the palace, the queen was in charge of the household, so naturally she had a bigger say than the king. And also, the king was very aloof, like a saint. He had his own routines and used to make sure that the routine went smoothly. And the queen used to look after all the things in the palace, like calling people for parties, making guest lists, ordering food, everything.'

One member of the royal family told us: 'Even though the late queen was strong, the king was not henpecked. He was the one with the opinions; she was the doer. He might say: "This garden was planted with this tree and that tree by my ancestors. I don't want it changed, I just want it to work." And she would take care of the details.'

'The reason the queen was seen as the tough one,' another relative observed, 'was that she was the mouthpiece, the safety net, a good check for him. He made the decisions but she enforced them, so he remained looking good.'

We sat under a pipal tree in Dilli Bazar, in eastern Kathmandu, waiting to meet the man perhaps most responsible for tarnishing Queen Aishwarya's image. It is only over the past two decades that the royal family has been exposed to any public scrutiny. Padam Thakurathi has been the one to bring them down from their pedestal and cause the first cracks in the family's veneer of perfection.

A bicycle and a motorbike had just had a small prang in front of us. We watched the Nepalese equivalent of road rage: two men staring blankly at each other for a few seconds, before moving on.

We were still chuckling at this – not considering what it said about the Nepalis' ability to forgive – when a man came towards us. He wore a cream *kurta suruwal* and had a thick head of black hair. He must have been in his fifties. From the left, his face was handsome and supple, with a few crow's feet. We knew it was the man we were waiting for because, on the right side of his face, there was a deep groove, about five centimetres wide, from his hairline to his brow. A huge chunk of his head had been blown away one night by an assassin's bullet.

Padam Thakurathi led us to his home behind iron gates and a guard dog. We sat in the television room and his pretty teenage daughter brought tea and biscuits. It was surprising how quickly Thakurathi's glass eye, lagging behind the healthy left one, ceased to seem abnormal.

A staunch pro-monarchist and *panchayat* member, Thakurathi got fed up with the palace's centralisation of power in the early '80s and turned critic. He made enemies and lost his seat. By then, however, King Birendra had introduced limited freedom of speech. So Thakurathi and seven friends started a series of newspapers, with Thakurathi taking the editor's role.

One of his newspapers hounded Queen Aishwarya for several months, publishing stories every day about a dodgy bank she'd allegedly set up in London with the government as guarantor. When she'd taken millions of rupees out in the name of 'the social work co-ordination committee of Nepal', the plan was that the bank would collapse and the people of Nepal would cover its debts. According to Thakurathi, she'd then pocket the loot.

'Queen Aishwarya has come from the Rana family, but her parents were very poor,' he told us. 'She was fond of money, and she wanted to make lots of it.'

Her power during the *panchayat* years was demonstrated, Thakurathi claimed, by the way she kept one prime minister in power despite two no-confidence motions against him. '[The prime minister] used to make money and give her very old diamond necklaces and other gifts.'

But Queen Aishwarya wasn't the only one to squirm under Thakurathi's glare.

The first time Thakurathi was thrown in jail was for publishing a column in which it was claimed some female police officers had been seen dancing with various unnamed politicians.

His jail cell was tiny, with somewhere between seven and ten other prisoners. They had to line up on the floor to sleep. 'And they did not give food. You had to ask your family to bring you food in the morning and evening. So many bugs. No bedding. You had to take your own bedding. Those prisoners without family in Kathmandu used to sleep on the cement. They were pickpockets, drunks.

'There was one toilet for all the people . . . The whole area was ankle-deep in piss and the other things. There were some bricks put there, so you could go to the toilet standing on them.' He was released after seven days without being charged.

If the authorities had hoped his detainment would dampen his ardour, they were mistaken. He was now a man on a mission.

Thakurathi couldn't write directly about the royal family, so he coined a name, 'the Underground Gang', to write about family members and the milieu of people surrounding them who were above the law. He just didn't know how far above it they were. Those who controlled access to the king were in many ways more powerful than the monarch himself. Thakurathi soon found himself in jail again, then again.

During one of his early incarcerations, Thakurathi was told he should talk to a prisoner who'd been brought in on drug charges. 'It is Prince Dhirendra who gave the drug in bulk to me,' the prisoner said. 'I distributed it to the small shop-keepers.' It was common gossip that royal family members used to bring drugs into the country, said Thakurathi, but this was the first time he'd ever heard it from the source.

'Whenever the royal family used to go abroad, their baggage was not checked. So they used to take hashish, heroin, temple idols and other things into foreign countries. And they would bring gold and heroin and other things into the country. Gold was cheaper in Nepal than in India so they used to smuggle it into India, avoiding duty. We used to write about it all.'

Prince Dhirendra was the indulged youngest brother of King Birendra. He was a naturally social person who was unhappy in his marriage, so he got out and about. The people saw a lot of him and liked him.

One day Thakurathi wrote a story highlighting a string of irregularities surrounding a biscuit factory owned by Prince Dhirendra, including that it was being used to smuggle gold to India. It created quite a stir. Thakurathi was telephoned at home by the prince's aide-de-camp, Bharat Gurung.

'My master is very, very angry with you.'

'What do you want?'

'You leave journalism and I can get you any amount of money you want,' the ADC promised. 'Whatever you wish for.

You can have any position in the government. The only thing you have to do is leave journalism.'

'I don't need even a single penny from your master.'

Thakurathi broke away from telling us the story to laugh at the absurdity of himself taking a government job: 'When he offered me money and the government post, I thought: I am right. I have hit the nail on the head. I was encouraged . . .'

Thakurathi stayed right in the government's face. The battle of wills stepped up a gear, however, in 1984 when, as chief of the Nepali Sports Council, Prince Dhirendra had gone to Los Angeles for the Olympic Games. Thakurathi received a clipping from a Los Angeles newspaper which reported that a member of the Sports Council who was very close to the Nepalese royal palace had been arrested smuggling heroin into the United States in a soccer ball.

'He was in jail. But the ambassador of Nepal managed to get him out to march in the opening ceremony. So they sent us the fax and we wrote the news.'

He felt the repercussions within days.

'I had been invited to dinner at my friend's house with my wife and kids. The next day was a very holy day for women. Tij, we call it. They fast all day for their husbands, not even drinking water. And because they have to fast all day, they eat a huge feast the night before. So we were invited for dinner and we got home at eleven o'clock, and went to sleep.

'My son was one year old at the time and he used to sleep with us. Our bedroom was on the ground floor. I slept on the right side of the bed, next to the window, my son in the middle, and my wife on the left. We used to keep a zero-watt bulb burning all night because my son was afraid of the dark. It was a hot season, so we had the window open and just the flyscreen there.'

He was lying on his back with his head next to the sill. The assassin cut the flyscreen and pointed his gun through it. The bullet entered at the top of Thakurathi's head, slicing down the right side of his forehead and exiting at the eyebrow. 'According to the police I was hit from eighteen inches away. My wife heard the sound and was confused. She turned the light on and saw a flow of blood pumping from my head with much force.'

A lot went right for Thakurathi over the coming hours. He was rushed to hospital and the next morning there were 50,000 people gathered outside the hospital in solidarity. His enemy the prime minister placated the mob by promising that Thakurathi would get the best treatment possible. King Birendra, who was overseas, made the same commitment.

When he woke up thirty-five days later he'd been moved to a hospital in Bangkok. His wife was by his side. She'd asked the doctor what her husband's chances were. The doctor gave three options: 'One, his left side will be paralysed; two, he will be mad; or three, he could be like a newborn child.'

When Thakurathi woke, he saw himself in the mirror with a bandage on his head. He thought he must have been hit by encephalitis. The doctor came in wearing a white apron.

'What is your name?' the doctor asked.

'I am Padam Thakurathi.'

'Do you know who is the president of the United States?'

'Ronald Reagan.'

The doctor patted him. 'Congratulations.' Somehow, he was okay.

We asked Thakurathi if he thought King Birendra was involved in the Underground Gang.

'No, no. The king wasn't a part of it. Because I'll tell you why, when I returned to Nepal after the treatment, the police came to my house and took my statement . . . I said, "It is the work of the Underground Gang."'

But Thakurathi was dismayed to find that after ten months,

the case had not even been filed. So he sought an audience with King Birendra.

'The king sat in a chair on a platform and I had to stand one step down,' Thakurathi recalled. 'I bowed to him. And because the king used to know me, he came forward to me. I was wearing a *topi* on my head so he could not see the scar. He asked, "Where were you shot?" I removed my cap. He was a little bit horrified.'

The journalist explained to the king the anguish of wondering if another attempt would be made on his life and knowing that nothing was being done to find the would-be assassin. King Birendra was sympathetic. He assured Thakurathi that the culprit would be found.

A task force was set up and soon the gun was traced. Decades earlier, the late King Tribhuvan had given it to a relative. This person's son then lent it to a martial-arts guru, who in turn gave it to the assassin, a cat-burglar of some renown.

While Prince Dhirendra escaped charges, a coterie of people close to him were arrested, including, most notably, his ADC, Bharat Gurung. Gurung was prosecuted in a military court for connivance in the attempted murder of Thakurathi, drug trafficking, gold smuggling, illegal foreign-exchange transactions and unauthorised possession of weapons.

He was sentenced to thirty-three years in jail, and all his property – about 6.5 hectares of prime land in different parts of the Kathmandu Valley – was confiscated. (In the early '90s, however, the new democratic government granted him a pardon amid much speculation of bribery, and all his property was returned.)

We had read an interview with Thakurathi in *Shopping for Buddhas* by Jeff Greenwald, in which he had implicated the then Prince Gyanendra in a host of nefarious deeds. Yet today we were only hearing about his younger brother Dhirendra. Was the new king, Gyanendra, not equally involved?

'It is very difficult to talk about him now. A king is very different from the brother of a king.'

We confined our conversation to Dhirendra.

So much of what Thakurathi claimed, though, we simply had to take on trust. He said that most of his information came from well-placed sources, but there was no documentary proof. We decided to revisit an acquaintance who was well up on the affairs of Kathmandu. We chatted in his car on the way to his physiotherapist.

Like other Kathmanduites we spoke to, he didn't doubt the basic truth of what Thakurathi had been writing, that Dhirendra especially was involved in the seedier side of things. Drugs, gold smuggling and probably antiques. 'That period in the late '70s, early '80s was when antiques smuggling was at its peak. There's nothing left to steal now.'

He said that while Gyanendra was known to have had an easy run with his businesses owing to royal patronage, his story wasn't as disreputable as Dhirendra's.

'I had a bit of experience in this. I was a court interpreter in the USA in the early '80s, and every single day there'd be some poor Sherpa woman or a Terai peasant hauled in after being caught with condoms full of heroin up their orifices. They all had the same story: that they'd been made to do it.'

By whom?

'Well, once I was asked to listen in to a taped phone conversation between two of the Nepalis and I was really shocked at the names coming up. These people went very high . . . Bharat Gurung and others in that crowd. But Gyanendra's name never came up. After a while I wouldn't do it any more because I had to come home and I didn't want these people knowing that I knew. I've never told anybody this before.'

While Prince Dhirendra's ADC, Bharat Gurung, had been a free man for almost a decade now, there was one man still left in prison over the assassination attempt.

A crumbling, puddled road led us to Central Jail. We passed one checkpoint with no gate and were still on what looked like a public road when we realised we were already in the visitors' area. Behind a cage door with a few padlocks hanging loose was a corridor with men sitting along the walls, disappearing into darkness. Inmates.

Outside the door was a guard, a bayonet on his rifle. A row of five men were talking to people over a metre-high concrete fence, the only barrier separating the prisoners from the road to freedom. We waited for our prisoner to be brought through the cage door.

Bikhash Gurung, the man who shot Padam Thakurathi, was led in. He was fresh-faced, his hair neat in a centre part. He wore a crisp short-sleeved denim shirt and tracksuit pants. He and Dinesh, our friend and interpreter, started to talk, and we could see from Dinesh's expression that it was quite jovial. We scoured the prisoner for signs of badness. His arms were thick with strong veins; a tattoo of what might have been a dragon was just visible under his sleeve. There were small scars on his forehead but his round face was friendly.

'He says he does not want to talk about his case,' said Dinesh. 'The people who arranged it are now in high places. If the government excuses him, he might be out in two months. When he gets out, he will meet Mr Thakurathi. They aren't enemies with each other . . . He doesn't want to say much because it may hamper his career in jail.'

How long has he been here? Fifteen years?

'I managed to escape three times,' he told Dinesh. 'I have been sentenced to 207 years.'

Gurung asked if we wanted a Pepsi. He gave the order and three bottles were brought out.

What's jail like? we asked.

'It's a very dark life . . . lots of people come to interview me. They are all interested in writing a book about me. But I will not talk about the shooting of Padam Thakurathi and who gave the order.'

Is Padam Thakurathi an honest man?

'Yes.'

Gurung would not take our money for the Pepsi. He said

it all went on his account so we presumed he must have an income from somewhere. We thanked him and left.

As we walked back down the rough road, Dinesh told us how important Thakurathi had been for Nepal. 'You know, at the time of his shooting, whenever someone criticised the government, people would joke that they should wear a helmet to bed.' Thakurathi, he said, was a hero.

As for Prince Dhirendra, the late 1980s weren't a good time. Not only was he bringing a lot of bad publicity to the family, he'd made the dangerous move of divorcing his wife in order to marry an Englishwoman, Shirley Greaney.

His previous wife hadn't been just any Rana cousin. She was Queen Aishwarya's sister, Prekshya. (Aishwarya's two younger sisters had married King Birendra's two younger brothers.)

Dhirendra had thus alienated himself from the woman many thought really ran the country. She certainly ran the palace, and with her as an enemy, Dhirendra was on the outer. He was stripped of his title, ostensibly for marrying a foreigner. In 1988 he left for England and was rumoured to have told the king, 'I will return when the country is ruled by a man.'

chapter 14

a royal affair

We were attempting to probe a tight-lipped young diplomat about his association with the royal family when he
suddenly brought up the name 'Barbara Adams'. She had
moved to Nepal from the United States forty years ago, he said,
and was a great source of stories about the royals. 'She was the
consort of a Nepalese prince,' he explained.

We were immediately eager to meet her. If anyone had an
insight into what Devyani was up against with Queen
Aishwarya, it would be Barbara.

When we'd first phoned her, one afternoon around three
o'clock, she'd replied in her New England accent: 'Could you
call back in an hour? I'm in the middle of some very exciting
luncheon conversation.' It had endeared her to us immediately.

During a subsequent phone conversation, she'd been
distracted by some bad news she had received, about the arrest
of a former student-activist friend of hers, before changing the
subject: 'A friend of mine is starting up a peace movement. Oh
my, I said I would do a hunger strike with her on Sunday,

but I can't.' We had a feeling we'd enjoy ourselves in Barbara's company.

Barbara drove us down Durbar Marg in a slightly battered, army-green Land Rover. She wore a brown *kurta suruwal* – a fashion habit picked up during her exile in India – and her long white hair was pinned behind her ears in the manner of a young girl rather than a woman in her sixties. We had expected some-one petite, a bit Grace Kelly even. But Barbara was more earth mother, passionate, with a big voice and a hearty laugh.

We pulled into the driveway of an old Rana palace, which was now the stamping ground of Kathmandu's well-heeled, the old stables having been converted into an elegant sanctum of shops and restaurants. Barbara led the charge into Chez Caroline's sunny courtyard, pausing to greet some of the glam-orous lunchers in a swoop of kisses, before finding a quiet table up the back. The waiter adjusted our wide cream umbrella and brought fresh ginger soda. And Barbara told us her story.

'I knew from the moment I could *think* that I couldn't live in America,' she said as she scanned the menu of blue-cheese salad, smoked salmon and imported lamb. 'I was born in New York, grew up in Washington DC. My father was a career government person. He joined the government with the New Deal in the Roosevelt era, so served in a lot of those ministries. My mother was a very wild, creative, intelligent, discontented lady. Very different.'

After leaving school – 'as soon as I humanly could' – Barbara travelled around India, paying her way by writing free-lance articles, until the opportunity to cover Queen Elizabeth's 1961 stopover in Nepal brought her here. As it turned out, the young American missed the royal visit but, she told us, 'The country was so fascinating, I couldn't leave it.'

In Kathmandu, she immediately found herself mixing it up with the city's best: 'The Ranas and Shahs were about the only people I could meet in those days. They all wanted to practise their English.' Barbara's introduction to her future royal beau, Prince Basundhara, came during her first couple of weeks in Kathmandu, on a night out with two American game hunters she'd met by chance. 'We all sat down around the bar after dinner, and this guy sort of plopped down next to me into the empty chair and said: "Oops! Sorry, I thought you were someone else." And that was he!' Barbara broke into delighted laughter at the memory.

Prince Basundhara was the youngest brother of King Mahendra. In his early twenties he had been married off to a twelve-year-old Rana girl, Princess Helen, and the following year, the first of their three daughters was born.

The couple separated in the early 1950s. They would never be allowed to divorce, but they lived apart and Prince Basundhara took on various lovers. He had a fourth daughter with another woman, and then created an international stir when he got engaged to an American in New York. His father, King Tribhuvan, would not agree to the marriage. The relationship fizzled and the prince returned to Kathmandu, where, that night in 1961, he met Barbara Adams.

Barbara continued: 'Then he invited us all back to his house and showed us slides of the queen mothers – he had two mothers, they called them the queen mothers – of their pilgrimage to the source of the Ganges. And it was very informal and cheerful . . . and that was it.'

Prince Basundhara was an elegant man, more attractive than handsome. Everyone always thought he was Italian. Beneath his debonair exterior, though, Barbara could sense a vulnerability: 'My heart went out to his loneliness . . . he had a sort of longing for the freedom in the west. Being in the royal family is always frustrating because they can never do exactly what they like. There's always this yearning . . . And the Shahs had all been prisoners in the palace for such a long time under the Ranas.'

Barbara soon moved in with Basundhara. The couple could never marry, but they lived as husband and wife. They occupied their time the way one did in those days, with hunting in the Terai in winter and camping trips by the lake in Pokhara. He took her on a royal trek to the kingdom of Mustang near the Tibetan border and gave her a racy Sunbeam Alpine convertible, in which she'd zip around Kathmandu.

As tourists began trickling into the country, they started what was possibly the first travel agency to open in Nepal. Barbara became a director. At first, there was just the rich, adventurous jet-set crowd and the mountaineering expeditions. But towards the end of the '60s, the hippies turned up.

Barbara's story was interrupted as an attractive Nepalese woman in western dress approached our table.

'Ketaki!' Barbara greeted her. We recognised the name immediately. Princess Ketaki was one of Prince Basundhara's daughters – the little girl who was living with King Tribhuvan when he brought down the Ranas. Barbara and Ketaki kissed and made promises to catch up for lunch. Ketaki was shown to her table.

That was your stepdaughter? we asked.

'Yes. How did you know? In fact, she and I have something in common. Ketaki had a difficult time when she divorced her Nepalese husband to marry an Englishman.'

Ketaki, we later discovered, had been another to struggle against palace protocol in the name of love. She had been married off to a young Rana man when she was twenty years old. Within the year she gave birth to a son, and three months later, she walked out.

Princess Ketaki was at a party in Kathmandu in the early '70s when she met an English helicopter pilot, Alan Chester. The pair fell desperately in love and wanted to marry, but Ketaki first had to ask the king's permission to divorce.

King Birendra procrastinated. He asked her to wait until after his coronation in February 1975; he didn't want a scandal before that. It was fair enough. But even after his coronation, the king wouldn't make up his mind. Princess Ketaki was young and in love, and waiting a year for the king's response was a long time. In the end, she and Alan simply ran away.

When King Birendra summoned Ketaki back, he granted her the divorce, but took away her privy purse and her title. Ketaki didn't mind. She preferred the life of a middle-class wife to that of a princess. She became Mrs Ketaki Chester.

She and Alan left Nepal for eleven years. When she returned, she was welcomed back into the family, but Queen Aishwarya never approved of what she had done. Even Ketaki's mother, Princess Helen, to whom she was close and whose own marriage to Prince Basundhara had crumbled, never accepted the union. 'Apparently,' Barbara told us, 'Princess Helen has largely ignored Alan and their two children.'

So how did the royal family react to Barbara? we wondered.

She hesitated for a moment. 'I don't know whether they can hear or not,' she whispered, nodding at the table where Ketaki was dining with another member of the royal family. 'We can talk about other things.'

The waiter brought our lunch, after which Barbara continued her story, starting with Prince Basundhara's death in 1977. Things turned sour with the Shahs. 'They were nice to me while he was alive, and turned on me when he died.' The palace took the travel agency away from her. So Barbara moved into interior decorating and craft promotion and design in an attempt to make a living. 'I'd lost Basundhara, I'd lost my life – the textiles were so beautiful they gave me something spiritual and some visual happiness.' But she was left almost penniless, and her plea for a share of her lover's property was soon stamped out by the king.

'It was all decided in the palace. But, of course, I was never an intriguer. All these people were into intriguing and they had choices and powers . . . Some Rana said to me: "You're more stupid than our maidservants. Even a maidservant would have gotten *something* out of this . . ."

'I think there's a certain narrow-mindedness, especially with the women in the palace, of always wanting the royalty marrying into their side of the Rana family . . . Of course, when King Mahendra's wife died – you must have heard – [his father] King Tribhuvan desperately wanted him *not* to marry another

Rana girl: "We want to get out of their control, not entrench ourselves further."'

'May I join you for five minutes?'

We looked up. It was Ketaki, a drink and a packet of cigarettes in her hand. She took a seat.

At the same time, a chic woman with broad olive features passed by. 'Ketaki,' the woman enquired, 'how's your arm?' The former princess smiled off the concern, but from across the table we could see a huge, grooved scar in the crook of her left arm, while she held her right arm stiff against her body.

Ketaki Chester was a petite woman, almost fragile. Fifty-ish, but she looked younger. She was bubbly, instantly likeable, and perhaps a little too straightforward for her own good. She and Barbara lit cigarettes.

'So how did Alan get his visa to get out of the country?' Barbara asked her.

'The king, of course,' Ketaki replied. It was strange to hear her refer to her first cousin as 'the king'.

Barbara turned to us. 'Ketaki's husband Alan has been a prisoner in Nepal for sixteen years. They wouldn't let him out of the country because he didn't have a visa. There were huge fines he would have had to pay – 60,000 dollars or something. But he had to go to England for medical treatment.' Barbara drew back on her cigarette and moved the conversation on to the Maoists.

'Well, it's going to go on till that king of ours does something,' said Ketaki.

'Do you think he will?' Barbara asked.

'Don't worry, he'll do something. He just has to wait out the year. The queen mother has asked him to do that and so he will.'

'Yes, but in that time 2000 people could be killed.'

Ketaki's food arrived and she left to rejoin her table.

After Prince Basundhara's death, Barbara found she had trouble renewing her own visa. 'They tried to get me to leave the country, they tried to confiscate my car that he'd given me – the little sports car. I had to hide it in a field for six months.'

Barbara dropped her voice to a whisper. 'It was basically the queen. The king was just run by the queen . . . she was very resented. The last time that I was kicked out [of the country] before this recent exile to India, it was supposed to have been [at the request of] the queen. She actually kicked her own husband's brother out, Prince Dhirendra . . .

'All I knew was that suddenly, hysterically, there was this great pressure on the government to get me out, get me out, get me out. The Home Ministry people were calling me all the time: "You must leave the country." And I'd have parties with all my VIP friends in case the police came, it'd be hard for them to grab me.' Finding an ally in the American ambassador, a six-month reprieve was granted her – a promise by the prime minister, no less. This meant nothing, however: she returned home from hiding to find herself under house arrest for ten days, after which she was forced out of the country. 'Evidently,' she summarised, 'when the queen wants something, every-body's hysterical.'

Barbara chuckled. 'These things are funny in retrospect but they're never very pleasant . . . Anyway, then the sweet, lovely ambassador said: "Barbara, I want to take you to the air-port. They have humiliated you so much, I will see that you leave in style." And he took me with my closest friends in his special car, with the flag flying, to the VIP room and we had champagne and caviar. That was so sweet. You remember these things.'

After that incident, and again when she was later kicked out accused of being a Maoist sympathiser, Barbara would return to Nepal to discover there'd been a smear campaign against her, presumably at Queen Aishwarya's instigation.

'Everybody would be so scared. Everyone here tends to go where the palace says, so people would shun me, some of my friends would shun me. Here – who wants a taste?' With that she broke off from her tales of palace machinations and pushed her lemon-basil sorbet towards us.

It struck us then that while King Tribhuvan had thrown off the official shackles of the Rana regime some fifty years ago, the Rana women in the palace still wielded the power.

chapter 15
we all are sufferers

Suraj Shamsher Rana greeted us at the front door of his modern brick home, about 100 metres down the driveway from the family's old palace, where he and his sister Queen Aishwarya were born. As much as we'd heard about Queen Aishwarya, we were keen to talk to someone who knew her more intimately, someone who'd observed her relationship with Crown Prince Dipendra.

We were starting to discover that, when you're a royal, very few people ever really know you. Even close cousins and palace employees who'd known the king and queen for decades would tell us that they never saw the royals interacting as a family. As one cousin said: 'I don't even know whether they watched television together.' Then, Queen Aishwarya's brother Suraj had agreed to meet us.

Suraj limped inside. One of his legs, he explained in a quiet voice, was shorter than the other as a result of a shooting accident which put him out of the army as a lieutenant-major in 1978.

In the hallway, Suraj stopped at a long picture of his and Aishwarya's ancestor Juddha Shamsher, jowly and moustachioed, flanked by his nineteen wives and a phalanx of sons. Our host guided us through the faces in the picture: 'This is Bahadur Shamsher and his son. This is my grandfather, and this is . . . and by the way, this is my wife.' He gestured to the real-life woman in a lilac *kurta suruwal* who was hovering around. She gave us a bright 'Hello.' Her name was Anju.

'It is very complicated,' she said, nodding at the Rana portrait. 'I think you ought to see a family tree or something to understand this.'

Suraj Shamsher was a short man, not much over five feet. He stood on a little lounge to bring the photo down. As he did so, a shining pistol lying loose on the cushions bounced around his feet. It was pointing directly at us, but he didn't seem to notice.

With the old photo laid on a table, he pointed at another young man in a bird-of-paradise hat. 'And this is [my wife's] grandfather.'

'On my mum's side, you see,' explained Anju. 'Close,' she said, as in, she and her husband were closely related. 'He is the queen mother's father. You need a chart,' she repeated.

She pulled out Percival Landon's *History of Nepal*, which included a family tree at the back. Suraj talked us through it. Just like Queen Aishwarya and King Birendra, Suraj and his wife were third cousins, descended from Juddha Shamsher's sons, the full brothers Hari and Agni.

'He had a lot of concubines,' said Suraj of Juddha. 'He had about seventeen or eighteen sons.'

So some of these brothers were from concubines, we confirmed, pointing at the names towards the end of the list of Juddha's seventeen official sons.

'Don't say that in front of –' Anju was silenced by a glare from her husband.

'It's on tape,' he said.

She looked at our tape recorder, surprised. 'Can you erase that?'

We rewound it to wipe off the name of this son of a concubine who was still alive.

She asked if we were going to write that inbreeding had something to do with what happened at the palace. Suraj glared at her again. Changing the subject, we asked what Aishwarya was like as a girl.

'She was a bright person from the very beginning,' Suraj replied.

Bright as in intelligent, or bubbly?

'Intelligent,' they answered together.

It soon became apparent that Anju was going to be far more illuminating than her husband, who had a certain shell-shocked distance about him. Pretty and petite, her jittery energy was working her hair loose from the clip tying it back. She spoke with her whole body. Chain-smoking, she held each cigarette between her ring finger and little finger, making a fist, through which she dragged the smoke, like blowing a bugle. The sweet floral smell of the room faded.

'She was like a big sister to me,' said Anju, scattering ash into a cut-glass ashtray and across the table. 'We grew up together. She was a very strong character . . . We hardly used to meet, but we used to write letters, to and fro. It was fun, you know. We'd talk on the phone, but not much. There was a certain restriction at the house. And whenever I had a problem I used to ask her advice. I'd complain about my mum, dad or sisters. Little things. I was more the same age as her sisters, Queen Komal [the wife of King Gyanendra] and Princess Prekshya, but she was always my big sister, because I didn't get along with my own sisters.

'She had everything that a woman could have. She was a very understanding person. She was very determined, and very, very sure. Anything she did, it had to be perfect. Everything neat, clean. She was good in art. She used to write poetry. She had beautiful English language. She was good in Nepali too. She loved literature.'

At the age of nineteen, Aishwarya found herself engaged to the future king. We asked Suraj what his thoughts were when he heard his sister was going to be queen.

'I actually had no feelings.'

'My husband's very different,' explained Anju. Suraj was in the army doing basic training. It wasn't a big surprise, he said. He knew 'talks were going on'.

Despite the fact Aishwarya and Birendra were related, lived a stone's throw apart and would often be at the same family functions, they were almost strangers. 'He was royalty so you just couldn't go and talk to him. They had seen each other, but that's all.'

Were there restrictions on young men and women talking at that time?

'Not in the family,' Anju answered. 'Absolutely everybody is related to everybody in our society. You will talk to a certain circle. You have friends and your cousins. But when it comes to royalty, you don't expect to go and chat with them like any other cousin. You treat them with respect, a little bit of separation.'

Traditionally, the couple would have remained strangers until their wedding night. But times were changing and in the year between the engagement and the ceremony, Aishwarya and Birendra talked a lot on the telephone.

Suraj was on duty at the royal wedding in February 1970. He was selected by the army as a security guard to protect the future queen. Despite the pomp and incense, the elephants and all the fuss, his memories of the day had faded. He thought there must have been 1500 guests.

His wife recalled that the crown prince and crown princess of Afghanistan were there. 'She was a beautiful lady, the crown princess of Afghanistan. I think Prince Charles was there, also Japan's emperor and empress. They were crown prince and princess then.' The procession stretched two kilometres from Singh Durbar, the parliament building, to Narayanhiti Palace.

Despite being the focus of such attention, Aishwarya didn't seem nervous. She was always ready to do what needed doing. She was strong – 'Very, very strong,' Anju reiterated. 'That is why people misunderstood her.'

After Aishwarya gave birth to Dipendra in June 1971,

there was a gap of five years before the birth of her next child, Princess Shruti. According to Anju, Aishwarya said she planned it that way so she could devote herself to grooming the crown prince.

'For the first few years she had her children, and then she joined the social work. And she gave all her children a normal upbringing. Normal, absolutely normal. And people are saying, "Oh, she didn't bother about the crown prince when he was sick in school." I don't know. She was a good mother, I knew that. What mother would like to spoil her young? He's not an ordinary boy. They are not *ordinary* children. They are public property, right? And it's difficult, I think, for a mother, to handle children like that who have never been said "No" to. It's always "Yes" to the royals. So only the mother can say "No" to him. Think about it. It's very difficult.'

We commented that at least they didn't have the tabloid-media attention that besieges the British royal family.

'The media had a lot of criticism for [Aishwarya's nephew] Prince Paras, even at that time. But the crown prince [Dipendra] was so popular with the youth of Nepal that even if he did something wrong, we would have never known. Maybe there was a cover-up somewhere, who knows? Prince Paras, everybody knows everything about him, how bad he is. But we didn't know what Crown Prince, er, King, Dipendra was actually like. Think about it that way, too.'

As Suraj filled heavy glasses with light French red wine for us, his wife stroked the fluffy dog snuggled against her thigh. We asked what breed it was.

'She's a Pekinese, but not a good breed. That's what we say in Nepal: even dogs need pedigrees.'

We commented on how easy it was for us outsiders to see their family's tragedy as something other-worldly, something in the public domain but not quite real.

'I think I will never be shocked in my life any more,' Anju said. 'My son died at the age of twenty-three and after that I got cancer – bone-marrow cancer – and now this [the royal massacre]. Then Princess Prekshya died in a helicopter crash.

One after the other. My father had three brothers and eight sisters and five of us have got cancer . . . Just recently my cousin-sister died. She had stomach cancer. My eldest sister had breast cancer. My dear other sister has sarcoma. And then the other sister has colon cancer, and when she had an operation it went into her liver. We all are sufferers.

'I felt: "Who am I?" Me dying makes no difference to anybody. It might affect my family, but *that* family is a complete loss to us,' she said, pointing at the royal-family portrait on the wall. She apologised that the official portrait of the new king, Gyanendra, and Queen Komal was not hanging in the most prominent position in the room. 'I couldn't bring myself to move the others . . . Look at them. They're all gone now.'

There was a long pause. We sipped our wine.

'When I was in London having my bone-marrow transplant, every night she [Queen Aishwarya] gave me a call. Every night. And she used to encourage me. She was so worried about me. She gave me life, you see. You know, you have your family, your friends giving you life when you're sick – and it was *her*, because she was my queen too, as well as being my sister-in-law. It was a big honour to me.

'People don't understand her because she was very intelligent, you see. If you know this is black and somebody tells you it is white, will you believe that? She had that character to say it was black. I get hyper when I talk about it because they don't say nice things about her, only rumour. And I get very put off when I hear interviews and everybody blaming her for it. Why would a mother want her child to do that? There are certain norms and traditions, and in our society, the Hindu society, the kingship has to form certain things, you see. It's not like me, an ordinary person. My child can get married to anybody, I wouldn't mind. But they have to follow certain traditions, norms.'

Did Aishwarya ever talk about the tensions between her and Crown Prince Dipendra over his marriage plans?

'Why didn't he talk to his father?' Anju answered our question with one of her own. 'Look, all children have a tendency to fight with their mum. When his mum said, "Go down to your father", why didn't he speak to him? He was going to speak to him on the Sunday or Monday, or whatever. Why did he have to go and shoot his father? His father was a gem of a person. He was a really good man.'

Was Dipendra afraid of his father, perhaps?

'How could he be frightened of a father who's trusted him so much? I think he was afraid of the answer "No" . . . He knew how to respect his elders. When I was sick he came to see me twice. I was nobody, he could have come or not come . . . He used to give me little presents. He did all that. I mean, I can't understand him.

'And when people talk about drugs, I didn't think he was on drugs. He used to do a little bit here and a little bit there. All the children do nowadays. That was no big deal. He was not addicted, not to that harder type. But you expect youngsters to be curious.'

'He never tried hard drugs,' said Suraj.

'We are all children of the '60s,' added Anju.

How well did they know Dipendra?

'From the very beginning he had two types of character,' Suraj answered.

'We kept our distance from him,' Anju said. 'The crown prince, Prince Paras and my son were all born in 1971. And we all used to say, "What's wrong with you '71 kids?" My son, he went to the States, he got paranoid and then he came back here and shot himself. My son.'

We were shocked into silence by her frankness. We had seen a single picture of him on the bar. His hand covered his face. Suraj didn't bat an eyelid. Just looked on blankly and sipped from his glass.

'Then, Prince Paras started throwing his tantrums,' Anju continued, 'and then Dipendra with his girlfriends, and this and that. We always used to say, "What's wrong with these '71 children?"'

As we stood to leave, Anju ran to the kitchen to get us a large jar of her homemade chilli pickle. Suraj insisted that we get in their car and be driven home, but we politely refused. Their hospitality was far too gracious. 'You are my guest,' Anju said, brushing off our compliments. 'I am a pious woman, like the queen.'

We walked into the night with a pervading sense of sadness for what they had been through. Anju's question rang through our brains: what was wrong with those boys of 1971?

It was a question to which we were beginning to see an answer. We had been in Kathmandu for three months and had started meeting palace insiders and survivors of the massacre. During the coming hectic months, as the temperatures rose, the roadside dope plants grew tall and leafy, and thunder seemed perpetually to threaten, we would meet more. Few of them would allow us to turn on our tape recorder or quote them directly, but Dipendra's story started to take shape. Simpler and sadder and far more compelling than the gossip imagined.

part two

'Madness was in the family.
Eccentricity was in their blood.'

Brigadier-General (retired) Rabi Shamsher Jang Bahadur Rana

chapter 16
the birth of a prince

The precise timing of Prince Dipendra's birth on 27 June 1971 was a secret. Unofficial astrologers must not be allowed to chart the course of the future monarch's life, and hence the future of the country. Not that any star could foresee the strange life ahead for him.

From the beginning Dipendra's chubby face and cheeky smile won hearts. His aunties thought he was the cutest baby they were ever likely to see. Just seven months after his birth, Dipendra's already exalted status was lifted a notch when his grandfather, King Mahendra, died of a heart attack while hunting tigers at Chitwan, in the jungles of the Terai.

The shy and thoughtful Birendra ascended the throne, promising his allegiance to the gods of development. For any other Hindu male, the death of a father requires thirteen days of stringent ritual to assist the departed soul into the afterlife. Kings, however, are not allowed to mourn. They are immortal, above religion. They do not shave their heads nor grieve in public.

In the confines of the Narayanhiti Palace grounds, however, the new king slept in a tent for the thirteen days and fasted
on a restricted diet. All the baby Crown Prince Dipendra might
have noticed was that his parents were suddenly a lot busier.

It was not until Dipendra was three-and-a-half years old
that the astrologers found an auspicious date for his father's
coronation – 24 February 1975. Columns of soldiers marched
out of the eerie dawn mist before the ceremonies began with an
hour-long ablution in which the king was anointed with soil
from all parts of the land. Representatives of the four Hindu
castes dabbed him with curd, honey, milk and liquid butter, as
priests maintained a continuous chant. The bird-of-paradise
crown was lowered onto his head at the appointed minute –
8.37 am – and he was paraded off in a train of bejewelled and
painted elephants.

Crown Prince Dipendra already knew this was his destiny,
but sometimes it was hard to keep to the script. There is footage
of him in his little military outfit with its red-striped navy-blue
trousers; his hand instinctively goes up to hold his father's, but,
when his father doesn't respond, he seems to realise his mistake
and stiffens back to attention.

When it came time to educate Dipendra, King Birendra
wanted to avoid repeating his own experience of isolation from
his family and from his people. He decided that, for the first
time, the future monarch of Nepal would be educated with his
subjects.

From the age of three, Dipendra was sent to a preschool.
The plain-clothes aides-de-camp who took him there each day
had no trouble getting him to go to school, but they had
tremendous problems trying to get him to come home. He'd
want them to keep driving, anywhere but home. They didn't
really know why. He just wanted to stay out. To make matters
worse, the crown prince had a difficult nature and wasn't
scared of them.

For a month or two each year, the king would move his
court to one of the regions. The entire government would live
in a tent city housing up to 600 people, often in districts with

no water, roads or phones. There, the king spent hours each day hearing petitions from his subjects. No person could be denied an audience and Birendra would dispense edicts to his secretaries on the spot, much as the Rana prime ministers had done before him.

Queen Aishwarya and the children would often accompany him, living in a five-by-five-metre 'Swiss-cottage' tent with separate pit toilet and shower. The ADCs were allowed to discipline Dipendra, but the king and queen insisted that they actually explain why he shouldn't do something rather than just tell him 'No'. Nevertheless, Dipendra understood his status from an early age, and when his parents were away, as they often were, he had a free hand.

On one of these regional tours, to Surkhet in the far west, a member of the royal staff, Major-General Bharat Simha, was watching Dipendra play on the wet grass around a temporary fountain set up at the front of the canvas court. Simha asked the Crown Prince not to run on the grass. But Dipendra kept running.

'Please, don't do it, you might slip and fall in the pond. I will get in trouble,' the major-general implored.

But the five-year-old would not listen.

'I will tell your parents when they come back. I'll tell. I'll have to pick you up and take you inside.'

Dipendra turned to Simha and retorted, 'As a general, you cannot command me.'

From the beginning, Dipendra had an intense need to win at games. Any games. One of his cousins would recall a family picnic at the former royal hunting ground of Gokarna where they were playing Twister. 'We were in a tight position and he couldn't do it. He fell down. So he was pissed with me because I won. Since that day I realised he couldn't take defeat. Other people just let him win.' It was a competitive streak that would later come to the fore with any pursuit, from karate to drinking bouts.

Much has been made of Dipendra receiving his first gun around his eighth birthday. Certainly it led to an ongoing obsession with firearms, but he was already older than most of his cousins when they got their first weapons. With the gun came strict lessons on how it was to be handled. From his parents' point of view, it provided a perfect lesson that with power came responsibility.

At the start of year four, in 1980, Dipendra was sent to a boarding school, Budhanilkantha, just north of Kathmandu. There, he would for the first time meet a genuine cross-section of his subjects. The school had been set up as a British aid project. It reserved a quarter of its places for scholarship students from the districts, whereby an untouchable boy who scored well in the entrance exam would be chosen ahead of a high-caste boy who did slightly better.

In order to create an air of egalitarianism in a country where a surname spells out one's class, all boys were referred to by their first name and a number. Hence, the future king became 'Dipendra 832'. He thrived in the relative anonymity of the modern orange-brick buildings.

King Birendra ordered the school to treat his son the same as all the other boys. He received ten rupees a week pocket money, just like them. And his security contingent of nine or ten officers was under orders to remain in the background.

He learned to mix easily with his subjects. Naturally outgoing, he picked up a distaste for overt formality. But, as much as he wanted it, he could never be just another student.

One of the teachers at the school during this time was Dharmapal Thapa. Some former students recalled him as the best history teacher they ever had. He wove the story of Dipendra 832's ancestors, as they went off to wars and slaughtered each other, into an engaging tapestry. But Thapa wasn't all he seemed.

He was at the school at the personal request of King Birendra. Thapa was in fact a senior army officer who saw it as a great honour that the king would give him the assignment of playing nursemaid to his son. (It certainly didn't hurt Thapa's career, because a decade later King Birendra made him the commander-in-chief of the army.)

Thapa would later demonstrate how Dipendra 832 was treated the same as other boys with the story of how, on his first day, the crown prince was mucking up, chatting to the boy next to him. Thapa knew if he didn't deal with it then, Dipendra would misbehave every day. So he picked up two blackboard dusters, went over to Dipendra's desk and gave him a dirty look. Then, with a duster in each hand, he clapped them on the cheeks of the boy Dipendra had been chatting to – staring down the crown prince as if to say, 'You're next.' Suitably chastened, Dipendra bowed his head and never gave him any problems again.

One of Dipendra's contemporaries remembers the crown prince as cheeky in his early years, but that he settled down as he got older. He had a wide circle of friends, without being particularly close to any one person or group. 'He was an extrovert,' the school friend recalled. 'He used to talk a lot. Make up stories. He was a very lazy but talented student. He had a very sharp mind, but at maths he was quite weak.'

His history teacher, Thapa, noticed in particular that the crown prince wrote beautifully. Each year on Mother's Day, he wrote a poem for Queen Aishwarya as a gift.

Dipendra's roommate recalled that they used to stay up talking and laughing into the night. He talked even then of a girl he liked, Supriya Shah. They were often up so late they'd sleep through the first bell and wouldn't wake until the breakfast bell rang at 7 am.

He was, it seems, an exemplary student. Those who went to Budhanilkantha with him would be unable to believe the accusations later levelled at him. Sure he was the best marksman in the school, but he also loved swimming and golf. He was a keen folk dancer, and his roommate would say that his happiest moments at the school were starring in school productions of *Julius Caesar* and *Macbeth*.

One of Dipendra's aunties used to say he had inherited the best of both his parents: 'King Birendra was a very wise person. He wasn't clever. I mean, you tell him a joke you would have to tell him twice or three times before he understood it. But he was very wise. He tended to be almost like a hermit. And I think she [Aishwarya] made up for that side of it . . . She was very intelligent, very sharp. And she understood something before you were halfway through a sentence.'

At home during his school holidays, Queen Aishwarya was a strict disciplinarian, and she was the only one who could say 'No' to Dipendra. Not that he needed it much. Around his parents he was always polite and respectful. If his father was walking around smoking a cigar, Dipendra would follow him with an ashtray.

Sundar Pratap Rana, an ADC at the palace, used to work with the crown prince during the holidays. Dipendra struck him as very intelligent and very sharp, with an obsession for 'hunting'. Young Dipendra would take a gun and go walking through the palace grounds, shooting pigeons, monkeys, rats, anything he could get his sights on. Rana, as an agile young officer who had come first in his rock-climbing course, used to scale walls or trees to retrieve the kills.

Dipendra spent all his spare time with soldiers. They became his role models. As a thirteen-year-old, each morning he'd give the ADCs his written schedule. If there was a picnic, he would plan it like a military exercise and present the officers with their orders.

A normal day's schedule during the holidays would see him walking until 10 am, then tutors would arrive for private classes until 1 pm. He'd have the afternoon free to perhaps go shooting, then at four o'clock he would visit the queen mother for fifteen minutes. After that, he'd play soccer with the ADCs and security personnel against soldiers from the royal brigade stationed at the palace. They'd play until it was too dark to see, then he'd go to the swimming pool, before his favourite part of the day, dinner at 9.30 pm.

Dipendra had a lifelong problem with food. He could never get enough of it and his ever-fluctuating weight became a real problem. At boarding school, the food was awful and there was little of it. It wasn't unusual for there to be late-night raids on the kitchen led by whomever was hungriest. Mostly, they'd wolf down bread and jam.

Dipendra put on a lot of weight around years nine and ten. His nicknames at school were 'Elephant' and '*Foxho*' – (literally 'lungs' – a Nepali way of calling someone fat). He didn't seem to mind the names and would later sign postcards to his Budhanilkantha friends with a drawing of an elephant.

Despite his increasing size, Dipendra was selected in year ten for the school football team to play in a national competition. He was a rugged defender who apparently warranted his spot on the side. The team did well, but when it was time to play outside the Kathmandu Valley, an edict arrived from the palace forbidding him to travel for security reasons. The crown prince took the news hard. His roommate in the little four-bed dorm remembered: 'He got very, very upset. He cried the whole night. I could not sleep that night. I felt very sorry for him.'

When the team came back to play in the valley, Dipendra refused to play again because he felt so humiliated. He watched from the sidelines as they played in the final.

Already, it was clear to those who knew him that there were two distinct personalities at work. There was an obstinate side which had to get its way – had to win – and there was the public side, the decent, intelligent Prince Charming.

No matter how much they tried to be egalitarian at Budhanilkantha, from the cooks who slipped him extra food, to the teachers who dusted the face of the boy next to him, Dipendra 832 could never be just another Nepalese kid. And so he was to be shipped off to the king's alma mater, Eton College.

First, he had to pass his O-level examinations (the equivalent of the school certificate in Australia). The first question in the Nepali language paper was: 'What would you do if you were king for a day?'

Dipendra 832 got an A.

chapter 17

eton

King Birendra's former tutor, Tom Holden, was now a housemaster at Eton, so he was brought over to Nepal to help Dipendra's transition from one arcane world to another.

Holden thought that if any Christian school could handle a Hindu deity, it was Eton. The school was used to dealing with the children of extraordinary people. Holden couldn't help but feel that Prince Charles would've had a much happier childhood if he'd been sent there. And perhaps Charles knew that too, because that's where he would send his own sons, Princes William and Harry, a few years after Dipendra attended.

The last time Holden and his wife had come to Kathmandu was to attend Birendra's coronation in 1975. This time, in 1987, after two weeks' sightseeing, the teacher was summoned to Narayanhiti Palace.

Holden had a session with Dipendra where the teacher made it clear there'd be no acting the crown prince at Eton. Dipendra seemed to accept that readily.

Holden knew Dipendra wasn't going to feel the same sort of isolation his father had experienced. Not only was Nepal far less remote and backward than it had been in 1959, but England, too, was now more multicultural. Still, they had to work through the cultural minutiae.

'Do you know what boxers are?' Holden asked.

'Yeah,' said Dipendra, raising his fists.

'No, no. Underwear.'

Holden knew boys were quite particular about such things and if Dipendra arrived in some sort of Y-front thing, he'd be in for a hard time. On returning to England, Holden alerted Lady Camoys – the wife of King Birendra's old friend and guardian Lord Camoys – to the problem. She got Dipendra's sizes and went shopping.

In September 1987 when King Birendra and Queen Aishwarya turned up at Eton with their son at the beginning of the first term, Holden showed them to Dipendra's new room. 'Would you like to see his clothes, ma'am?' he asked the queen.

On the top of the first box she opened was a pair of strawberry-patterned boxer shorts. 'Goodness me!' she said.

Holden well remembered the religious restrictions placed on Birendra during his time at the school, and so asked the king if Crown Prince Dipendra could attend the carols service coming up at Christmas. 'That's perfectly all right,' the king replied. 'Provided you don't convert him.'

During his time at Eton, Dipendra was placed into the care of three guardians: Holden, Lord Camoys and Bharat Simha. The last of these was the general who had been unable to order the five-year-old crown prince away from the fountain and who was now the Nepalese ambassador in London.

The troika decided that the key to Dipendra's adjusting to his new life was that he be kept away from the embassy, where there'd be all the familiar bowing and walking backwards. The crown prince's ADC was ordered to stay in London to make his time at Eton as normal as possible.

The king didn't perceive any threat against the boy, but

Britain's Special Branch came out to the school and fitted a panic button in his room. It would set off a gargantuan racket in Holden's side of the house and alert the local police, who had a plan to cut off every route out of the school. (When Prince William came to the school some years later, Special Branch added the measure of taking boys' names off their doors.)

It was difficult for Dipendra arriving as a sixteen-year-old when the other nine boys in his 'block' had already had two years to settle into their own little groups. He had to work hard to make friends. There were those who toadied up to him, while some didn't want to be too friendly in case others thought they were being obsequious.

Naturally gregarious, Dipendra slowly broke the ice. He soon had the nickname 'Dippy', and began to make his mark, big-noting as best he could. He blabbed that, back in Nepal, he had his own concubines and could bed any woman he desired. He also went on about how much he loved brandy. Drank it all the time, he told them.

This last boast led to his first great lesson in public relations when one of the boys took him up on his claim and asked him to get some liquor. Dipendra was nabbed buying the stuff and sent to the headmaster. The school had a standard system of punishments: he received a fine amounting to just over twenty dollars and was 'gated' for three weeks. No big deal, until somebody at the school stole the form detailing the misdemeanour and sold it to the notorious *Sun* newspaper. 'Eton Prince flogs booze to toff pals' went to print at the end of his first term.

Such news could never be reported in Nepal, where his father still held a tight rein on the media, but people such as newspaper editor Padam Thakurathi took great delight in photocopying the *Sun* story and distributing it privately. Nepalese people still remember their shock at seeing the illicit copies which multiplied throughout the kingdom. Strict Hindus aren't meant to drink (although it is a popular pastime in Nepal) but what caused more indignation was a quote from an unnamed boy about Dipendra's boasts of bedding any woman he wanted.

Tom Holden put the episode down to rotten luck and tried to use it for the betterment of the future monarch. 'Now this is a terrific lesson for you,' he told the crown prince. 'You've got to learn who you can trust.'

Dipendra appeared contrite.

'What are you going to do if you find who leaked the story?' Holden asked.

Dipendra looked down to his clenched fist.

The crown prince was already making his mark in the school's fledgling karate team. He was a black belt before he arrived, having been trained in martial arts by palace soldiers since he was a little boy. The master in charge of karate, Mike Town, noted how strong and very quick the new boy was. The school only had one other black belt and so from the beginning, despite being quite short, Dipendra took on the best boys from the other schools.

Word came from the embassy that he wasn't to fight any Nepalese boys. It wouldn't be proper for him to beat up his subjects or, far worse, that he might be beaten by them. But Town thought it highly unlikely that any of them would have got the better of Dipendra: 'He could out-punch virtually everybody. Very accurate, very fast.'

Whereas other boys tended to be more circumspect, this teenager went in with fists flying. Winning a fight required two controlled hits to the torso. Dipendra would normally have his first point within seconds, so matches that would usually last three minutes were over in one. Town would not remember him losing: 'He was certainly one of the most impressive fighters we've had in my twenty years at Eton.'

The ambassador, Major-General Bharat Simha, came to see one of his bouts. Despite Dipendra's comfortable win, the old envoy didn't like what he saw. Legs and fists flying everywhere. What if one hit the crown prince in the eye? Afterwards,

160

the ambassador told Dipendra that karate was too risky. He was going to write to the king about it.

'My God, this is one thing I like and you're going to tell my father. Thank you! Thank you!'

Dipendra's pleas must have had some effect because he wasn't stopped from competing. In his final year he became captain, and his team won virtually every match.

The crown prince was a good prematch motivator, but when the team fought poorly, he became irate. Town recalled one particular occasion: 'The team had not performed as well as they might. He waited until the next week, then Dippy gave them a real dressing-down. He was pretty cross. He was quite frightening when he was cross. Told them what's what in no uncertain terms. And he would have continued doing so but the boys saw me come in and they quietened down. They would have got a lot more verbal abuse if I wasn't there.'

Town was also witness to Dipendra's temper outside the sports arena: 'I happened to look out the window and saw him walking down Common Lane [near the school] with a couple of friends, when some wretched youth threw a bucket of water on them from a window up above. Fortunately it just missed. He roared into the house. I think he thought his pride had been slighted. The other two restrained him, otherwise he might have done some real damage. There were rumours about him using his skills outside the ring, but I don't know how much of that was just schoolyard banter.'

As a senior boy, Dipendra sometimes came around for a beer with Town to discuss karate. The teacher always found him courteous to the point of being old-fashioned. He had been instructed on how to act by his father, who had been at Eton when it was a far more formal place. Town found him to be a great chap.

Another teacher, American Kevin Nevers, was in charge of the Clay Pigeon Shooting Society. Nevers knew nothing about shooting, but believed he was recruited into the club by the boys because he was a smoker and they hoped he'd let them smoke. He did.

Nevers would later write that on winter afternoons he and some of the boys would travel in a minivan to a country estate one of the boys' fathers owned. 'And there we'd have a bang. Dippy was a crack shot. Of course he was.' As Nevers pointed out, he was nominal commander of one or two Gurkha regiments. The crown prince showed Nevers how to hold his gun, sight it, and how to lead the clays. While Dipendra instructed Nevers, they'd talk.

He once told Nevers 'that he didn't especially want to be king', as Nevers put it, much as a plumber's son might announce he didn't want to follow his father into the family business. The crown prince also told Nevers that when he succeeded the king 'his first order of business would be to clean the government of the corruption which was fouling it.'

The crown prince may have been a superb marksman on the shooting team and a martial-arts star, but, as writer Patrick French explained, 'in the arty, laid-back world of Eton boyhood, these were low-status hobbies, and many of Dipendra's contemporaries found him peculiar'.

After he became infamous, many would describe him as dark and sullen. Daniel Kruger, a few years below Dipendra, recalled teasing him once while he was skipping in the school gym. Dipendra lifted him off the ground by the jaw. 'Don't laugh at me,' he told the younger boy. 'Don't ever laugh at me.'

One of Dipendra's best friends, Ed Demetriou, would recall to the BBC: 'He was quite rough, really. He wasn't clever with words like most boys were. Most boys, it was cool to be a little sharp with your wit. And he wasn't sharp with it . . . [he] became more marginalised socially as time went on at school.'

Ben Elliot, the nephew of Prince Charles's consort Camilla Parker Bowles, thought Dipendra was 'a freak . . . really emotionally odd . . . He was always smashing people's watches and punching people in a "humorous" way.' Another classmate recalled that people 'were either wowed by him or thought he was an army ninja . . . We thought he was a psycho, very scary.'

This idea of there being two sides to the crown prince's character very much echoed the opinions of those we'd spoken to in Nepal. There certainly seemed to be a duality about Dipendra in his school days, because others at Eton just remembered him as a sweet-natured guy with a smile stitched on his face.

Before arriving at Eton, Dipendra had spent six months being intensively tutored at the palace. Professors had been trawled out of Tribhuvan University to spend an hour every day with the crown prince for virtually no pay. His geography tutor, Dr Bal Kumar K.C., never usually taught below masters level, but had agreed to take on the then fifteen-year-old for the honour.

Two years later, K.C. was forced to cut short his post-doctoral work in Boston to return home because of the death of his father. He was in his all-white mourning clothes in the middle of the strict thirteen-day death rituals when some people from the palace came to his house.

'Change your clothes,' they told him.

'Why?'

'The crown prince is coming from London. You are going to do his project.'

The doctor soon found himself in a helicopter flying to Ilam in eastern Nepal, which, the previous year, had been devastated by an earthquake that killed 1000 people. Dipendra had decided to do his big A-level geography assignment on the disaster. With the doctor's help, he compiled questionnaires, and together they interviewed victims of the quake.

As poor villagers told their tales of woe, the crown prince wasn't always happy with the answers, especially on government aid. 'It looks like there are a lot of communists here,' he told the doctor. 'They say they are not being helped by the government, but the government is giving them thousands of rupees.'

K.C. was in an awkward situation. He didn't know how to tell Dipendra that there was corruption in his father's government; that just because someone had been allocated 10,000 rupees, it didn't mean that's what they received. 'You know, there are many different types of people in the government,' he began. 'Some of the people might be stupid enough to give only half the money to the recipient, and half the money to their own pocket . . .'

The original government plan had been that the recipients of the money had to repay half of it, but the doctor made sure the crown prince realised the people's plight. When Dipendra went home, he was instrumental in the government wiping the debt.

And he got an A for the project.

When Tom Holden wrote letters to the parents of his boys, he always kept a copy of *Debrett's Correct Form* by his side in order to know how to address dukes and earls and Hindu kings. And so it was that he had sat down in March 1988 to inform His Majesty King Birendra of Nepal that his son was doing well, but that – as delicately as he could put it – Dipendra was increasingly anxious about not communicating enough with his father. It wasn't that Holden thought he was unloved. More that royal families in general are different from other people. As a result of that letter, the crown prince got a fax machine in his room. It was the first one Holden had ever seen.

Not all family contact was being encouraged by his mother, however. In 1988, Dipendra's uncle, the wayward Prince Dhirendra, had been stripped of his title and exiled from Nepal after divorcing his wife, the queen's sister Princess Prekshya.

Dhirendra came to London with his English wife, Shirley Greaney. He had lost much of his wealth, but he was comfortable in a ground-floor flat in Paddington with a garden, six cats and three dogs. Many of his nephews were arriving in London for their studies, including Prince Paras, and they would stay there at weekends. Dhirendra was charismatic and cool, something of a guru figure to the teenage boys. Crown Prince Dipendra, however, was forbidden by the queen from seeing him and she sent orders to Tom Holden that her brother-in-law was not to visit Dipendra at the school.

One of Dipendra's cousins who was in England at the time would recall that the crown prince's senior year at Eton was perhaps the happiest of his life. 'Particularly in London, away from the spotlight, doing his own thing.' He was coming to the city more often and they were getting out and enjoying themselves.

When he went out with his cousin, the ambassador had to be informed. 'We used to say, "We're going this way," and then go the opposite way. "We'll be back by eleven." We'd be back by four in the morning.'

Ambassador Bharat Simha would be sitting up waiting for them like a nervous mother. They sometimes exchanged heated words about it, but the thing that struck Simha about the crown prince was the way he'd come in the next morning to apologise: 'I am sorry. Whatever you did was for my own good.' He was such a disciplined lad. The ambassador was certain that Nepal was going to be in good hands.

The cousin, however, remembered how the crown prince used to grab liquor bottles from the embassy bar to take back to school with him. He was drinking straight Scotch by this time, no ice, no water. And he could handle it too.

The cousin also remembers lying for Dipendra to get him out to see his 'girlfriends': 'Once, he went to some park with his girlfriend. He said, "I'll be back in two hours." I was waiting in McDonald's for five hours.'

One such 'girlfriend' was Rossella Scarcella. She'd met the crown prince when he came into the clothes shop where she worked, Skin Appeal, in Windsor, across the Thames from Eton. She kept an eye on him, thinking he might be a shoplifter, because he looked scruffy in his combat jacket. When he came up to pay for a leather jacket, she noticed the letters 'HRH' before his name. He told her, without arrogance, that he was the crown prince of Nepal. They talked while he played with her Yorkshire terrier, and he asked if he could drop by again. The twenty-two-year-old from Florence already had a boyfriend but she said yes, anyway.

They started taking walks by the Thames, which is narrow and serene around Windsor, his ADC keeping a respectful distance. To Rossella, Dipendra was a polite, kind and funny young man. 'We would talk about all sorts of things and he never suggested or said anything improper,' she would later tell the *Mail on Sunday*. 'I had a partner already so I do not think he was looking for romance. I think he valued the time and space to talk to someone without it being at Eton or in his royal family.'

She asked him about his love life, whether he had anyone in mind. He said he was looking. Dipendra admitted that he'd probably have an arranged marriage, but that he'd prefer it if he was in love with the girl. He wanted romance, but knew his duty came first.

As for a casual fling, he told her: 'My father would not approve if I did something not right and he got to know about it. He can be quite hard on such things.' To her, Dipendra seemed to have an immense respect for both his parents, and only spoke of them with affection.

There were those who believed that the crown prince never felt this affection was reciprocated, however. A long-serving ADC heard the young royal say as much when they were on a flight to Germany. They were sitting in the smoking section and both were drinking. The ADC, 'Bim', noted how well the teenage crown prince could hold his liquor, but it loosened their tongues and they ranged over all sorts of subjects. At one point, Dipendra turned to the soldier and said, 'You know, I have never known in my life what love is.'

Bim believed him. In the palace, children are looked after by governesses and maids, with little close attention from their parents. 'He was not looked after as a child with caring, tender love,' the veteran ADC would recall. 'He had a feeling that he was not very much liked, that he didn't get love from his parents, and in the last couple of years he was on his own.'

In the early months of 1990, Dipendra's fax machine was reaming out updates on Kathmandu's growing democracy protests. Other students could see the concern on Dippy's face and would watch as a black car with 'NEP 1' numberplates whizzed him away to the embassy.

As housemaster, Tom Holden would talk to each boy individually every night, so Dipendra kept him informed of the unfolding events in the mountain kingdom. The possibility of the monarchy being deposed started to become very real to the crown prince.

He told Holden that the queen had suggested King Birendra should abdicate in favour of the crown prince, to act as a circuit breaker to the protest movement. But Dipendra strongly opposed her plan and told his mother she should never speak to him like that. He was absolutely loyal to his father.

But that's not to say he didn't see a Machiavellian role for himself. A cousin would recall that they were skiing in Switzerland when the demonstrations began: 'I remember him calling his father and saying, "Let me come back and handle things." But the late king didn't want to kill his subjects, he wanted to empower them, which the crown prince didn't like. [Dipendra] was of the view that you had to direct the people because our people are not really educated to make democracy work. He genuinely wanted to crush the top leaders who were heading this movement. He thought once he did that, the whole situation would come under control. I remember him saying, "The head of an elected government can order his troops to kill his people, but the king, if he orders his troops to kill his own subjects, then there'll be a black mark on the whole dynasty." So I remember him telling his father: "*Da*, If you don't want to take the blame in history, let me do it. I'll come back. I'll order my generals. I'll do the dirty work." He was a cunning guy.'

As the protests escalated and his father caved in to the popular will, the cousin could feel a growing sense of frustration in Dipendra, directed against his parents. When Dipendra heard that he was destined to be a mere figurehead monarch, it was said that he was so furious he smashed a hotel door.

'At that time Dipendra was more of an extremist, and when he came back [to Nepal], he tried to fit in and adapt to the system,' the same cousin remembered. 'He was pretty successful. One could never say what his ulterior motives were. Because of the actions he took on that fateful night [the palace massacre], one could feel he was trying to do away with the system as well. He didn't like the way democracy was going in Nepal. He didn't like the way his father was doing nothing about it. I think he wanted to do away with the system.'

Tom Holden's last letter to the king and queen, in April 1990, congratulated them on their son's 'considerable statesmanship and maturity' during their country's crisis, which had ended only days earlier. Despite all the troubles, Dipendra had worked hard and improved academically. Not only had he sat his exams in the same month that his father handed over power, he'd also got his second dan in karate on his final weekend.

Holden was invited to a dinner at the Nepalese Embassy that was to be attended by the prince of Thailand, a Japanese prince and all sorts of ambassadors. He was anxious about Dipendra showing off or just appearing ill-informed. But the young crown prince turned out to be the perfect host, charming and dignified.

The Nepalese ambassador prided himself on being able to read character. Already a fan of the fast-maturing crown prince, the ambassador believed that after the way Dipendra had performed that night, he appeared set for a stellar career: 'He just dominated everyone. He was brilliant. You could talk with him on any subject: politics, economics, global current affairs. I was complimented by my dinner guests. They said, "My God, you are lucky to get such a bright crown prince." '

Shortly before Dipendra left Eton, he visited Stonor Park, the stately home of one of his English guardians, Lord Camoys – otherwise known as Tom Stonor. Inside the red-brick walls, surrounded by a wooded deer park in the Chiltern Hills, he was to meet some other visiting Nepalese dignitaries.

Pashupati Shamsher Rana, like King Birendra, had been looked after by the Stonor family during his school days and had remained firm friends with them. Soon to negotiate his country's change to democracy, Pashupati was visiting with his wife and his stunning daughter, Devyani, just a few months younger than the crown prince.

What impact the gregarious Dipendra had on the Rana girl is unknown, but he is reported to have told her very early in their acquaintance that she was fit to be queen. He told a mutual friend, Payal Kohli, that she was perfect and he had fallen in love with her there and then.

But Devyani was a modern woman who wasn't necessarily going to fall for the first prince who came along. She was beautiful and intelligent, a born organiser, and she was going to have to be won. Besides, she'd probably already heard that the crown prince had professed his love to another.

Just before his return to Nepal, Dipendra had given his friend Rossella Scarcella a white-gold bracelet encrusted with sapphires and moonstones. She gave him a diamond ring. He told her how sad he was to be losing his freedom.

They kept up a correspondence for a time, but his letters changed from being lighthearted to quite strained. She thought he was under pressure, that perhaps the palace didn't approve of their friendship.

Dipendra wrote to her once he'd received his A-level

results – an A in geography, a B in economics and a C in English. He admitted that the marks were not 'that great, but in view of the fact that the situation in Nepal distracted considerably, I think it is OK . . . Well, it is decent enough (I think! I don't know about my parents!!)'.

He finished the letter by hinting that perhaps he had been seeking more from their relationship: 'It was really sad that I didn't get to know you earlier when I was there. I was really getting to like you! Maybe we could have got up to something!! Lots of Love & Kisses, Dippi.'

The correspondence with Rossella petered out as the prince was swallowed back up by his own world.

Since his days at Budhanilkantha, Dipendra had a thing for his third cousin, Supriya Shah. They talked on the phone, but dating in the western sense wasn't an option. On the crown prince's return to Nepal, he declared his love for her and asked his parents if he could marry her. Permission was denied.

Most accounts of this claim that it was because the couple was too young. The queen's brother, Suraj, would maintain it had more to do with inbreeding, since Supriya's grandmother and the queen mother were sisters: 'The only thing my sister said was, "Don't you think it's too close?" She never said "No."'

Dipendra was not put off by the refusal and continued to see Supriya, his uncle told us. 'They were in love and there was nothing wrong.'

chapter 18
the hindu world's most eligible bachelor

When Dipendra turned up for officer training at the Kathmandu military academy, he had already spent much of his life around soldiers. There was little his instructors could teach him; he knew tactics, weapons and drill. He wasn't the best in terms of physical condition, but in all other areas he was top of his class. Especially on the rifle range.

Dipendra didn't have to do military training. His father became head of the army without ever learning anything more than how to salute and inspect troops. But again, King Birendra wanted his son to experience the real world.

The crown prince got yelled at like everyone else, recalled one of his instructors, Ananta Simha. He mixed easily with the other recruits, but he could never be their equal. He was already colonel-in-chief of the army, and as such didn't have to sleep in a room with two or three others like the rest of the cadets. He got his own quarters, while his new personal ADC, Raju Karki, slept in an adjoining room.

As a public-relations exercise, Dipendra's spell in the

army worked a treat, and he would remain immensely popular with the military. But he only did six months of the eighteen-month course before he was pulled out to begin a university degree in geography.

Tribhuvan University had been a hotbed of anti-monarchy sentiment in the democracy movement of less than a year earlier, so it wasn't an option for him to attend classes there. Again, his old tutor Dr Bal Kumar K.C. was called upon. Dr K.C. organised other professors to go to the palace to teach various subjects required in a bachelor's degree, such as English and Nepali, while he handled the geography.

Each day the academic would be picked up by a royal car and driven in his formal Nepalese clothes to the palace. It had been strange for him in the beginning. He saw himself as a 'basic man who came from the mountains and walked on the street'. But he got used to the palace. He accepted the woefully inadequate remuneration as an honour. At first he'd even tried to give the money back. One thousand rupees for five months work was hardly worth collecting, but he was told that it had already been allocated so if he didn't take it, some palace bureaucrat would.

When it came time to give Princess Shruti and Prince Nirajan extra tutoring, Dr K.C.'s name came up, but Dipendra made sure to scuttle that. He told his siblings that the doctor taught such complex things they'd never understand him. The real reason, however, was status: he wanted the best geographer in the country as his own personal tutor. It gave him a psychological edge.

There was a little truth to his excuse. When the doctor had been tutoring Dipendra in preparation for Eton, he taught material from the master's curriculum, years ahead of the academic level required. Dipendra had seemed to soak it up and never said he didn't understand anything. 'There were concepts that would take me one week to make my master's students understand, but he would pick them up in half an hour,' said Dr K.C. 'He was very lazy in writing, but if he edited other people's writing he'd make a masterpiece.

He loved writing very simple, active words. Unambiguous language.'

Dipendra cruised through his bachelor's degree towards the top of his class with a 72 per cent average, and went straight into his master's. Once again, Dr K.C. took over as course co-ordinator.

During the professor's first stint as Dipendra's tutor in 1987, he had found the crown prince childish and hyper-active, always wanting to be outside. And he knew who was boss: 'He had a sense of commanding officials, and all his military assistants, making sure everything was put in its proper place. Very good organisational ability.' But Dipendra had matured tremendously since then, and had learned to exercise subtlety in his commands.

An example of this came in 1994, when Dr K.C.'s wife was diagnosed with breast cancer and the professor took her to Bombay for a mastectomy. Gone for two or three months, he had not planned for the crown prince's studies. He was concentrating on saving his wife's life. One day, as the final exams loomed, Dipendra called him in his Bombay hotel.

'Look, I can't do it . . . I'm a little bit lost and you're the only one who can help me.'

'Yes, Your Highness.'

'On the one hand your wife is sick and you are with her. I wouldn't really ask you to leave your wife to come here. On the other hand, I am in trouble. You are the only one who can help me out. How can you solve this problem?'

The tutor was in a bind, but when he told his wife of the call, she had no hesitation: 'Go, go, go. I am not dying right now, so go. This is the right decision. There is nothing you can do to help me.' She had high expectations that when Dipendra became king, her husband would be rewarded with a pres-tigious diplomatic or government position. Dr K.C. never expected that, but he returned to Kathmandu all the same.

Each day he would arrive at the palace at 7 am and they'd do a four-hour exam. He'd dictate the answers for an hour per question as the crown prince transcribed in longhand before the doctor went home for lunch. Then they'd resume at 2 pm and do another exam. This went on for a month.

Dipendra sat the exam at the university like any other student, writing his name, 'Dipendra Shah', on the top of his papers. The crown prince topped the year with 86 per cent.

Dr K.C.'s wife's cancer spread to her brain. Dipendra used his influence to get her into the military hospital but she died the day after he handed in his master's thesis in 1996. He helped out with logistical support for the religious rites. 'He was very kind,' the tutor recalled.

When King Birendra was growing up, he had been allowed little freedom by his father, who had been allowed none by the Rana regime. But the king was determined to give Crown Prince Dipendra's life a degree of normality. Dipendra was allowed to drive and go to restaurants and clubs. 'Once he is king, he'll have to abide by certain norms,' King Birendra reasoned to one of his senior aides. 'So before he has to shoulder that responsibility, we have to let him go.'

But it wasn't as though the palace was a monastery. From the age of eighteen, young royals were required to attend palace functions and could be seen with a mug of beer in their hands. 'They gave us all the privileges, the good, the bad and the ugly,' recalled one of Dipendra's cousins. 'They never said, "Don't do this," or "Do this." [During the Holi] festival we drink *bung* – marijuana seeds ground together – and my first experience drinking that was in the palace . . . And at Shiva Ratri you smoke weed. Every once in a while we used to get a lecture from our mum: "Hey, today isn't Shiva Ratri."'

If a cousin came visiting from western Nepal, he might bring a block of hash as *prasad* (a gift to a god which has been blessed at a temple). The weed from the renowned Manakamana temple, in particular, was reputed to be very good in both spiritual and potency value. So if one of the 'brothers'

(Nepalis call their first cousins 'brothers') brought some back from there, they'd call the others and all go around for a smoke. The same applied to alcohol – a A$150 bottle of Johnnie Walker Blue Label, for example, being another valid reason for a royal knees-up. 'While growing up we were never denied the pleasures of life. It's there. You make your own decision.'

They were young men who were stuck in a cultural void, no longer children but not accepted into the adult world of the senior men. While their fathers might meet to discuss politics and ways of influencing the floundering new democratic leaders, the hierarchy left the young men with no role. So they partied. Prince Paras might have done it with more vigour than the rest, but they all lived a decadent lifestyle alien to their country's traditions.

To his Uncle Suraj, Dipendra became a different person when he drank – aggressive. 'He used to pick on me.'

Suraj had been quite a drinker in his younger years, and had also been a crack shot with both pistol and rifle. But Dipendra always wanted to prove himself and, with a few whiskies under his belt, he'd pester his uncle, challenging him to drinking bouts and shooting competitions.

Suraj had no choice but to demur: 'No, I can't do that,' he'd tell his nephew. 'You are great. Who the hell am I?' That would calm the crown prince down, his pride intact.

Certainly, Suraj wasn't going to take him on in a drinking competition. He knew Dipendra could drink half a bottle of spirits and still be sober.

The new democratic politicians were doing such a poor job of running the country that, by the mid 1990s, the people began to look back at the *panchayat* days with nostalgia. The royal family, removed from the tawdry business of government, found its popularity steadily rising. Even the image of Queen Aishwarya had softened, helped by a decision that she be allowed to smile in public.

Ordinary Kathmanduites started seeing the royal couple driving around town together with no fanfare or walking the streets with their uniformed ADCs following well back to avoid attention. And each year at Badha Dashain, when the public could enter the palace grounds to take *tika* from the king, the queue grew longer.

King Birendra had always tried to convince Dipendra and many of his sceptical cousins that a constitutional monarchy was the only way forward. The crown prince appeared to slot easily into the new meet-and-greet monarchy. He was far more gregarious than his father and always maintained an impeccable front. If he saw someone he'd known at Budhanilkantha, for instance, he'd stop the royal Landcruiser to talk to them.

Even though Dipendra had kept a wide circle of friends at the school, he'd chosen to stay in close contact with only a small group of them after he returned from Eton. His gang would meet at his place in the palace grounds, Tribhuvan Sadan. They'd be required to wear a *topi* to get into the palace but Dipendra did not put much stock in formality. He insisted that his younger siblings address his friends as '*dai*' ('older brother'). And his friends no longer called him 'Elephant' or '*Foxho*'; he was now 'CP', short for 'Crown Prince'.

They'd drink and play billiards and talk about school life. Or they might listen to music and play the board game called carums, which involves flicking disks like casino chips across a powdered board.

Unlike the get-togethers with his cousin-brothers, Dipendra never smoked dope in front of his school friends, just Shikhars, the local cigarettes. He drank a lot but always seemed in control. Far from being aggressive when drunk, he became more interesting, his friends believed. Sure, he dominated the conversation, but 'he had more ideas, more knowledge of the country, more information, more reasoning powers than us . . . Yet he would listen and then argue . . . The arguments sometimes became heated. Personal politics. We used to say vulgar words, but he never got angry . . . if it was his mistake he would say sorry to us also. He never behaved like he was the crown prince.

'He was very, very much optimistic for the country . . . And he had visions also. He used to say, "I will bring a drastic change to the country." . . . He was frustrated with the work of the politicians and government officials, because everywhere there was corruption . . . He didn't talk about taking power back. He wanted to be the constitutional king. He knew the people around him at the palace were not very honest, so what was the use of taking power when the palace officials are more powerful than the king?'

Dipendra had stayed in touch with Devyani Rana after meeting at Stonor Park towards the end of his time at Eton. She hadn't been particularly keen on him, but increasingly she was dominating his thoughts.

A close friend of Devyani's, 'Sita', was in London in 1995 when she heard a rumour that Devyani was involved in some sort of relationship with the crown prince. She got straight on the phone to her friend back home in Kathmandu.

'Rubbish!' Devyani told her. 'You know what Nepal's like.'

'Yes, I know.'

'It's just a rumour that started because the crown prince asked me for a dance. I told him I was only allowed to dance with my brothers.'

Sita believed Devyani, and she may well have been telling the truth, because the story of her refusing Dipendra is retold by close family friends as an example of her fortitude. 'I think very few girls would have had the will or courage to refuse the crown prince,' one said. Yet the rumours persisted, and so did the crown prince.

In that same year, Devyani caught up with a former teacher, Rena Sewak, from her old school in India. The teacher asked if she had any marriage plans. Devyani brushed off the question: 'Oh, ma'am, there is no chance of getting married here yet. One's life is so protected . . . it's not like Delhi where we could go to Connaught Place or Greater Kailash whenever we wanted. One can only go anywhere with our parents, and that too to our family friends' places.'

Dipendra's relationship with his first love, Supriya Shah, had lost steam during the early '90s, but never petered out entirely. Denied permission to marry Supriya, he had continued to phone her, but the more outgoing and vivacious Devyani Rana became his obsession.

Devyani Rana was an independent young woman and didn't need a barrage of calls from a crown prince on heat. She was very bright and well educated, and had begun to help her father as a political organiser, winning herself a reputation as a dynamic worker. She could handle the logistics of an election campaign, moving five truckloads of supporters from one rally to another, making sure they were fed and the drivers paid. She'd also screen constituents before they got to her father.

On one occasion a friend walked into her place and there she was, in a chair surrounded by twenty villagers cross-legged on the ground, all having tea. She was down to earth and generous to a fault, another friend would say. She knew how to talk to people.

According to some, she also knew how to get her way: 'She used to draw the schedule for her father: "Meet this man, meet this man." She was pretty dynamic. "If you meet this man from this side, you have to go and meet this guy from the other side." She'd manipulate people, maybe pull some strings and ask people to put some pressure on certain people to get her way. A typical politician.'

Gradually, however, Devyani gave in to Dipendra's persistence. One can deny the advances of the Hindu world's most eligible bachelor for only so long. As he pushed it from friendship to something deeper, the romance remained a secret and, by western standards, innocent affair.

'She has always been a very sober young lady, even as a young girl,' said a family friend. '[Devyani] was always considered to be very careful and proper about the way she conducted

Rashmila Shakya, aged twenty-two, with a portrait of herself as the child goddess Kumari.

'Cosmically unsynchronised'… Our friend and translator, Dinesh, with his forbidden fiancée, Shanti.

Dinesh Shrestha

Royal astrologer, Dr Mangal Raj Joshi.

A reluctant Balami bride … Radhika (centre) with her new husband and her friend Gita, who at thirteen has already been married a year.

Amy and Mark in Bhaktapur in the Kathmandu Valley.

The granddaddy of them all...
Prime Minister Juddha
Shamsher Rana.

Where did she come from?
A portrait of Juddha
Shamsher's controversial
mother.

Brigadier-General Rabi Shamsher Rana, royal in-law and one of the last surviving sons of Juddha Shamsher.

Three-year-old Gyanendra is crowned king in 1950, with Prime Minister Mohan Shamsher Rana and eight-year-old Pashupati Shamsher watching on.

Courtesy of Min Bajracharya

RIGHT: King Birendra atop an elephant at his sumptuous coronation ceremony in 1975.

BELOW: Queen Aishwarya on a royal trek in the Himalayas in 1979.

Australian Picture Library/Corbis

Brig. Gen. (Ret.) Dr Khagendra Bahadur Shrestha

LEFT: Guns were a lifelong passion… Crown Prince Dipendra in 1982.

BELOW: An official royal family portrait, taken at Crown Prince Dipendra's coming-of-age ceremony in 1991. From left: Dipendra, King Birendra, Prince Nirajan, Queen Aishwarya and Princess Shruti.

A more relaxed royal family photo taken at the Barahi temple opposite the royal holiday house in Pokhara. From left: Crown Prince Dipendra, Ketaki Chester, Princess Shanti, Princess Sharada, Queen Aishwarya; seventh from left: King Birendra; sixth from right: Princess Jayanti; and second from right: Dhirendra Shah.

King Birendra and Queen Aishwarya in worship in 1997.

Princess Shruti in 1996.

Prince Nirajan in 1996.

LEFT: Crown Prince Dipendra's first love, Supriya Shah.

BELOW: Crown Prince Dipendra in a favourite photo.

Crown Prince Dipendra at an arms factory in 1998. The publication of this
photo would later cause a riot.

RIGHT: Devyani's father, Pashupati Shamsher Rana.

BELOW: Crown Prince Dipendra after a para jump in 2001.

Courtesy of Min Bajracharya

Brig. Gen. (Ret.) Dr Khagendra Bahadur Shrestha

Crown Prince Dipendra's forbidden love, Devyani Rana.

King Birendra and Queen Aishwarya on their morning walk.

Gyanendra ascends the throne for the second time three days after the 1 June 2001 massacre.

LEFT: Journalist Padam Thakurathi still bears the scar of an assassin's bullet.

BELOW: King Birendra's katto brahmin, Durga Prasad Sapkota, at home in Kathmandu.

Dinesh Shrestha

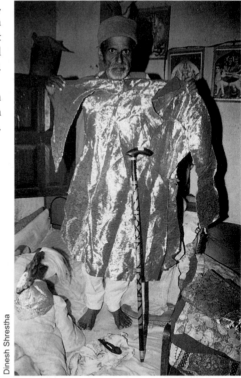

RIGHT: Dipendra's katto Brahmin, Devi Prasad Acharya, at home in Kathmandu, shows off the outfit he wore for the traditional ceremony.

BELOW: King Gyanendra and Crown Prince Paras in their new roles.

Dinesh Shrestha

Courtesy of Min Bajracharya

herself. I heard that when the crown prince fell for her, he had the means and so made it a point to check out her reputation. It was found to be impeccable.'

The timing was good, because in 1995 the palace was starting to send out feelers to the handful of suitable families in Kathmandu that might produce a bride. Pashupati Shamsher Rana and his wife knew that their daughter had met the crown prince, but were unaware of any budding romance when they sent Devyani's picture to the palace as a marriage proposal.

Dipendra was receiving dossiers on potential brides from all over the Hindu world. There was a pile of them six inches high. He showed them to his cousins and they had great fun scouring the photographs for likely mates, joking about marrying the lot of them like their great-grandfathers would have done.

But Dipendra only had one pick. If it had been up to him, it would have been all over when he came to the photo with Devyani's huge dark eyes. He'd have been married and pumping out heirs in quick time. But the decision was not his.

Queen Aishwarya and her mother were in charge and they had a thick veil of problems with the daughter of Usha Raje and Pashupati Shamsher Jang Bahadur Rana.

Sitting in the living room of Queen Aishwarya's brother Suraj in April 2002, the issue had been straightforward. 'Devyani was not to their class,' he said, perking up from his otherwise stilted responses. 'So, naturally only my sister could have said "No". She said: "No, this is not right. But if you still want to do it, you go and ask your father." But he didn't have the guts to ask his father.'

Suraj's wife Anju joined in: 'Before he even got into this, he had asked Her Majesty Queen Aishwarya whether he could marry Pashupati Shamsher's daughter. And she said, "No." So why did he continue that relationship? He *knew*.'

There was no doubt in their minds – and in the minds of other royal relatives we later spoke to – that caste was the only issue at hand. Talk of feuds between rival Rana clans and a personality clash between Queen Aishwarya and Devyani didn't wash with them. That Devyani's father was a politician and her mother Indian also appeared inconsequential.

'Devyani's only problem was that she was not to this standard,' Anju said, pulling on a cigarette.

'He was told, "If you want to get married to her, you have to leave your title,"' said Suraj.

'It was not the queen's choice, you see,' said Anju. 'It was his choice. So they showed photos of different girls. If he had anyone in mind, it was up to him. He could have got married to anybody, but he was after Devyani.'

So what, exactly, was wrong with her caste?

'Her father's side is okay. It was her mother's side . . . Her great-grandmother, she was from Nepal. She was not A class, she was C class.'

On the surface, Devyani Rana appeared to have an impeccable pedigree. Her father was the grandson of the last Rana prime minister, Mohan Shamsher Rana. He was from the Chandra Shamsher branch of the family, known for being wealthier and more sophisticated than the rival Juddha branch, from which the royal family was descended.

Her mother, Usha, was the daughter of the Maharaja of Gwalior – 'the Scindia' – one of the richest and most powerful of India's former royal dynasties. Her uncle was the high-profile Indian Congress leader Madhavrao Scindia.

Devyani's parents raised their daughter with the dignity, discretion and flawless manners for which they were respected. But, as Anju said, the problems went further back than that.

chapter 19
poor relations

I n 1885, Nepal was under the rulership of a gentle, pot-smoking Rana prime minister, Ranaudip, the last surviving brother of Jang Bahadur. The second generation of Rana men were eyeing off the order of succession. By rights, Jang Bahadur's eldest son, Jagat Jang, was at the head of the prime ministerial line. But he had dozens of cousins behind him, and waiting patiently at the back of a queue wasn't a Rana trait.

On top of this, Jagat Jang had not endeared himself to his cousins with his ostentatious displays of wealth. For his marriage to the eldest daughter of King Surendra, a tax was levied on every household in Nepal, raising a fortune for Jagat as a dowry. He'd inherited his father's palace and built his own (complete with a zoo), at which he threw lavish parties. Jagat was generally despised by his jealous cousins but especially so by a group who became known as 'the seventeen brothers', the sons of Jang Bahadur's youngest brother, Dhir Shamsher Rana.

Dhir had died in 1884, and after his sons had waited out the obligatory one year's mourning, the plotting began. They had to meet away from the prying eyes of the capital, where two was company and three a conspiracy. So they chose the Dakshin Kali temple on the southern outskirts of the Kathmandu Valley, a place where, more than just having privacy, they could receive the blessing of the bloodthirsty goddess.

Returning to Kathmandu, the conspirators approached their family astrologer seeking the most auspicious date for a coup d'etat. On 22 November, the day chosen, the five oldest of 'the seventeen brothers' proceeded to Narayanhiti Palace, then the residence of their uncle, Prime Minister Ranaudip.

They whispered the day's password to the guard at the gate and entered. The eldest brother, Bir Shamsher, waited downstairs with his father-in-law, Prince Upendra (brother of the late King Surendra), who had been brought along to convey royal legitimacy on the bloodshed to follow. The other four brothers, Dambar, Khadga, Bhim and Chandra, continued on with carbines concealed beneath their black overcoats – their 'British warms'.

As they passed the various layers of security, they declared in commanding voices that they had an important message from the British resident to be presented to the prime minister without delay. A maid guided them to the door of his private chamber, where they again called out that they had a message. Inside, Prime Minister Ranaudip was lying in bed writing holy scriptures. A man sat on the floor reading him the newspaper and two 'maids of honour' massaged his feet while his wife, the maharani, lay on a velvet bed. Ranaudip asked a young boy to open the door.

'*Ke ho?*' he asked as the conspirators burst in. 'What is it?'

'This!' Khadga replied, as he pulled out his short rifle and fired two shots into his uncle.

Khadga and his four brothers went from the murder scene to the royal residence inside the same palace, where the ten-year-old King Prithvi Bir was living. They dragged him and his mother into a carriage and took them across town to confer more royal legitimacy on the assassination. The Queen Mother then put the royal seal on the document declaring Bir Shamsher Rana the new prime minister. In return, the first order he gave was to immediately dispatch troops to murder her brothers, the sons of Jang Bahadur.

The troops arrived at Jagat Jang's mansion and called to him from below. He appeared at the window and was cut down by a volley of bullets. Jagat's son was shot fleeing across a field, jewels stuffed inside his cummerbund.

News of the murders burst through the ruling elite. By dawn, most of them had gathered as much of their jewellery as they could carry and arrived at the British Residency seeking asylum.

Kathmandu was placed under martial law. All shops were closed and the streets deserted but for army patrols. The only activity was outside Bir's palace, Bag Durbar ('Tiger Palace'), so named for the two animals kept caged out the front. A military band was playing martial music and soldiers periodically fired volleys of celebration into the air, spooking the listless cats. Letters were dispatched to district officials advising that Prime Minister Ranaudip had died of natural causes.

The Shamshers had been the poor relatives within the Rana clan, so poor that before the events of 22 November 1885, all seventeen brothers still lived at home in their late father's only palace. But now Bir, as senior clan member, appropriated the entire fortune of Prime Minister Ranaudip, which included a horde of gold, silver and jewellery, as well as 100 elephants, eight Arab stallions, thirty-five thoroughbreds, nineteen English hounds, sixty Australian cows, 8000 sheep and various estates and plantations.

His brothers took the mansions of their murdered or exiled cousins, but none of them felt like living in Narayanhiti Palace, home of the genial old uncle they'd murdered. The royal family could keep it. This was still an intensely superstitious society where ghosts and demons were real.

Henceforth, the Shamsher branch of the Rana family would dominate Kathmandu society. Devyani Rana was descended from the trigger man, Khadga, on her mother's side, and one of the other murdering brothers, Chandra, on her father's side. That, however, was not the crime for which Devyani would be asked to pay.

After the assassinations, Khadga Shamsher became commander-in-chief of the army. According to historian Adrian Sever, he was an extrovert, who tended 'to overrate both his own capacity and the value of the services he had rendered to the new regime.' In quick time, he was accused of plotting to overthrow his brother Bir, the new prime minister, and was exiled first to Palpa in the far west, then to India. All his sons were stripped of their rights to inherit the prime ministership. But this was not Devyani's problem either.

It took months of begging by Dhan Kumari Devi, Khadga's wife and Devyani's great-great-grandmother, for her to be allowed to follow him into exile. When she was at last granted permission, she travelled over 'fern-filled goat tracks crawling with leeches, in a mile-long caravan of mules and palanquins carried by a hundred or so bearers. In the upholstery of these palanquins she somehow managed to secrete much more of the family's gold, jewellery and other valuables than her permit allowed her to take out of the country.'

She had thus saved her husband from a life of modest means.

But Dhan Kumari Devi was a mere junior wife, or a concubine, according to some. *This* was Devyani's problem, because all Dhan Kumari Devi's progeny were tainted, and it was this flaw in Devyani Rana's ancestral history to which Queen Aishwarya and others would so strongly object. One hundred and ten years later, royals across Kathmandu would cite this marriage as Devyani's fatal problem, conveniently forgetting that their own ancestor, Juddha Shamsher Rana, came from an equally low-status 'wife'. There were, however, further compromises to Devyani's ancestral purity still to come.

Khadga always believed that when the prime minister died, he would be summoned to Nepal to be crowned maharaja, but when it happened, another brother, Deb, took the job. Deb was soon ousted in a coup by his younger brother, Chandra Shamsher, who would reign for twenty-eight years – accumulating all the wealth and sophistication for his descendants (Devyani included, through her father's side).

So Khadga settled in to a low-key, princely life in a huge mansion he built thanks largely to his junior wife's booty. Something of a tyrant to his family, 'he was above all a Rana of Nepal', wrote his grand-daughter. 'He revelled in the dominance of his sex; he was a soldier and a hunter, a strutting egocentric . . . attired in the gaudy uniform of an officer of the Nepalese Army.'

While other exiled Ranas were marrying their children into top-notch Indian families, the daughter from Khadga's junior wife was betrothed to a Rajput of no great means.

The horoscopes of the bride and groom were analysed by astrologers and found to be well matched, so the marriage proceeded. But according to family legend, the young woman – well educated and able to read Sanskrit – discovered that her stars were in fact totally at odds with her new husband's. Their union was doomed to be short-lived. As she read on through the chart, she realised it foresaw that she would give birth to a daughter, then die within days. Her daughter wrote that her mother was so convinced by the prophecies that, when she went to Sagar to have her baby, she took jewellery and other valuables as a nest egg for her unborn daughter's upbringing and dowry.

Nine days after the birth, the young mother died. The baby girl, Bijaya, born in 1919, was destined to become one of the most enigmatic figures of late-twentieth-century India.

Bijaya grew up in the house of her grandfather, Khadga, where she recalled there always seemed to be far too many servants. These resembled poor relations, 'with ties of loyalty, of shared adversity and even, I suspect, of blood, for the Rana menfolk, as a class, were not known for celibacy'.

Men having multiple wives, concubines and affairs with attractive maidservants were common, 'and their progeny invariably attached themselves to the main household.'

Bijaya grew into a slim and striking beauty.

Her uncle was given the task of arranging her marriage. He started thinking about aiming for the very top, the Maharaja of Gwalior, one of only five maharajas termed '21-gunners' – denoting the size of salute given them by the British.

The Scindia family did not normally marry outside its Maratha caste, but Bijaya's uncle managed to get her photograph slipped into the pile.

Unlike other Indian princes, Marathas did not pretend to be gods. They took pride in their peasant origins. They came from hill-hardened folk, not unlike the Gurkhas, who rose up and rolled back the Muslim Mogul empire, capturing the Mogul capital, Delhi, in 1771.

In the course of their empire building, there were famous massacres of Rajputs which have kept the two groups despising each other ever since. Rajputs, literally 'sons of kings', would not normally accept a lowly Maratha in marriage. But the Scindias got mighty rich and even in this most rigidly caste-bound society, that goes a long way.

There was also Maratha resistance to the maharaja's Rajput bride, but he'd seen her photo and he wanted her. His mother was unable to dissuade him, 'and after a while she had taken it all in good grace'.

Bijaya, now a maharani, entered a world of fabulous wealth. Her new palace was a 900-room edifice – 'a massive Milanese wedding cake air-dropped in to the jungles of central India', as writer William Dalrymple described it. It boasted a chandelier said to be second in size only to one in the royal palace of St Petersburg. In order to test that the structure was strong enough to hold it, a ramp had been built up to the roof, then twelve elephants were walked across it. Only then would the architect install the chandelier.

Bijaya would recall miles of velvets and silks, emeralds in their thousands, and gold being weighed like grain. She had far more servants than she needed, about a dozen cars and a dozen chauffeurs.

It was into this world that Devyani's mother Usha was born in 1943 – Bijaya's second daughter.

Nine years after the British were booted from the subcontinent in 1947, Bijaya entered politics and won Gwalior with a massive majority. She would become, as described by Dalrymple, the 'doyenne of India's growing army of militant Hindu revivalists'. Her daughter Usha was an active and zealous campaigner, often hitting the hustings with her sister. They were 'cheered wherever they went as though they were film stars'. While the family lost its title, then its tax concessions, and the palaces sagged and crumbled, they remained one of India's premier dynasties.

At the end of June 1967, Usha married Pashupati Shamsher J.B. Rana, who also aspired to a political career.

Even though they were both from families whose considerable glories had faded, they were still extremely wealthy. Much richer, it is said, than the Nepalese royals. Indeed, a widely circulated story about why Queen Aishwarya forbade Crown Prince Dipendra to marry Devyani was that Devyani's mother, Usha, had once quipped to the queen that the Shahs were not wealthy enough to keep her daughter in the style to which she was accustomed. It is almost inconceivable that anyone would say such a thing to Queen Aishwarya, however. As one friend of Usha's explained to us: 'Mrs Rana is a cultured, dignified lady with an excellent upbringing and background. She would therefore never dream of ever making remarks in such poor taste and I know for a fact that she has certainly not done so. They have always held the royal family in the highest esteem. This is pure rumourmongering.'

As the friend explained, if you want to find a reason to oppose a marriage on the basis of some obscure point of caste, 'then I guess it isn't difficult to find or even create a problem or situation in order to see it does not take place'.

chapter 20
the future queen

evyani Rana had won the crown prince's heart, but he couldn't let Supriya Shah go. He carried pictures of both in his wallet. The two women each knew who the other was, but they didn't speak.

One of Crown Prince Dipendra's cousins, 'Krishna', threw a lot of parties during this period, the end of his wild bachelor days. Dipendra would always want to be called beforehand and given the guest list, in case both Supriya and Devyani would be attending. But they were always there because Supriya, as a cousin, was automatically invited, as was Devyani who was a friend of Krishna's girlfriend. There was no way Krishna was going to exclude one of them just because it made the crown prince a little uncomfortable. Indeed, he may have got some pleasure out of it.

Often, Supriya would set herself up in one room, while Devyani – the 'outgoing bachelor woman' – would be working another. Dipendra would bounce between the two. It was all part of the fun, as far as Krishna was concerned: 'Three of my girlfriends used to be there also. There'd be five, six models running around, my married brothers running around them, my sisters-in-law nagging me, "Why are you bringing them here?" '

The parties were haywire affairs with seventy-odd people going hard till 5 am. People left after breakfast. It was at one such gathering that Devyani and Dipendra first 'close-danced'. While this would be considered outrageous behaviour in the wider Hindu community, it was perfectly acceptable to the racy, westernised crowd – as long as it was kept in-house. 'We always tried to protect him,' Krishna said.

'Don't decide now; have ten girlfriends and decide later' was the advice frequently given to the crown prince by his cousins but, as each of his generation was married off, Dipendra became increasingly frustrated. 'Look at it,' he'd complain. 'All my brothers [i.e. cousins] are married, they all have kids, and I'm not even settled down. I still can't decide who to marry.'

At one point he even brought up a reversion to the good old days. 'I think I'll have two wives,' he told two of his cousins, and they were like: 'Yeah, man. Go for it.'

This sort of arrangement had been the norm until his grandfather, Mahendra, became the first king to take only one wife at a time. The tradition had faded, but Dipendra knew that when he was king, he could do as he pleased. Such talk was known throughout the family. One older relative thought Devyani, being such a strong character, 'would have been senior queen, of course. Maybe he would even have three or four wives. The atmosphere would probably have inspired him'.

In quieter moments, the crown prince rationalised his infatuation for the part-Indian Devyani to his cousins: 'Think about how much control I could have with India, just by one marriage . . . It doesn't have to be her. It could be any [suitable Indian woman], but particularly this one.' A strategic alliance with Devyani's family – with its powerful Indian political connections – could do away with the possibility of a repeat of the trade embargo of the late 1980s, which led directly to the fall of the absolute monarchy. The marriage would 'neutralise' India, he said, just as he boasted of neutralising Britain by awarding it an arms contract.

As the official quest to find Dipendra a bride ground on, the field was cut back to such an extent that there was only one name left: Supriya Shah, the crown prince's first love whom the queen had forbidden him to marry only a few years earlier. While Queen Aishwarya had stopped that match the first time around – because they were too young and too 'close' – Supriya was now seen as the best alternative to the unpalatable Devyani.

The choice caused many to speculate that the queen was being bloody-minded, that she was simply exerting her power. The crown prince would argue that they were no longer in the Dark Ages. He could draw on the fact that King Mahendra had abolished the caste system back in the '60s and therefore the main objections to Devyani were invalid. But all this was to no avail. The queen wasn't budging and neither was he.

'Devyani was such a player,' Dipendra's cousin Krishna said. 'Once she got in, she made him feel she was indispensable. She used to give him expensive gifts. Every day she used to cook for him and send the food over. The ADCs would go and pick it up. She was a good continental cook . . . Sometimes she sent food here. She was trying to win us all over. That's how she worked.'

When Dipendra gathered with his old Budhanilkantha school friends at Tribhuvan Sadan, he would talk a lot about girls. One of his friends recalled it as Dipendra's great weakness: 'All day, all night, he'd dream about girls. That was the environment that others created. He had nothing else to do.' When the crown prince introduced Devyani to this group, they were mightily impressed. She was so friendly and obviously talented. But as time went on, they came to dislike her and would exchange stories about her ambition. The old school friends were pleased that Queen Aishwarya was holding out against the union and couldn't help thinking that Supriya had been the better choice all along.

'What I have heard, but not seen,' one friend recalled, 'is that whenever Devyani used to go out of the country, she used to bring presents for each and every person who surrounded the crown prince, from the very lowest to the highest . . . I don't think it was necessary. When we came to know about these things, we realised there was something mysterious going on.'

'Kiran', another of Dipendra's cousins, could see an important difference between the two women: 'Supriya was taught the proper way of dealing with people. She dealt with his ADCs as an employee, she dealt with the secretary as a secretary. But Devyani started becoming friends with all the ADCs, drinking partners, private home parties.' Indeed, Devyani already knew one of the ADC's wives, who was a college friend and cousin. She therefore didn't have to wait for the crown prince to tell her what he was doing.

Sometime around 1998, Dipendra told Supriya he was going to marry Devyani. Still, he demanded Supriya's total fidelity. He forbade her from working and told her that if she married anyone else, he would 'finish the guy off'. It all led to speculation that maybe he did intend to marry them both when he became king, which probably wasn't going to be too far off. King Birendra suffered a heart attack in November 1998, aged fifty-two. Considering that King Mahendra had died at the age of fifty-five and King Tribhuvan at forty-nine, both from heart attacks, Birendra was on borrowed time.

Just weeks before the heart attack, Kirti Nidhi Bista, a former prime minister, was at a dinner with the royal family when Queen Aishwarya pulled him aside and asked if he could have a word to the crown prince. She was worried that there was no royal heir. 'Dipendra has to marry,' she told Bista. 'Go and tell him.'

The tall Brahmin politician didn't find it a difficult topic to broach – Dipendra's marital status was public property. 'Are you not going to marry?' Bista asked. 'It's time for you to marry.' But the crown prince laughed the old man off. He wasn't going to engage in that subject.

The crown prince's royal duties – sitting in on King Birendra's meetings to learn the ropes of the family business, overseeing security at Narayanhiti Palace, and the occasional trip overseas – left him with a fair amount of time on his hands.

Dipendra liked the idea of becoming the first person in his family to have a PhD, so as soon as he'd finished his master's he went to see Dr Bal Kumar K.C. Excited as he was at the prospect of being the supervisor to Nepal's first royal doctorate, Dr K.C. knew it would take four or five years, so he wanted to make sure that his student's heart was in it.

'Why don't you concentrate on the situation of the country?' the professor asked him. 'You don't *need* a PhD.'

'Yes, sir, you're right,' the crown prince replied, 'but this is modern Nepal, and the people and the government have to deal with the country's problems. We have less to do with it.'

'What did your father say? Did he tell you to do a PhD?'

'The king said I can do it, but not at the expense of my royal duties.'

Dipendra wanted to do an extension of his master's thesis, comparing fertility rates of people who had lived in Kathmandu for generations to those who had migrated to the capital from other regions. Student and tutor would wait for the 2001 census data, which would not be released until 2002. They also wanted to take their time because if Dipendra did it too quickly, people might think Dr K.C. had done all the work himself.

The professor was asked to keep Wednesdays free so that he could hasten over to the palace whenever Dipendra called. Could be any time. During these sessions, they'd spend hours brainstorming and discussing academic concepts, as well as just chatting about the state of the world. Dr K.C. couldn't help thinking that Dipendra was teaching him more than he taught Dipendra. The crown prince had visited more of the remote areas than the teacher and had been briefed from the grassroots up to the level of world leaders.

Dipendra talked of his dreams of one day creating a constitutional monarchy with 'less power but more influence', of going into the houses of the people, visiting development sites and praising those doing good work. He would share their experiences and become the heart and soul of the nation. He had a clear vision for the country.

Although there was a growing undercurrent of tension with his mother, Dipendra continued to be the dutiful son. Every day, when they weren't otherwise busy, he visited his parents at their residence at about 10 am. At 1 pm, they lunched together, and at 9.30 pm, they'd sit down to dinner.

When the crown prince was travelling with Her Majesty, he would act as her bodyguard. He'd tell her ADCs he could do a better job than them – not just because he was such a crack shot and a karate expert, but because he was free to manhandle her to safety whereas they might hesitate.

Palace security became one of Dipendra's growing obsessions. Being something of a gadget freak, he had organised the computerisation of the security forces. He programmed the ADCs' walkie-talkies and always carried one with him. To many, he was a hardware bore, talking incessantly about technology, guns, helicopters and radios.

All his cousins had grown up with guns and were interested in them. They talked about them a lot, but less so as they got older. Dipendra, on the other hand, seemed to get deeper into it all. He knew the thickness of springs, the drop of a bullet over certain distances, the impact at fifty metres, at 100 metres.

He even boasted that he had advised an arms manufacturer on how to improve a particular gun, and that some of his ideas had been implemented. When he'd move the conversation on to specialist security weapons, about which his cousins had no knowledge – Israeli-designed Uzi submachine-guns and other such things – they'd find themselves making polite excuses to leave.

One of his uncles, Prabhakar Rana, who was generally impressed by the crown prince's intelligence, remembers whispering to him once at a social gathering, 'Sir, as a crown prince, should you only talk about that subject?' It was usually not such a big faux pas because Dipendra always gravitated towards military people at these functions anyway.

At an extended family party, Dipendra was getting drunk with Krishna when Devyani whispered to the now-married cousin, 'Stop serving him drinks.' She had already started acting like his wife and it was out of hand as far as Krishna was concerned. 'It's my wife's family's party,' he told her. 'If you don't like it, you leave.'

Like many of the crown prince's friends, Krishna didn't like the way Devyani was starting to control those in the crown prince's circle – the way people made way for her when she walked into a room, clearing a space next to Dipendra as if she was already queen. He had it out with her: 'You are my [cousin] brother's girlfriend. You are just a girlfriend.' That ended the conversation and pretty much ended his social connection to the couple.

Once it had become known to Dipendra's cousins that Devyani was not approved by the queen, it became difficult for them to remain neutral. Even if they supported CP's desire to marry whomever he chose, they couldn't voice that support without fear of upsetting the king and queen. As a result, the crown prince started moving away from his family-based circle.

He started telling little fibs to avoid their social gatherings. Devyani's young professional friends were far more understanding of his aching heart.

'He hung around a group of people who accepted Devyani,' Krishna recalled. 'He wanted people around him to recognise the fact that she was his woman, and for people to treat her as the future queen.' They were 'Yes-Sire' types, by Krishna's reckoning. Where a cousin-brother might be able to give him a reality check, these new friends never would. Instead, they provided their houses for the couple to keep up their secret rendezvous. But as the 1990s drew to a close, the couple started playing a more dangerous game. Dipendra would send his ADCs out to sneak Devyani into the palace.

It was a game in which Devyani had the most to lose. Not only were they defying the queen, but if such behaviour became widely known, it would rule her out of marrying anyone else in Nepal. Time was no longer on the couple's side, they were playing for all or nothing. 'This talk about Devyani and CP had gone all over India,' remarked Krishna. 'If she didn't get married to CP it would be a big blow for the whole Gwalior family, you see.'

chapter 21

the games

hile Dipendra's generation of cousins had all been crazy drinkers and potheads, it seemed to Krishna that they settled down and sobered up by their late twenties. All except Dipendra, who 'became more haywire'.

'This guy was like an overgrown baby. We used to try to talk to him about starting up royalpalace.com, and he would be talking about playboy.com. "Grow out of it. You're nearly thirty, man." He had a *Penthouse* spread as his screensaver. We presumed he would grow up, because knowing him, he had all the potential. He was like two different personalities. Outside he played out his duties beautifully, he had a wonderful public image, but inside you could see his frustrations.'

One of his cousins involved in the Nepal Sports Council remembered coming to Dipendra with the news that some of the best shooters in the west of the country had gone over to the Maoists. 'I cannot control the shooters in the west,' the cousin told him. 'They have seven weapons over there. With those weapons, do you know how many people can be trained [as snipers] in one-and-a-half years' time?' But Dipendra just seemed interested in chatting about what was hot on TV, the internet, the top line of watches, and clothes. The cousin thought this was a reflection of the tastes of the crown prince's new friends.

The hours he was keeping were getting more extreme. He would sit in his room late into the night, a ball of restless energy, trawling the internet and smoking joints. Often he'd call whichever of his two senior ADCs was on duty and they'd drink whisky and chat into the early hours.

One night in June 2000, Dipendra had just returned from dinner with his parents at about 10 pm when he summoned Colonel Sundar Pratap Rana, the ADC who used to scale walls to retrieve dead pigeons for the then-teenage crown prince. Sundar Pratap was now a senior ADC for the king, but with no further duties to be performed that night, he hurried along to the crown prince's residence. Such calls weren't unusual; they'd talk about military matters, politics or anything else they felt like.

On this night, however, Dipendra's marriage plans were the only item on the agenda. The soldier had never met Devyani Rana, but he'd heard palace whispers about the conflict between the crown prince and the queen over his choice of bride.

Dipendra looked despondent. 'I don't think I will get permission to marry her,' he said.

'Your Highness, your parents cannot do that to you,' the soldier replied, simply trying to put a positive spin on things. 'Most probably, at your birthday they will announce the marriage.'

The ADC would later think back that maybe Dipendra had been trying to sound him out on the king's feelings, and perhaps he was hoping something of his unhappiness might be conveyed to his father. If that was his intention, it failed. Sundar Pratap would never talk to His Majesty about such personal matters.

The ADC was from a humble background, and no relation

to the former ruling Rana family. His positive thinking had got him to where he was, and so he continued to make confident noises about the crown prince's birthday party, which was only a couple of weeks away. What else could he say?

As a result of the pep talk, Dipendra may have awaited the 27 June palace soirée with unusual anticipation. The party kicked off at 7.30 pm with the crown prince playing the good host, greeting his guests – ambassadors, government officials, military brass and all the royal relatives – as they arrived. Five of his old Budhanilkantha friends were also there, as usual. They found it easy to mingle because so many of the top military people had been undercover teachers at their school.

At such functions, the elders take their food first, leaving the younger generation to stand around for up to an hour, getting steadily more merry as they wait their turn. So by the time the older ones were ready to cut the birthday cake, the young people were still eating.

'Call him to cut the cake,' ordered the queen, as word went out to find the birthday boy. 'He's twenty-nine years old. Do I have to hold his hand to cut the cake?' she quipped. Such a comment was regarded as quite a slur within the delicate confines of palace etiquette.

One of Dipendra's closest school friends, 'Tej', noticed he looked depressed. As the prince mingled, Tej took the opportunity to find out why.

'I'm very upset,' Dipendra told him. 'I have drunk a lot. I'm out of control. I just went out and vomited.'

This mood seemed unusual to Tej. They'd been on plenty of drinking bouts before, but usually it just made Dipendra cheerful. Tej wanted to ask more but other people were nearby – diplomats and officials.

Dipendra called over one of the king's senior military aides, 'Bim', whom he had known since he was a boy – the same aide to whom Dipendra had once confided that he'd never known love. The crown prince looked irritated and angry as he launched into a rant. 'You know, I'm twenty-nine. Next year I'll be thirty. I'm not married. Is it my problem? Is it your problem?

Whose problem is it?' He was aggressive, almost threatening. Bim didn't know what to say.

The party reached its scheduled end at eleven o'clock without the announcement Dipendra had hoped for. As the bulk of the crowd went home, the crown prince worked his way through the younger family members, inviting them all back to his place, Tribhuvan Sadan, for a more relaxed celebration.

His brother-in-law, Gorakh, wanted to go home because Princess Shruti, his wife, was five months pregnant and he had to work the next day at Grindlays Bank. 'Let's just stay for a little bit,' Shruti said to him. 'If there's a problem, we can leave anytime.' So, like the others, they made their way through the palace grounds to the billiard room attached to Dipendra's residence.

Guests were pouring themselves drinks at the little bar near the door when Dipendra asked them to gather around. He had something to say.

'Well, as you all know, it's been difficult for me to reach a decision as to who I should marry,' he told them. 'I've toyed with the idea for six or seven years, but I've made my choice. I have decided to marry Devyani and if anyone has anything to say, speak up now.' The crown prince scanned the crowd, daring anyone to protest.

There was a murmur of assent. 'No man, it's your choice.' But most were silent. The younger generation tended to be supportive of, or at least ambivalent towards, his plans. It was up to him, he was an educated man. 'Okay then, let's have a drink and party,' he said at last.

Most of the men went back to the bar. Some started a game of pool while Dipendra went up to his room to change out of his formal clothes.

Gorakh and Princess Shruti went with some of the women out to the lounge chairs on the verandah, which fronted onto a little courtyard garden. Among the younger generation, they were the most open about supporting Queen Aishwarya on the marriage question. They both thought Dipendra had just made a big mistake announcing his intention to defy her. Dipendra had always been rational to his brother-in-law about his plans to marry Devyani so when the crown prince reappeared wearing a tracksuit, Gorakh took the opportunity to pull him aside. They had known one another since attending school at Budhanilkantha together, and Gorakh was Devyani's fourth cousin and good friend, so he felt in a position to say something.

'Why have you done it this way?' he asked. 'Why not ask your parents first? People will go around talking about it now. Why do you want to put yourself in such a bind?'

Dipendra's expression changed to a sneer. 'Well, I've made up my mind. If you're not with me, you're against me. You're sitting on the fence.'

This struck Gorakh as odd, since he clearly wasn't sitting on the fence. He knew the conservative nature of their society and felt the gossip would be harmful. 'You know you have to be careful about these things,' he tried to reason. Gorakh had told Dipendra as much before. In fact, he'd gone further, saying that one had to marry whomever was considered appropriate. This time, however, his words sent Dipendra off.

'Anyone who gets in my way – I don't care whether it's my father, my mother, my grandmother – I'll kill them. I'll finish the monarchy and bring down the whole institution with me.'

Princess Shruti was listening from about ten metres away. She made a peculiarly Nepali exclamation, '*Oof*!', to signify that she was sick of all this nonsense.

Dipendra heard it. He suddenly turned and ran at her, grabbing the mother-to-be by the throat and throwing her to the ground. She was on all fours. He stood over her like he was about to kick her in the stomach, but her female cousins came running across: 'What are you doing to your sister? She's pregnant!'

Gorakh stood and watched, helpless, knowing he couldn't raise a hand to a crown prince. Dipendra threw one of the cousins up against a wall, and another onto the floor. He then karate-kicked a large flowerpot, which toppled and smashed.

Gorakh pulled his wife to her feet as Dipendra raved, 'Get out of my house, now.' Gorakh didn't know how to leave appropriately. Dipendra was jumping up and down like a spoilt brat, high as hell on alcohol and grass, Gorakh thought.

'And if you go now don't ever bother coming back,' the crown prince's tirade continued. 'I will never do anything for you. Consider yourself gone.' The other men had rushed out from the bar and were trying to coax Dipendra away, saying, 'Relax, man, relax.'

'You're either with me or against me on this,' he repeated. 'What's it going to be?'

The threat to kill anyone who got in his way greatly unsettled Gorakh. Coming from anyone else, it could easily be ignored, but Gorakh had previously heard about his old school friend's threats to kill any new boyfriend of Supriya's, and he tended to believe that the crown prince was capable of it. He had visions of Dipendra turning up at their house with the army in tow, walking inside, blasting away and then being saluted as he came out with a smoking gun.

Even after the birthday incident, Crown Prince Dipendra had his supporters within the family. Some of the male cousins thought that it had been inappropriate for Princess Shruti to comment on his affairs. In Hindu culture, when a woman marries, she leaves her family and becomes part of her husband's clan, free to play a role in her new family as her seniority grows with age and each baby. But she no longer has a say in what goes on in her old family.

Part of the reason Dipendra resented Shruti's opposition to his marrying Devyani was that he thought she owed him some support. A few years earlier, the beautiful princess had attracted no shortage of marriage offers from the princely families of India; she, however, wanted to stay in Nepal. Cousins recalled that the crown prince stood up to his parents, demanding they listen to Shruti's pleas to be allowed to marry a Nepali. 'My sister has already said no to India,' he told them. 'Why are you taking more offers from India? Take some from Nepal.'

After she married Gorakh Shamsher Rana, in May 1997, Dipendra couldn't help feeling that his support had not been reciprocated as his own struggles with their parents intensified. She was a close friend of Dipendra's first love, Supriya, going back to their school days, and this probably influenced her leanings. The relationship between the two siblings became tense. Dipendra saw his mother talking to Shruti, but never to him, and Shruti had always been the king's favourite. He felt increasingly left out.

Gorakh was a little surprised then, when Dipendra came to his house on the Friday following the birthday fracas. He wanted to apologise. Gorakh accepted, of course, and like everyone else in the family, just wanted to forget it had ever happened. But Dipendra refused to apologise to his sister. This created a problem, since Father's Day was approaching and the royal children always attended this day of celebration together.

The queen stepped in, asking Princess Shruti to apologise to her older brother. 'I know it's his fault,' she told Shruti, 'but he's your brother. Just make up and come to Father's Day together.'

Shruti agreed. When she said sorry to her brother, he reacted like he had scored a major victory. 'So now we're friends again,' he said.

As patron of the Nepalese Olympic Committee, Crown Prince Dipendra found himself with a job to do in September 2000. The Sydney Games also provided him with the opportunity to strut on an international stage.

Dipendra flew to Australia accompanied by his two aides-de-camp, his personal assistant, a doctor and a servant. He had a local driver. Three Australian Federal Police officers provided added security, and a staffer from the Australian Embassy in Kathmandu was seconded to his entourage.

At dinner on the first night, the crown prince was, as

usual, the life of the party and had everyone laughing. He was in great form. Throughout the trip, he appeared to maintain firm discipline with his drinking, and on most mornings, he was the first to wake. He'd go into his ADCs' room. 'Wake up! Wake up! Let's get moving.' He was invigorated by the activity.

They were staying at Quay West, a hotel in the heart of the city, with the Opera House just a javelin's throw away, out the huge windows.

A friend of Dipendra's, a fabulously wealthy Kuwaiti prince, was also staying at Quay West and invited him up to his room. Dipendra had thought his own accommodation was impressive until he saw the Kuwaiti's lavish suite on the hotel's top floor. He felt humbled, but this was nothing a little bullshit couldn't fix.

On the flight to Sydney, ADC Raju Karki had been telling the crown prince about a VIP protection course he had recently attended where he'd learned, among other things, that most fire-brigade ladders didn't extend beyond the tenth floor. So Dipendra told the Kuwaiti that the only reason he was staying in such a low-level room was because his ADCs insisted on it for his safety.

From the start of the Olympic visit, though, his security team was given a very real safety concern. Dipendra was keen to go skydiving while he was in Sydney, and ordered his ADCs to organise it. This presented them with a huge headache: they were responsible for His Royal Highness's safety and here he was, ordering them to endanger it. It was like so many things the ADCs had to do. They would later be criticised for allegedly getting drugs for him, but they had little choice in such matters. Their job was to serve him. The permanent ADCs were like good Hindu wives, loyal, obedient and in it for life.

The two aides were forced therefore to go through the motions of organising the skydiving, all the while delaying and trying to think of a way to avoid it. Eventually, they went into cahoots with the embassy official to say that the Australian Government wouldn't allow him to jump. Dipendra accepted the 'decision' politely.

The crown prince handled his range of official engagements with his usual easy charm. At dinner with the Nepalese athletes, he showed why he was so adored by his people. He was full of encouragement for everyone. 'Even if you don't win, it doesn't matter,' he assured them. 'But if you can get the Nepalese record, I will give you a medal when you get home.' With the judo team, he got up and demonstrated techniques, and regardless of how useful his instructions were to his country's best martial artists, they thought his involvement was a great boost.

Yet the crown prince also showed the other side of his personality. At an International Olympic Committee reception at Darling Harbour, he was to be met by an official at the door and escorted upstairs. But when Dipendra arrived, no one was there to greet him. A complete change came over him. An obvious anger welled up inside, but he contained it in the most focused way. And as the minutes ticked by with still no one coming down to meet him, the intensity and focus of his unblinking rage scared those who saw it.

Early in the Australian trip, an old school friend of Dipendra's, now resident in Sydney, got in touch with him. The friend came to the hotel and the crown prince was at his most relaxed, readily accepting an invitation to visit the friend's modest home in Sydney's western suburbs.

In the privacy of the home, however, Dipendra let his guard down and drank a few too many Dimple Scotches. The friends talked loudly and happily, exchanging stories about school and the times since. Dipendra spoke of smashing a car at Eton.

But as the drink took hold, others listening in couldn't help but notice that the crown prince was depressed. He complained that no one in his family understood him, that he was alone, and openly admitted it was the issue of marriage that was causing his melancholy. He felt he might go crazy, he said; he could do anything at any time. He felt his family was against him and he was on his own. He was especially upset with his mother.

Dipendra told his friend not to worry, though; by *Baisaakh* (the Nepalese month from mid April to mid May) the following year there would be some news on the marriage front. Everything would have settled down by then. Despite his openness with his old school friend, the crown prince was still shrewd enough to withhold the details of a rendezvous he had planned with his lover.

Coinciding with the Olympics, Devyani told her circle in Kathmandu that she was off to London for a holiday.

Her close friend 'Sita' was a little suspicious. She asked Devyani, 'How come every time the crown prince leaves the country, you leave the country?'

Devyani immediately picked up on what was being insinuated. 'No way, I wouldn't have the guts,' she insisted. 'It's just that the only chance I get to leave is when he's not here.'

Satisfied, Sita gave her a shopping list for London.

Devyani flew into Sydney on a flight from Moscow on the day the crown prince had finished his list of official engagements. Her arrival was top secret, kept even from Dipendra's personal assistant. ADC Raju Karki was sent to pick her up at the airport. She greeted him like a friend.

Arriving at the hotel, she was whisked into the crown prince's room, where she stayed. No one else was allowed in. When they'd leave the hotel, those few people in the know would go ahead to check that no other Nepalis were in the foyer. 'It was like a big secret that everybody knew,' said one of the staff.

Dipendra and Devyani enjoyed the sights of Sydney as young lovers, visiting Taronga Zoo and Darling Harbour, taking a lunch cruise on the harbour, and dining at various restaurants. They were always holding hands and kissing, 'in a very decent way'. Dipendra had talked about shaving off his beard so he would be less recognisable, but didn't go through with it. Instead, he just pulled his white Nike cap low over his eyes, which were hidden behind a pair of dark sunglasses. It had the desired effect.

But a volatility in the relationship was lurking just beneath the surface. At an Italian restaurant at Circular Quay, heads turned when the crown prince suddenly gesticulated and knocked a fork off the table. His voice was raised: 'You always drive me crazy at lunchtime with all these questions. You always piss me off when I'm eating, nagging me. Stop it!' Devyani looked embarrassed by the sudden attention, but they seemed to get over it quickly and were soon chatting again.

The couple spent almost two weeks together, sightseeing and shopping in the anonymity of a foreign city. Devyani did not accompany Dipendra to the Games, however. Instead she'd go out shopping again, often buying little gifts for the staff. All from her own money, of which she seemed to have plenty. They weren't sure why she did it. Maybe it was to buy their silence, maybe she was just a generous, down-to-earth person. They didn't mind.

Those within the royal party thought very highly of Devyani, and when told that the crown prince was going to marry her, they could allow themselves to respect her despite the scandalous nature of her accommodation. They knew she would become a great queen. She'd talk politics with them and was never overbearing. She was a good listener and had a mind of her own. And like the ADCs, she seemed very concerned for the prince's welfare.

Devyani left Sydney three days before the Games' closing ceremony. The crown prince sent an ADC off with instructions that he wasn't to leave the airport until he had seen her plane take off. This was interpreted as a sign of how much he loved her.

After that, a staff member presented him with a bottle of

Dimple. 'You bought this bottle thinking I will drink it myself?' the crown prince asked him that evening. 'I will drink it with you. You should not buy these expensive gifts.' Together then, they drank, talked and watched television.

The crown prince spoke of his father and brother, but not his mother. He talked about the time his parents came to an open day at Eton when his brother was in a boxing match. Prince Nirajan was so badly beaten he cried, and his father had too much to drink. 'My dad was so drunk he nearly fell over,' he said of King Birendra. 'They were all laughing. He couldn't understand what people were saying to him.'

But Dipendra also talked about his dreams for Nepal, about opening up the palace – 'It can't be a dinosaur any more.' His ideas came bursting through but they were all tempered by the fact he could do nothing. He was frustrated.

chapter 22
the arm wrestle

δ evyani Rana had returned home from Australia without any of Sita's London shopping. But her friend still didn't suspect a thing.

Whispers of the trip were said to have filtered back to Kathmandu, creating quite a ripple. It was reported that when Australian officials confirmed Devyani's visit, it drove a further wedge between the lovers and Queen Aishwarya. As the *New Yorker* later put it, the trip 'suggested a degree of intimacy that in itself would have ruined Devyani's marriage prospects'.

Meanwhile, talk of the birthday-party incident months earlier had slowly wound through the upper echelons of the palace staff. It resonated with some who'd heard Crown Prince Dipendra make similar, 'If I go down, everybody goes down' comments.

One of Dipendra's ADCs, Gajendra Bohra, even told others that he wanted to leave the crown prince's service. They were great friends – almost best friends – but Dipendra was too demanding, too moody, fickle and cunning. Bohra wanted a life of his own, but once inside the golden cage, the crown prince would not allow him to leave.

One day, Dipendra called his father's senior aide, 'Bim', for a chat in his office. The crown prince still hadn't told his father of his intention to marry Devyani, despite having made the public vow. Time was against him. Dipendra could expect his first heart attack within twenty-five years since only one of the Shah line since Prithwi Narayan Shah had lived beyond fifty-five years of age. He had to get a move on, for the sake of his own love and the continuation of the line. He wanted Bim's help.

'Do you want me to talk to His Majesty?' asked the aide.
'Yes.'
'How would you like me to present your case?'
'That's up to you.'
'Have you asked other people to do this too?'
'Yes.' The crown prince listed several ex-generals close to His Majesty. But Dipendra thought about it for a while, then changed his mind. He asked Bim to hold off for three months. 'I will do it my own way first,' he told the ADC.

Bim waited, as instructed. Once the three months had passed, in which time the crown prince had said nothing more on the subject, the king's aide asked if he should go ahead and approach His Majesty. 'No, I changed my mind,' Dipendra told him. 'You are still working in the palace so it would be inappropriate that you take my case to him. You may get in trouble.'

Dipendra continued networking, though, trying to build a coalition of support. Shortly after this, in early May 2001, his former guardian and Birendra's old friend Lord Camoys sent a fax to the king urging him to allow the marriage to take place. The Englishman had known Pashupati Rana even longer than the forty-two years he'd known the king, and Devyani and Dipendra had met at his home. From a western perspective, there was no reason why the marriage should not proceed. But whatever influence Lord Camoys might have had with King Birendra, he couldn't sway the queen. 'The queen was very strong, intelligent,' Bim recalled, 'and the crown prince was the same. Very similar types. His Majesty was just a spectator between them. He couldn't really stop it. He was so gentle.'

Certainly, Dipendra wasn't handling it too well. He was stacking on weight. He got rid of his beard, but then went about unshaven, and his eyes spoke of heavy nights. He was smoking more ganja and drinking more whisky than ever. Often he wouldn't get out of bed until 9 or 10 am – a freakishly late hour for a Nepali. He and Devyani were talking a lot on the phone, late into the night. Then he would call her again at about 2 am, every night, presumably for a quick goodnight, because the calls never lasted more than a minute.

Outside, they had started to flaunt their affair more. Since his announcement the previous June, they had begun to be seen at restaurants like Fire and Ice, an Italian place on the edge of the tourist district of Thamel with the horn-tooting ambience of any Nepalese street. It is opposite the entrance lane to Gorakh and Princess Shruti's house. So public had the affair become that the winner of the Miss Nepal pageant was asked if she thought the crown prince should marry the woman he loved. When she said he should follow his heart and marry for love, the audience reacted with a standing ovation.

Devyani's mother had visited Queen Aishwarya at the palace some time in 2000. An ADC led Usha Rana into the queen's chamber on what was billed as a social call. He left the two women alone and the subject of the discussion has never been revealed.

Sita and Devyani had been close since childhood, but Devyani was always uncomfortable talking about Dipendra, and so Sita wouldn't ask. Even when he rang Devyani while Sita was there, Devyani would avoid the issue.

It had only been since late 1999 that Devyani would even admit to having a relationship with the crown prince, four years after her friend had first quizzed her. When at last Devyani did come clean, Sita wondered how she could tolerate Supriya Shah always being around. 'Well, she was in the picture way before me,' Devyani said of Dipendra's first love. 'They had such a strong relationship.'

'I don't care,' Sita said. 'I would never put up with another woman.'

Devyani just seemed to accept it.

One day in early 2001, however, she turned up at Sita's with a black eye. 'It looks like a punch,' Sita's husband joked. He would never have said such a thing if he suspected it were true. Then there was a second incident, which she claimed was the result of falling down the stairs. 'I was upset,' she explained.

Devyani's grandmother – the prominent Indian politician Bijaya Raje Scindia – had died recently, and her mother Usha had been suffering heart problems. There was enough going on in Devyani's life to cause her to be falling down stairs, Sita reasoned.

According to her family's version of events, a bruised Devyani joined her mother in the United States, where Usha's brother-in-law, a heart surgeon, performed an angioplasty. Devyani stayed on to look after her. Sita, however, heard that Devyani broke her jaw and flew to the States for treatment. When she returned, she still had bruising.

'I guess she wanted to create this image in front of me that everything was perfect and happy,' Sita would recall. 'She was very emotional and I guess this [pressure from Dipendra] was all happening. She changed quite a bit. From what I saw, they had become quite desperate. Come what may, she had to get married.'

Devyani was getting ever more short-tempered. If a waiter was a bit slow bringing a meal, she'd create a scene. Her friends felt she had become arrogant. Sita even had fights with her where she'd blurt out, 'You're not the queen yet.' At other times, though, Devyani could still be her old self, generous and kind. 'She was always there when I needed her,' Sita remembered. 'But she used to be very irritable, shouting at everybody . . . she would never tell me what was wrong. From what we've heard now, he used to abuse her.'

After a fight with Dipendra, Devyani often used to turn her mobile phone off and go into hiding. Dipendra would ring all her friends, trying to find her. He never had anything to say to Sita, just 'Where's Devyani?' Dipendra's ADCs noticed that when he'd had a fight with Devyani, the crown prince would dress up in full combat gear, with camouflage jacket and cap. He'd grab a few guns from the arsenal he kept in his room and go out driving in his souped-up Toyota Landcruiser. It was stress relief, as far as they could tell.

On one occasion when Dipendra was looking for Devyani, he heard she was at Sita's house. Soon he arrived in the grey Landcruiser. Sita's husband didn't know Devyani was hiding out, however, and so called to her, 'Hey, your boyfriend's here to pick you up.' Weeks later they learned that Dipendra thought they were all accomplices in some game of cat and mouse; that he was angry with them for hiding her. From then on, they'd never tell him if Devyani was there.

At public functions, the crown prince would arrive with the king and queen. If he spotted Sita, he'd go over to her and whisper, 'So where's your friend?' Everyone would crowd around her with interest – 'What's he saying?' they'd all ask. Sita hated the attention, and hated his little games.

One observer who knew Dipendra better than anyone, and had come to know Devyani through the relationship, didn't deny that the affair sometimes got violent, but was adamant that Dipendra was deeply in love. They would have their fights one day, but be affectionate the next.

The observer presumed that Devyani genuinely loved the crown prince, but she was getting desperate. She had invested seven or eight years in the relationship without an engagement and it was becoming well known that she was Dipendra's girl.

When her parents had tried to get her married elsewhere, she told them she was in love with the crown prince. They agreed to wait for a year for a proposal to come from the palace. As each year passed with no offer, she'd ask them to wait some more. 'And it wasn't like they could say, "Forget him, we'll find someone better." He was the Crown Prince of Nepal.' As the years went by, her parents put more pressure on her and so she, in turn, put more pressure on Dipendra.

Not only had she gone so far that if she didn't marry him her reputation was in tatters, but the reputation of her whole family was at risk. Typical of the gossip, one royal relative noted: 'Apparently her mother was going around India saying her daughter was going to get married to the Crown Prince of Nepal. It had become common knowledge here. Everybody talked about it. I think she got too exposed . . . In a society like ours, once it's public knowledge that a girl is involved with some guy, it would be very difficult to find another guy who's willing to forget that. This is a small society.' According to one of Dipendra's cousins, she had to hang on to the crown prince at all costs: with everyone saying she'd be queen, anything less would have destroyed her ego.

It was by no means one-way traffic, as Dipendra's family portrayed it. Devyani's family have claimed that she wasn't desperate, just fed up with the uncertainty, the gossip and the constant tension.

Devyani tried to end the relationship several times. On one occasion she applied to Brown University in the United States where her brothers-in-law had helped arrange admission for further studies. But the crown prince simply would not let go. His persistence succeeded in breaking her resolve time after time.

Devyani's family had received proposals from some of India's finest families – reportedly the houses of Jodhpur, Bhagalpur, Jaipur and Baroda. One resolute young Indian royal set himself up at the Yak and Yeti hotel determined not to leave until he had Devyani Rana's hand. But Dipendra threatened to take poison unless she stayed true to him. Her family had to tell the Indian that they were sorry but their daughter could not marry him.

'It was the crown prince who pursued her from the beginning and would not let go,' a family friend pointed out. 'When the most eligible (or so we thought) young man like the Crown Prince of Nepal was so persistent in his affections, it does become hard for any young lady to resist.'

Queen Aishwarya's great ally in this battle of wills was Queen Mother Ratna. She was, by this time, the most respected person in the royal family, but fifty years earlier Ratna had been despised by King Tribhuvan for what she represented – the ascendancy of the Ranas.

If King Tribhuvan had had his way, the end of the Rana regime would also have seen the end of intermarriage between the two powerful clans. But some months before the Shahs had fled to India in 1950, the Rana wife of Crown Prince Mahendra, Indra, died, having produced an heir and five other children. Following their glorious return home in February 1951, Mahendra found himself in love with Ratna, his dead wife's sister.

By then, the democracy campaigner B.P. Koirala had become home minister in one of the unstable early governments. In his autobiography *Atmabrittanta*, Koirala would recall how Crown Prince Mahendra dropped in unannounced at his house one evening. Koirala's baby daughter had died that same morning and his family had just returned from her funeral, but the prince was too tied up in his own affairs to care.

Mahendra announced he was about to resign as crown prince and pulled out a letter of resignation with his royal seal. He said that he wished to marry his sister-in-law but his father would not permit it.

Koirala advised him to try to reach an understanding with his father rather than taking such drastic action. But the prince replied that he was being asked to marry a woman the king had chosen, and to disregard the woman he loved. 'I will become a commoner so that I can marry her.'

'But this is also a democratic right, and Your Highness should not have to abdicate on that count. I will say this to His Majesty.'

'Please try and resolve this matter quickly,' Mahendra urged the minister.

When Koirala next met with King Tribhuvan, at a party, they went out onto a balcony to talk. The king's other two sons, princes Himalaya and Basundhara, followed them out. Koirala told them what the crown prince had said, and the king replied that he would accept the prince's resignation.

Koirala protested: 'But that is not proper, not allowing him to marry someone of his choice. It goes against democratic norms and my own beliefs.'

'He wants to marry into the Ranas, whereas I am saying that we must sever our relationship with them.'

'How can a girl be rejected for the fact of being born into a particular clan? It was the Rana regime that was evil, not individual Ranas.' Koirala continued to plead his case, then asked, 'If you do accept the crown prince's resignation, who will take his place?'

'Here. He will,' the king replied, pointing to his son Himalaya.

'No, it will have to be Birendra,' said Koirala, referring to Mahendra's first-born, still an infant. 'He will be the king, not Himalaya.'

It appeared that King Tribhuvan had not thought about the correct line of succession. Given the family history, he was reluctant to contemplate another child on the throne. Minister Koirala, whose romantic side had been touched by the abdication of King Edward VIII of Britain to marry American divorcee Wallis Simpson, brokered a deal whereby the king agreed to a six-month cooling-off period.

After the allotted time, plans were made for the wedding, but King Tribhuvan made sure he was out of the valley at the time. What would normally have been a huge show of colour and wealth was a quiet and private affair at the royal holiday palace at Nagarjun.

While democratic rights may have helped Queen Mother Ratna marry into her post, it was caste nitpicking that would motivate this granddaughter of Juddha Shamsher to give a lot less than she was given. Her story did, however, give Dipendra inspiration. 'When my parents are away,' he told Bim, 'I can get married. I can go to Nagarjun and ask the district chairman to give us a certificate.' Or maybe, he thought, they could go to the family bungalows at Chitwan or Pokhara and not come back until his parents accepted their new daughter-in-law.

But Dipendra knew from the way the queen used to say, 'I have two sons' that he was placing his accession on the line. He had already been told he could marry the girl he wanted, but he'd have to leave the throne for his brother Nirajan, seven-and-a-half years his junior.

According to one senior member of the family, it was well known that Prince Nirajan, who had always been in awe of his older brother, had offered to help Dipendra in such a situation by becoming crown prince and then abdicating in favour of his brother when King Birendra died. But Dipendra's ego was too large to accept this. 'And Nirajan was a very shy, quiet kid. He smoked more hash than any of them and you just couldn't imagine him as a king,' the family member said.

Queen Aishwarya also had a lot to lose, and, as one relative pointed out, once she had drawn the battle lines and made an enemy of Devyani, she could not go back. Since King Birendra's first heart attack, the queen knew that she probably didn't have long before she became a widow – a low-status being in this Hindu society. The queen mother escapes the stigma of widowhood, but if Devyani became queen she would take Dipendra away from his mother, thus destroying Aishwarya's influence as a venerated queen mother. She'd be nobody.

'By the end of it, he hated his mother,' a cousin recalled. 'We could see them not even looking at each other, not even acknowledging each other.' Echoing the words of other royal insiders we'd spoken to, this cousin believed that the crown prince simply couldn't handle being given 'No' for an answer. 'And it was a pretty strong "No". From his point of view, he would say: "I have done everything they ever asked me to do. I ask them for one thing and they say, 'No.'" Education-wise he was top of the line. In his performance in military aspects, he was top of the line . . . He did all the religious rites, he didn't question . . . He did everything he was asked and he did it at his very best. So when he was told "No", he got into the thinking, Whatever I do, I can never please them. I think that slowly built up over a few years. You could slowly see the rift between the mother and the child.'

Still Dipendra played the dutiful son in public, while inside he seethed. The kid who couldn't stand to lose at Twister was now facing defeat in the biggest arm wrestle of his life.

chapter 23
wedding season

*T*he raucous thumping of wedding processions invaded Dipendra's head. The thrashing of bass drums, tubas and trombones, led by Arabian Nights clarinets snaking through the melody, were inescapable. Small cars smothered in garlands were followed by dancing processions clogging traffic on their way to houses lit by a thousand globes.

Dipendra had told his friend in Sydney to expect an announcement on his wedding by April or May 2001. But these auspicious days of the wedding season came and went with no news.

As the crown prince's state of mind steadily unwound, whispers through the Kathmandu elite started to hint that the issue of Dipendra's marital status was just the tip of the iceberg. One person seemingly in the know was Dipak Gyawali, the intellectual who helped us out with details of Dipendra's birth chart.

Dipak received some information from an ex-palace employee friend around this time, concerning an incident that took place ten years before at the royal family's summer palace in Nagarjun. Crown Prince Dipendra was visiting his mother's chicken hatchery when he learned that things had not been going well – five chickens had died the previous night. Rebuking the hatchery keeper for not doing his job properly, Dipendra then instructed the man to prepare three chickens for a picnic. 'Your Royal Highness, how do I account for them?' the hatchery keeper asked as the prince's vehicle was being loaded up. Rather than let his mother know he'd taken three birds, Dipendra told the man to lie to Queen Aishwarya: 'You said five chickens died? Add three more and say eight died.'

'Here's someone who's due to be the King of Nepal and he cannot get up and say, "I ate three chickens." It's a tremendous weakness of character,' Dipak Gyawali insisted. 'The later problems came about because he couldn't even say, "I'm going to marry this girl I've been going out with for eight years." . . . It's a flaw in character that showed he was very weak-willed. Not like his grandfather. When [Mahendra] decided he was going to marry the bride of his choice, he did it no matter what his father thought.

'Here [with Crown Prince Dipendra], you have a weak-willed character and on top of that you bring him up in a tradition that says he is next to a god and can do jolly well what he likes . . . On top of that, he was also into drugs . . . He's a thirty-year-old, with nothing to do. Very late for a Nepali to be single – even an ordinary Nepali who has to earn his living – but for a king, that's absolutely unacceptable because the job of a future king is to produce more kings. And he hasn't done that. You put it all together and you've got a dangerous cocktail.

'Schoolteachers said Aishwarya used to scold Dipendra so, at school when they were drawing with crayons, he used to draw his mother like a demon. Apparently she used to scold him, "You stupid fool, you're not going to be king," in the sense that [the sage] Goraknath had already said, "You are not going to be king." This kind of dialogue was always there . . .'

But if Kathmandu was already seeing rational omens of things to come, the cosmic world, too, was apparently screaming disaster. West of Kathmandu, the frightened villagers of Dolakha prayed as their famous Bhimeshwore idol began to sweat. As far as the chief royal priest, Ramesh Prasad Pandey, was concerned, everything that could be done to pacify the idol was done. Ramesh Prasad had also received word of the mysterious rain at the old palace in Gorkha. Another department in the palace had sent the necessities for worship. He just prayed for peace.

Then there is the well-known story about a Russian psychic who was more specific with her forewarnings. The woman often travels through Nepal, and sometime in the first half of 2001, she was staying at the Radisson in Kathmandu. Walking through the restaurant, she was drawn towards a table of young men. One of them in particular caught her attention, so much so that she went and asked a staff member who the fat, bearded guy was. 'That is the crown prince,' he told her. The psychic woman held her fingers to her head and pulled an imaginary trigger. 'He will self-destruct within six months,' she said.

'You mustn't say that,' the waiter whispered. 'He is the crown prince.'

But the woman shrugged. 'He will self-destruct.'

Around May 2001, the entire royal family gathered at the Hyatt Hotel for the eightieth birthday of one of their elderly Rana aunts. As a relative, Devyani was there also, but she and Dipendra kept a low profile through the early part of the evening.

'In front of His Majesty he was like a mouse,' a cousin recalled. 'He always had his hands in his lap, his eyes down with respect. But the moment his father wasn't around, it was just like a personality change.'

As usual, Dipendra went around asking his cousins to stay back with him after the elders were gone. Devyani stuck around too and when the last of the older generation had left, they went for it. 'They were just openly hugging and dancing,' one relative reported, 'which is just not appropriate at all – grabbing on to each other and dancing extremely close.'

The talk around the bar was that Devyani had given him the ultimatum: 'Marry me or I'll leave you.' Shocked onlookers took the performance on the dance floor as an emphatic 'I will'. At the end it got even more scandalous. They kissed outside the hotel where thirty or so drivers were lined up waiting to take the remaining guests home.

A few days later, Devyani said to her friend Sita: 'They're really pushing him. He's cracking up.'

'When is he going to marry you, then?'

'He does want to marry me, but at the same time he wants their approval as well.'

'Then what's he going to do? Why are you making such public appearances? People are talking about you. They're not saying nice things.' Sita knew that Devyani was the sort of person who cared about her image. This out-of-character behaviour showed how drastic the situation had become.

Devyani was going to stand by Dipendra regardless of whether he became king or not. That's what she said, anyway. Later, Sita would realise that Devyani hid so much about the relationship, she couldn't be sure what to believe. At this point, though, it really did look like the couple would just go ahead with a secret ceremony. He would take her to the palace and say, 'Meet my wife.'

In mid May there was a family get-together at the house of Princess Helen, mother of Ketaki Chester. The family always tried to gather one night a month, but had been unable to the previous month, so Princess Helen's was an unscheduled dinner to make up for it.

The elders were inside and the young generation stayed outside by the pool. Dipendra seemed more cheerful and attentive than he had in years. Ever since the affair with Devyani heated up, he'd been distant with his cousins, unsure where they stood. But that all seemed behind him this night. CP appeared interested in what the others had to say, which was unusual in itself, but he was also open to whatever questions they had for him. He spoke of losing weight and getting fit for a demonstration karate bout. He would begin his new regimen in a few weeks, he said.

One of the cousins, 'Shyam', presumed that given his buoyant mood, Dipendra must have come to an understanding with his parents. The crown prince seemed quite relaxed about the Devyani situation, even to the extent of talking to Shyam about a possible abdication: 'I have a younger brother. Why should I be worried?'

'We'll support you whatever you do,' Shyam told him, glad to see his cousin in such good spirits.

A few days after the gathering at Princess Helen's, one of Dipendra's closest friends from school got married. Devyani hadn't been invited, so the crown prince had his ADCs put pressure on the groom to have her asked along. But his group of school friends hadn't liked Devyani for some time now, and the pressure was resisted.

The mood at the reception was nevertheless relaxed. The crown prince went up to the roof with a crowd of friends to get some fresh air and smoke cigarettes. They were standing in a circle, when the groom asked him, 'When are you getting married?'

'I don't know. In a year or two,' Dipendra replied. The answer seemed very noncommittal compared to his strong position of recent years. He'd always been so upbeat about marrying Devyani that now his friend Tej thought he was putting the idea behind him. He didn't seem to be despairing.

Unbeknown to them, Dipendra was suffering under the

extra burden of knowing that his younger brother was already engaged. It was one thing to watch all his friends and cousins marry before him, but his little brother was seven-and-a-half years his junior. The imminent announcement would be another humiliation.

Another person to find Dipendra in an excellent mood in this, the last month of his life, was Dr Bal Kumer K.C., his geography tutor. The professor had his usual session with the crown prince in late May. They worked on a whiteboard, making plans for the year ahead, brainstorming for the PhD, which was starting to click into gear.

Dr K.C. was about to go to North Carolina for three months, where half his time would be taken up with his own work and half with helping with the research for Dipendra's thesis. He wasn't going to do the crown prince's work for him, he would insist, just help by finding texts that were unavailable in Kathmandu.

On 31 May, after dinner with his parents, Dipendra swung by the office of the king's ADC, Sundar Pratap Rana, who was working at his computer. 'Let's go,' he said, asking Rana over to his place for another of their late-night chats.

'Your Highness, I cannot go today,' the ADC replied. 'His Majesty might call me.'

'Okay.'

The prince was unshaven and didn't look too fresh. Something was on his mind, and Rana would forever regret that he never got another chance to ask what it was.

chapter 24
jestha 19

It was the morning of Jestha 19, 2058 – 1 June 2001 – the third Friday of the Nepalese month. Colonel Sundar Pratap Rana, clean-cut in his trim khaki uniform, was still in the office below King Birendra's private residence. The mild-mannered colonel had been on duty all night.

His Majesty appeared soon after 8 am and the pair stepped out for the king's morning constitutional. The air was warm. It was the build-up to the monsoon. For the next two hours, Colonel Rana shadowed the king as he walked through the grounds of Narayanhiti Palace.

The forty-four-year-old ADC had been with King Birendra for sixteen years and would always be proud that he got the job on merit. The way the palace operated in the 1980s, it was unusual to actually work your way up. Colonel Rana had never had connections with any top brass; his people were Magar Ranas, a tribal group from Gorkha.

Colonel Rana's Gorkhali ancestors had gone to war with Prithwi Narayan Shah. Then, eight generations ago, they migrated to Kathmandu to serve Jang Bahadur. One forebear served as an ADC for Jang's son Jagat, the heir to the prime ministership murdered by his cousins. Rana's family had served in the Royal Nepalese Army ever since.

Colonel Rana joined the army as a second lieutenant in 1977. Finishing second in his course, he was posted to the elite commando unit. From then on, he never finished less than second at anything. He was in outstanding physical condition; he topped the army mountaineering course and was selected for Ranger training in the United States.

Surpassing all that, though, was when the commander-in-chief shook his hand in 1985 and told him he'd been chosen to serve as an ADC. Rana underwent a course in VVIP security, taken from the British Close Protection Unit. He studied body-guarding, vehicle escort drills, anti-ambush techniques, and was instructed in protocol.

Royal ADCs are both aide and bodyguard. They are the last line of palace defence behind two battalions of 800 soldiers, and a 200-strong military security unit which specialises in close protection.

Rana might have worked with the king for the best part of twenty years, but he'd never pretend they were friends. His Majesty wasn't like the presidents or prime ministers he'd met. He was a god. A simple god with a propensity for simple foods, words and clothes. Colonel Rana would be with him until he retired.

That morning of 1 June, they finished the morning walk and headed to the indoor pool. The king disappeared into the sauna for twenty minutes before hitting the water. Colonel Rana watched the fifty-five-year-old monarch swim his laps. King Birendra was a good swimmer. He used to swim on his own, but since his heart attack, the ADCs made sure he was never alone. A heart attack or the Maoists. They were the two obvious threats to His Majesty's life.

The king emerged from the pool and Colonel Rana escorted him back to his residence. It was 11 am, Rana's shift was over. He briefed the next ADC on duty and left.

Over in the western quarter of the Narayanhiti complex, Crown Prince Dipendra was in his office making phone calls, finalising the guest list for dinner that evening. On the third Friday of every Nepalese month, the Shah clan gathered for a family do. It was Dipendra's turn to play host.

Over the past couple of days, his ADCs had rung around to check who'd be coming. When they phoned Dipendra's Aunt Ketaki, the former princess, on the Wednesday, she'd been surprised to hear from them. 'The palace has finally learned how to be polite,' her husband commented when she got off the phone. Normally, the queen's ADC would phone on the Friday afternoon, anytime between 2.30 and 6.30, to confirm that night's dinner was on. Family members knew to keep the night free. If Their Majesties had other plans, however, the get-together was off.

Princess Prekshya, the ex-wife of the former prince Dhirendra and sister to Queen Aishwarya, was also called that Wednesday. She said she'd try to make it but wasn't sure. The ADC called her back on Friday: she was down with a cold, she said, and wouldn't attend.

There were still a few other calls left to make, and Dipendra wanted to make them himself. He phoned his cousin-brothers to ensure that they were coming. They thought it unusual that he would call personally. Late in the morning, Dipendra spoke to his old flame Supriya, but didn't have anything in particular to say.

The crown prince also telephoned his uncle, Prince Gyanendra, in Chitwan. Gyanendra was busy with some VIP guests and had plans to fly to Pokhara that afternoon. He told his nephew he couldn't make it. 'I'll see you tomorrow,' Gyanendra said, and hung up. If the crown prince had insisted, he would, of course, have changed his plans.

Meanwhile, Queen Mother Ratna had decided that

because the younger generation had all come to dinner at Princess Helen's two weeks earlier, she would let some of them off the hook tonight. The queen mother phoned her step-daughters, the king's sisters, to tell them that their children no longer need attend. Prince Gyanendra's and Dhirendra's children would, however, still be required.

To those around him, Crown Prince Dipendra had been un-usually quiet that morning. His once-handsome face was bloated, his eyes tired and dull. He carried his bulky frame as a burden.

He joined his parents at their residence for lunch. Queen Aishwarya had come from a morning of *puja* with the royal priest. By the time Dipendra returned to his own quarters at 2.30 pm, his friend and ADC Major Gajendra Bohra had reported for duty.

An hour later, the pair drove out of the palace gates, Dipendra behind the wheel of his Landcruiser. His driving seemed even more erratic than usual as he headed south towards the sports complex in Satdobato, where he was due to check on preparations for the upcoming National Games. The king would inaugurate the games that Sunday, and Dipendra, as patron of the National Sports Council, wanted to make sure a rehearsal ceremony scheduled for Saturday was ready to go.

A parade of media, sports officials, government men and hangers-on awaited the crown prince when, at around four o'clock, he pulled into the sports complex. He strolled through the usual crush of obsequiousness to inspect the athletics arena, the volleyball courts, the pool and the shooting range. Dipendra turned to the head official: 'Everything okay?'

'Of course, Your Highness,' the official replied. He con-firmed that King Birendra was expected at 8 am the following day.

Dipendra said he would show up at 7.30 to ensure that everything was in place for his father. Then he got back in his four-wheel-drive, made a quick call to Devyani and headed back to the palace. He didn't relish what he had to do next.

It was late afternoon and Devyani was at the gym with her cousin Maya.

The young women were close. Maya was one of the few people Devyani still seemed to confide in these days. They chatted until the conversation rolled around to the crown prince.

'What's happening?' Maya asked.

'Nothing's happening,' Devyani snapped. 'What should be happening?'

Dipendra returned home in time to join the royal motorcade setting out for Dilli Bazar. Nepal's first family had an appointment with the former royal guru, Nayan Raj Pandey. It was now 5.30 pm.

For security reasons, the crown prince rode separately from the king and queen, who were travelling in their bullet-proof Mercedes.

Princess Shruti wasn't expected to join them, and Prince Nirajan had also been excused as he had just that day finished his final university exam. Their older brother would similarly have preferred not to be there.

Nayan Raj Pandey was guru to both King Birendra and Crown Prince Dipendra. He had led each of them through their coming-of-age ceremonies, during which he had given them their secret mantras.

But more recently, according to author Jonathan Gregson, the old guru had betrayed Dipendra's trust. During an earlier visit, the crown prince had smuggled his and Devyani's birth charts to the old man for comparison. Nayan

Raj knew a little astrology and told his royal guest that he and Devyani were an excellent match. Better than most, in fact. Dipendra was thrilled.

After the meeting, however, the old guru – who apparently felt he had a greater duty to King Birendra than to the crown prince – alerted the king and queen to the clandestine exchange and tweaked the reading to suit his audience. From his interpretation of their birth charts, the guru told Their Majesties, Dipendra and Devyani were completely incompatible.

Dipendra found out about the guru's deceit. It was a betrayal of the worst order. And now he was being forced to attend Nayan Raj's seventieth wedding anniversary.

The crowd surrounding Nayan Raj Pandey's house hushed as the royal motorcade drove up the short alleyway. Devotees spilled from balconies and street corners, hoping for a glimpse. A red carpet had been rolled out from the front door of the three-storey brick house. As King Birendra and Queen Aishwarya emerged from their Mercedes onto the carpet, they were showered with rice and flowers, worshipped as gods.

The king wore a simple white *kurta suruwal* and an open beige waistcoat, a pale *topi* on his head. His thin grey moustache curved over his lip. The queen followed in a red sari, her black hair in a neat, full bouffant. The perfect Hindu wife, she wore red bangles, red beads around her neck and a red *tika* in the middle of her forehead. Crown Prince Dipendra, overweight and sullen, joined them.

Bowing down before them was the old guru. Below his rumpled grey hair, his brown forehead was covered in age spots. Nayan Raj's grin revealed blackened teeth. It was difficult to judge whether he was more proud that he'd achieved seventy years of marriage, or that the royal family was honouring him with such kindness. When, aged twelve, he had married his wife, King Tribhuvan had been a guest. Now King Birendra was here.

The retired royal guru's ancestors had served the Shah kings since Nayan Raj's great-grandfather, Bijay Raj Pandey, was elevated into the lucrative position for his role as Jang Bahadur's palace spy. A century and a half later, Crown Prince Dipendra might well have thought that the job description had changed little.

Nayan Raj guided his honoured guests upstairs and into his pink-carpeted lounge room. It was a formal room, with a huge deer head on the wall and a glass cabinet filled with ornaments, including a portrait of Queen Aishwarya on a plate. The room was a memorial to the Shah kings and their royal priests. Photographs fading back through the generations covered the walls.

Their Majesties took a seat on the brown floral sofa. Their son sat off to one side. Nayan Raj presented the king with two gold coins.

'Your Majesty, it is the custom I offer two gold coins,' said the old guru.

The king lightly touched the offerings. The priest already knew His Majesty would not take them.

'You don't need gold coins,' Nayan Raj continued. 'You have everything. There is nothing I have to offer you – except one thing. One thing you don't have.' The old priest clutched his chest. 'I offer my heart to your feet. Please accept.'

King Birendra smiled. Nayan Raj was delighted.

'Your Majesty, with your permission, I would like to recite a devotional poem.'

'Yes, yes,' the king nodded.

'Thou owner of jewel-studded palaces . . .' Nayan Raj began narrating in Sanskrit. But over in the corner, he noticed the crown prince stewing. His Royal Highness was not a gentleman like his father, thought Nayan Raj. It had been two years since Crown Prince Dipendra had granted him an audience. In that time, Nayan Raj had submitted six requests. He wanted to advise the prince against marrying Devyani, but Dipendra refused to see him.

Nayan Raj finished his poem and delicacies were served.

The crown prince, eyes downcast, refused everything. 'Please, Your Royal Highness, take something,' Nayan Raj pleaded. Dipendra took a sip of Coke.

The royal family stayed an hour. On their way out, they passed the priest's prayer room. The tiled alcove was swamped in religious images and golden idols sprayed with vermilion. Queen Aishwarya entered the room, sat on the floor, and prayed. Nayan Raj Pandey felt blessed.

The royal chauffeurs pulled into Narayanhiti Palace. Queen Aishwarya returned to her bungalow and King Birendra to his office. He had an interview scheduled with a magazine editor.

Crown Prince Dipendra went back to Tribhuvan Sadan and changed into slacks and a bush shirt for dinner. Then he walked down to the billiard room and called his ADC, Major Bohra, to join him.

The crown prince played a lone game of pool. Major Bohra arranged the balls. Shortly before 7.30 pm, when the guests were due, the ADC poured Dipendra a tumbler of Famous Grouse whisky and left the room.

chapter 25
a family affair

Ĩn the fifth century AD there was said to have been a great drought which threatened to destroy the ruling dynasty of Nepal. The desperate king consulted a Tantric priest, who told him the only solution was to sacrifice the most pious man in the kingdom – someone who would conform to thirty-two traits of integrity. The king immediately sent emissaries to every corner of the kingdom to find this model of virtue, but no such man could be found.

The king knew what had to be done. He summoned the crown prince and told him that, in order to save the kingdom, he must go to the Narayan temple north-west of the city at dawn the next day. There, he would find a man sleeping in a blanket. He must lop off the man's head.

The prince did as instructed. He found the sleeping man in the temple compound next to a desiccated pond and a dry water spout. As the man's head rolled away, water burst from the spout. Thunder shook the valley, and the rains came. It was only then, as water washed the sacrificial blood into the pond, that the prince realised he had killed his father.

The temple is now a well-tended little oasis of two ponds. Three ornate spouts still deliver cool, clear water. Across the road stands the south gate of the Narayanhiti Royal Palace, which takes its name from here – '*Narayan*' being a form of the god Vishnu and '*hiti*' being the Newar word for pond.

The bar had been stocked and the dining room set for a buffet. Alone in the billiard room, Crown Prince Dipendra nursed his whisky and played a few shots. The ceiling fans whirred.

In the kitchen, the royal chefs were preparing a spread of continental and Nepalese dishes. The food would be kept in a warmer until the king was ready to eat, sometime after 10 pm. The family would serve themselves. On nights like these, the servants didn't intrude; even the ADCs withdrew to a nearby office. As head of palace security, Dipendra carried a walkie-talkie and could call for help if needed.

Outside, it was cloudy and warm. The odd rumble of thunder rolled through the valley. Royal in-law Maheshwar Kumar (M.K.) Singh strode along the garden path towards the billiard room. He was on his own tonight; his wife, one of King Tribhuvan's daughters, was ill. At sixty-seven, Singh was still a handsome man, tall and elegant. His dark, feathery hair had just a whisper of grey. Family dinners being informal occasions, the only dress requirement for men was a Nepalese cap. But Singh was a respectful man and he liked to wear the full traditional outfit.

Singh had married into the family forty-nine years earlier. His father was an Indian prince who, during the British Raj, ruled over the state of Sarguja for thirty years. They were decadent times. Singh's father was reputed to have shot 1150 tigers, earning the distinction of killing more than anyone else in India.

The wedding between the eighteen-year-old M.K. and

King Tribhuvan's daughter Bimala took place in Calcutta in March 1952. Four years later, Singh accepted a job looking after the interests of Nepal's two queen mothers, and the couple moved to Kathmandu.

Singh continued down the hallway that skirted the front of the billiard room. He looked at his watch: 7.27 pm. The invitation was for 7.30. Singh always made it a point to be punctual at the palace. The usher standing by the billiard-room door looked at Singh as if to enquire, 'Do you want to enter, sir?'

'No, no,' Singh assured the servant. 'Wait.'

Singh could see through a window into the billiard room. The lounges by the windows had been arranged into two semicircles; behind them, three low-hung lamps lit the full-size billiard table. He watched as Dipendra played a controlled game.

When he glanced back at his watch it was 7.30 exactly. The usher announced his arrival and Singh strode across the white marble floor to greet Crown Prince Dipendra with a humble bow.

'What can I get you to drink?' Dipendra asked.

'Nobody is here yet, Your Royal Highness. There's no hurry.'

'I'm tending bar tonight, so you'll only help me if I can get you something now.'

'Okay, if it will help you, of course,' smiled Singh.

The crown prince walked over to the bar, tucked just around the corner of the L-shaped room. He looked full of life, Singh thought.

'So what will it be?'

'Whisky,' the old man replied, scanning what was on offer. 'I'll have Famous Grouse.'

'Ah, I'm having Famous Grouse too,' said Dipendra, holding up his half-empty drink. He scooped a couple of ice cubes into a glass and poured a peg for Singh.

Just then, a white-haired gent shuffled in. It was Brigadier-General Rabi Shamsher Rana, one of the last surviving sons of the naughty old Prime Minister, Juddha.

This was the first get-together General Rabi had made it to in months. He'd fallen and hurt his foot, and could only now get a pair of shoes on. But while the seventy-four-year-old's tattooed body was falling apart, he was full of spark and wore an impish smile.

Like Singh, General Rabi had been married to one of King Tribhuvan's daughters. He wed Tika in 1941, when he was fifteen years old, but his beloved wife had passed away some years ago. Rabi was not only an in-law, but a blood relative: uncle to Queen Mother Ratna, and great uncle through two of his brothers to both King Birendra and Queen Aishwarya.

'What would you like?' Dipendra greeted the old soldier as he approached the bar.

General Rabi pointed at the bottle of White Horse. 'That one.' It was his favourite drop. He used to drink it with King Mahendra. Dipendra poured with a heavy hand, but seemed stone-cold sober to Rabi.

Princess Helen walked in. Now in her late sixties, Helen was the estranged Rana wife of the late playboy prince, Basundhara. Her eldest daughter, Princess Jayanti, a dwarf, had also just arrived. There was only thirteen years between mother and daughter, and they were close. Both being single, they lived together.

Another of Princess Helen's daughters was then making her way from her car to the billiard room. It was Ketaki, petite and pretty, the princess who'd given up her title for love. She was, of course, alone. Her English husband had never been welcome in the palace.

Ketaki hadn't been excluded from the family after she divorced her first husband, but it was only recently, twenty-five years on, that the last of the resentment towards her seemed to have thawed. Queen Aishwarya had cleared the decks when she told Ketaki, 'I feel like now we can get along, but I never agreed with what you did.' Ketaki had thought, 'At least ask me why I did it before you judge me. I'll be happy to explain.' It had been the same for Dhirendra when he divorced his Rana wife to marry an Englishwoman.

Ketaki walked along the path that ran along the glass side doors of the billiard room. She knew Dipendra's quarters well. This was where her two grannies – King Tribhuvan's wives – lived. She knew the place was haunted. There was a ghost in the corridor there. You felt its chill behind you and were too afraid to turn around. You walked faster and it sped up too.

As Ketaki entered the billiard room, she glanced at the glass door to the dining room on her right. If you saw an old harpy in that door you'd be dead in six months. Ketaki's father, Prince Basundhara, had seen the horrendously ugly old hag, dressed in rags. He died soon after. Devyani Rana's grandfather, Bijaya, was also meant to have seen the old woman. Soon afterwards he took up an ambassadorial appointment in Delhi, where he was electrocuted in the bath.

The Narayanhiti Palace of Ketaki's childhood had been full of ghosts. One time the little princess snuck into a service area where a maid was having a gangrenous leg amputated. She watched as grown-ups forced alcohol down the woman's throat and continued watching as the maid went totally still.

The spirit of the dead maid returned to haunt her. The apparition would wait at a particular staircase and taunt her if she tried to descend alone: 'I'll kill you if you come down these stairs.' There was no way Ketaki would go down by herself. And nobody made her either, because everybody knew ghosts were real.

The little girl was well aware of what happened after Prime Minister Ranaudip was murdered here by four of his nephews in November 1885. It didn't matter how many coats of paint were put over Ranaudip's blood, the stain wouldn't go away until that part of the palace was destroyed by earthquake in 1934.

Inside the billiard room, Ketaki said hello to her mother while the crown prince got the former princess a drink. She then joined her sister Jayanti – always good for some witty conversation.

King Birendra's three sisters arrived, Princesses Shanti, Sharada and Shobha. Princess Shanti, the eldest, was alone. Her husband, the Raja of Bajhang in far-western Nepal, had died in 1984. Her adult children were among those Queen Mother Ratna had let off this evening.

Princess Shanti was a pious woman. Like her sisters, she had devoted much of her life to charity, as founder and patron of the Nepal Leprosy Association. She was also strictly traditional. She held on to principle and understood what her brother King Birendra was going through over Dipendra's marriage plans. Shanti had opposed her own youngest son's love marriage. When he went ahead with it regardless, she forced him and his new wife to leave the family home and live in an apartment for three years. It was only over time that Shanti had come to welcome her daughter-in-law into her home.

The king's next sister, Princess Sharada, arrived with her husband, Kumar Khadga Bikram Shah. Like Shanti's children, the couple's grown boys had stayed home on the queen mother's orders. Princess Sharada and Kumar Khadga had a relaxed air. In their late fifties, they were perhaps more liberal than others in the family of their vintage.

Kumar Khadga's ancestors were the rajas of Jumla in far-western Nepal, but his grandfather had frittered away the family wealth on gambling, politics and a brotherly feud. Money was tight for Khadga growing up, but he was an honest, hardworking young man and got a job to pay his way through an international law degree in Calcutta.

When he returned to Kathmandu, the palace assigned someone to follow him around. Satisfied that Khadga could be trusted, King Mahendra sent out feelers to gauge whether Khadga and his parents were agreeable to a royal marriage. Not that one could say no to the king's daughter.

King Mahendra had grand designs for the union. Out of the shadows of the Ranas and with a nationalist zeal, he gave all three of his daughters to men whose families came from western Nepal. The move bound the distant, populous west to Kathmandu.

For Khadga and Sharada, the marriage forced them to give up their personal ambitions. Khadga was prevented from practising law and Sharada from pursuing her dream of becoming a nurse. Instead, Khadga turned his efforts to establishing a mountaineering commission and a sports council. He was later employed to finetune King Birendra's speeches, and was now director of the Centre for Nepalese and Asian Studies at Tribhuvan University.

The 1960s, though, had instilled social awareness in both. It had been a time of great change in Nepal: King Mahendra theoretically abolished the caste system, the hippies turned up, and love marriages were gaining their first iota of acceptance. While the young couple respected the traditions by which they were bound, they were inspired by this movement. From walking to remote regions as emissaries of the king, to establishing orphanages or simply touching an untouchable, they made what small efforts they could to encourage the momentum.

Chatter and laughter started to fill the billiard room. Standing with Princess Sharada and Kumar Khadga was Princess Shobha, the king's youngest sister. She had left her husband at home recuperating from a knee operation. They all greeted their nephew the crown prince, and he returned to the bar to pour drinks.

Dipendra's brother Prince Nirajan had also wandered in. His sister Princess Shruti arrived with her husband Gorakh. The young couple had left their little girls, seven-month-old Surangana and Girwani, almost three, at home, just across the road.

Gorakh was a softly spoken gentleman in his early thirties. He was descended from Prime Minister Chandra Shamsher, an ancestor he shared with Devyani Rana. Like her husband, Shruti had a quiet elegance about her. She walked like a model, as though she had a book on her head. But beneath her pretty, demure demeanour, she had inherited her mother's fierce determination and firm convictions. When it mattered, she said what she felt and didn't mince her words. She'd proven that with her vocal objection to her brother's marriage plans.

That same determination also went into her talents. Just twenty-four years old, she was already a respected oil painter, having held her first solo exhibition when she was twenty. She was also a black belt in judo.

What her husband loved most about her, though, was that she was a normal, playful, caring person. And she was tough, too. At home, she'd practise her judo holds on him and he couldn't break them.

Shruti and Gorakh had an arranged marriage only in the sense that they married within the acceptable pool of candidates. They found each other and then let the elders know so the 'arrangement' could be made.

The last of the crown prince's guests were milling towards the billiard room. The king's youngest brother Dhirendra, the former wayward prince, was there, looking laidback in a loose *kurta suruwal* and *topi*. He'd arrived from England for a visit home a couple of months earlier, and was soon due to fly back to his wife in the Isle of Wight, where they'd moved from London. Dhirendra had arrived at the party with his three daughters and son-in-law, Dr Rajiv Shahi, an army doctor, while his ex-wife stayed home with a cold. Many thought his visit was an attempt to get back into Queen Aishwarya's good books and open up some business opportunities. The queen had made him pay for divorcing her sister Prekshya, and, with no royal backing, Dhirendra had struggled as a commoner in England.

The youngsters went and hung out around the corner of the L-shaped room, beyond the bar. There, they could smoke and drink without disrespecting their elders. These parties were always split into age groups, the crown prince being the only one of his generation to mix with everybody.

At the billiard table, some of the younger men started a game similar to Kelly pool, and Dipendra noticed his cousin Paras had arrived. The bad-boy prince, whose father, Prince Gyanendra, was away in Pokhara, was accompanying his mother, Princess Komal, along with his wife and his sister.

Paras walked over to greet the crown prince.

Across the palace grounds, ADC Major Ananta Simha was escorting Her Majesty Queen Aishwarya to the gathering. The queen was still in the red sari, bangles and beads she had worn to visit the guru.

Major Simha accompanied her to the hallway entrance. The stocky young man then withdrew to the nearby office, where he would wait until Their Majesties were ready to leave – probably sometime around midnight.

As the queen entered, Princess Helen and M.K. Singh rose to pay their respects. Singh apologised for his wife's absence, explaining that she had been unwell.

Over at the bar, Dipendra was getting his cousin Paras a drink.

'What would you like?' he asked.

'I'll just have a Coke.'

'A Coke? I've been drinking whisky,' Dipendra told him.

Paras thought the crown prince seemed a bit drunk. 'What happened?' he asked.

'We've been discussing marriage,' Dipendra replied. 'I spoke with *Mua* [Mother] and with *Afumuma* [Grandmother]. Both have said no. I'll talk to my father on Sunday.'

Dipendra joined Paras, Dr Rajiv and his brother-in-law,

Gorakh, in the game of pool. He turned to Dr Rajiv: 'I think I'm a little high.' It was 8 pm. Dipendra, still looking prim despite his comment to Dr Rajiv, obtained permission from his mother to leave in order to drive to the queen mother's residence across the palace compound and escort her to the party.

When Queen Mother Ratna arrived, she went straight to a sitting room across the hallway from the billiard room. She would never join the main party. As the senior-most family member it was more fitting that she remain here, where the guests would file in to pay their respects. She was joined by her sister-in-law Princess Helen, who would stay with her all night. The women were also second cousins through their Rana blood.

Dipendra returned to the billiard room, and word spread that the queen mother had arrived. Following protocol, the guests put down their drinks, stubbed out cigarettes, and made their way across the hallway to formally greet her in the sitting room.

The older generation lingered there while the others returned to the billiard room or moved further down the hallway to a deep verandah which overlooked the courtyard garden. Dipendra served another round of drinks, after which he, Paras, Gorakh and Dr Rajiv continued their game of pool. Dipendra was playing well.

At 8.12 pm, the crown prince pulled out his mobile phone and called Devyani. She was at home, getting ready for a party at a friend's house. Devyani would later claim that Dipendra only called to ask if she'd be going to the inauguration ceremony of the National Games on Sunday. But judging from what she did next, the call worried her.

The conversation lasted little more than a minute and Dipendra returned to the game. At 8.19 pm he picked up his mobile again. This time he phoned his ADC, Major Bohra. The conversation was brief: 'Send my cigarette case with the black and green.'

Within minutes, a servant appeared at the billiard-room door. Paras happened to be standing nearby, and received the black leather case for his cousin. Inside were at least five joints the servant had prepared earlier. He'd been rolling the marijuana leaf and sticky black hash into the crown prince's cigarettes for the past year.

Paras carried the cigarette case over to Dipendra, who immediately lit up a joint. Oh God, Gorakh thought. What if the elders return? What if His Majesty comes now?

It was approaching 8.25 pm when King Birendra wound up his magazine interview. Colonel Sundar Pratap Rana, the king's loyal ADC, was back on duty after spending the sunny afternoon shopping with his wife.

Rana took His Majesty's briefcase, and escorted him through the sprawling palace grounds. The path was unusually dark. Flashes of white threatened a storm that wouldn't come as thunderheads rose from the icy mountains surrounding the valley.

'That streetlight isn't working,' the king remarked. 'Tell the crown prince's ADC to fix it.'

Colonel Rana made a mental note of it.

In the billiard room, Dipendra's walkie-talkie crackled to life, announcing that the king had left his office. His Majesty was walking; he should arrive at the billiard room in about five minutes.

Dipendra's mobile phone rang around the same time but he let it go. The call diverted to ADC Bohra. It was Devyani. She and Major Bohra spoke for over four minutes. Devyani would later claim she made the phone call because, after her earlier conversation with Dipendra, she was worried about the crown prince. She thought the crown prince might be unwell, she told Bohra, and asked the ADC to check on him in his bedroom. Which was odd. Dipendra wasn't in his room, he was at the party.

Devyani was apparently so concerned that she then made a call to an off-duty ADC, Major Raju Karki, at his home in Patan. She asked him to go to the palace and check on the crown prince. Karki, due to leave for the United States the next day, told her he wasn't working; he would, however, call the on-duty ADC, Major Bohra, and check it out.

Devyani then travelled to the home of Indian businessman Sanjay Dugar and his wife, who lived very close to the palace. She would go with them to her friend's party, rather than arrive alone.

It was at the time of her call to the ADCs that a radical change came over the crown prince. Still playing pool, he began missing easy shots. He suddenly seemed very drunk, bumping into furniture, stumbling into his cousin. The young men stopped the game. This was weird. Dipendra could usually drink them under the table and still stand to attention.

Ketaki and her sister Princess Jayanti were also watching the crown prince. To them, it looked fake the way he was banging into things. 'He's not drunk,' Ketaki remarked to her sister. 'Why is he acting drunk?'

Through the glass side doors of the billiard room, the youngsters who were gathered around the floppy crown prince saw King Birendra coming up the garden path with Colonel Rana. A major embarrassment loomed as they watched His Majesty enter the hallway. Fortunately, he went straight to the sitting room to pay his respects to Queen Mother Ratna.

In the billiard room, Dipendra fell to the ground. He appeared to have passed out. The only thing the young men could do was get him out before the king saw what was going on. 'His Majesty has come,' Paras told the crown prince. 'We're taking you to your room.'

Dr Rajiv and Prince Nirajan hoisted Dipendra up. Gorakh lifted his legs. He felt awkward about grabbing his brother-in-law's feet, so he tried to hold onto his trouser-cuffs.

Prince Paras, who had a bad knee, opened doors for them as they heaved the great bulk of the semiconscious crown prince outside, across the verandah and through the courtyard garden. Shortly before reaching his sleeping quarters, they had to cross a pond. 'Don't fall in, don't fall in,' Dipendra mumbled as they carried him over the small bridge.

Reaching the crown prince's sleeping quarters, they lugged him up the stairs to his bedroom. There, exhausted and sweating, they dropped him onto a futon-like mattress on the floor.

Gorakh had never been to the crown prince's bedroom before, and felt uncomfortable being there. Prince Nirajan took off his big brother's shoes and belt, then asked Dipendra if his gun was hurting him. Dipendra always carried a pistol and the young men expected the holster to be pressing into his skin. 'I'm not carrying anything today,' Dipendra replied.

The four men left the room in silence. Nirajan turned the lights off and they returned to the party.

In the sitting room, King Birendra had paid his respects to the queen mother. His relatives had in turn paid their respects to him.

It seemed that His Majesty wanted to talk in private with the queen mother, Queen Aishwarya and Princess Helen, so the others excused themselves and moved back into the billiard room. General Rabi and M.K. Singh joined Dhirendra and Kumar Khadga, smoking out on the verandah.

'So what's the army up to now?' Khadga asked the old brigadier-general.

Word of Dipendra's behaviour filtered through to the ADCs in the nearby office. Following Devyani's worried phone call, Major Bohra sent an orderly to check the crown prince in his room.

Then the off-duty ADC, Raju Karki, phoned, as he had told Devyani he would. 'Everything's okay,' Major Bohra told Karki. His Royal Highness just had a bit too much whisky, he said. It was nothing serious. 'I've sent a boy to check on him.'

Karki decided to drive to the palace anyway.

The two palace servants sent to Dipendra's room found the crown prince on the floor, struggling to take off his shirt. They helped him out of his clothes, then waited while he went to the bathroom.

They heard vomiting. He emerged from the bathroom and ordered them to go to bed.

For whatever reason, Devyani must still have been anxious about the crown prince. When her friend Sita rang to ask for a lift to the party, Devyani snapped, 'Leave me alone!' before hanging up.

At 8.39 pm Devyani's mobile rang again. This time it was the crown prince calling from his bedroom. They were on the phone for thirty-two seconds.

'I'm about to go to sleep,' Dipendra told his lover. 'I'll call you tomorrow. Goodnight.'

chapter 26
ke gardeko?

The king and queen drifted back across the hall to the billiard room at around 8.45 pm, leaving Queen Mother Ratna and Princess Helen alone in the sitting room, where the door and windows were shut and the air-conditioning hummed.

The four older gents – Rabi, M.K. Singh, Dhirendra and Khadga – smoking on the verandah came indoors and topped up their drinks. They joined King Birendra near the billiard table. The king, with a Coke in his hand, approached his old uncle, General Rabi.

'What's new, Rabi?'

'Nothing new, Your Majesty.'

M.K. Singh had just got his second Famous Grouse. He joined the semicircle forming around Birendra. Holding his glass between his palms, prayer-like, he bowed to the king. It was a formal gesture, seeking permission to drink. Birendra nodded the okay.

The sweet smell of the crown prince's joint had been dispersed by the ceiling fans. If the king knew about his son's little episode fifteen minutes earlier, he didn't show it. He asked where Singh's wife was. Singh explained that she couldn't make it because she had gout.

'Yes, I also have gout,' said Birendra.

'Gout is in your family,' General Rabi pitched in, 'my wife had it too.' At this, they launched into a conversation about the family's various inherited ailments.

The queen and the older women were sitting to the left of the door. At the farthest possible corner from them, at a second cluster of sofas near the stereo, were the younger generation, many smoking like teenagers down the back of a school bus.

Ketaki and her sister Jayanti had just got a fresh drink and were standing near the bar. They hadn't even said 'Cheers' when the former princess saw Dipendra enter the room from the courtyard, wearing full military camouflage gear, with black gloves and a camouflage baseball cap.

'Isn't he getting a bit too old to dress up like this?' Ketaki quipped to her sister. They paid him no more attention. Ketaki would have been more scared had he carried just one gun. The fact he had one in each hand and two others hanging from his shoulders seemed to make him less threatening, as if he was just showing off to his father.

M.K. Singh was still standing in the king's semicircle, his back to the door and the courtyard, when he heard footsteps. He glanced over his shoulder and saw that the noise came from Dipendra's heavy black boots.

Singh saw only one gun – a little machine-gun in the crown prince's right hand – and, like Ketaki and Jayanti, didn't give it much thought. This was a family comfortable around firearms. Singh turned back to the conversation (still on cholesterol and high blood pressure). As Dipendra drew up next to Singh, the king stepped forward, smiling to greet his son.

Two explosions sent a jolt of pain into Singh's right ear. He instinctively stuck his index finger in it. The elderly gent saw that Dipendra had fired the gun into the ceiling. Singh shut his eyes.

A short blast of automatic gunfire followed, and the old man thought his buzzing eardrums had burst. He opened his eyes and was almost surprised to see everyone in the semicircle still standing. Then the king began to sag. Blood streaked the right shoulder of his white *kurta suruwal*.

Near the bar, Ketaki had heard the shots and spun around. In slow motion, she noted how the ceiling seemed to absorb the first bullets without any plaster coming down; the surprise written on King Birendra's face.

Nobody paid Dipendra much attention as he retreated from the room. They were all trying to digest what had just happened. The logical conclusion was that it was a prank – fire crackers, surely. But the growing bloodstain on the king's neck and right shoulder didn't support that. And the monarch was sinking ever so slowly to the white marble floor. '*Ke gardeko?*' he asked. 'What have you done?'

Ketaki heard screams from some younger family members. Singh nudged General Rabi as if to say, 'Look at the king'. Rabi started screaming, 'Doctor! Doctor!'

Dr Rajiv Shahi, Dhirendra's son-in-law, was running to the scene. He had been standing near the stereo in the far corner, but in response to Rabi's shouts, reached King Birendra just before he hit the ground, and eased him onto his back. The doctor put a finger in the bullet hole in the king's neck, then took off his coat and pressed it to the wound.

'Rajiv, I have also been shot in the stomach,' Birendra told the young doctor.

'Don't worry about that, sire. Stopping the bleeding is much more important.'

Queen Aishwarya rushed barefoot from her corner, assessed the situation, then raced out of the only unlocked door in the room – the same door Dipendra had just left through. She was yelling for an ambulance.

The room fell into empty silence. The crown prince was nowhere to be seen. The witnesses would look back at this interlude – twenty or thirty seconds, perhaps – as the last chance they had to flee or call for help. Instead, they looked at each other for cues. Looked at the king.

The crown prince reappeared.

Ketaki, still standing near the bar, was struck by the look on his face. Dipendra usually had spark in his eyes, but this night there was nothing. It was a look that would haunt her. *Terminator 2.* Absolutely expressionless, but concentrated.

The prodigal uncle, Dhirendra, stepped past Ketaki towards Crown Prince Dipendra. Dhirendra was a karate black belt too. The one person in the room who could have physically taken the crown prince on.

'*Baba*, don't you think you've done enough damage?' he asked, reaching out to grab the little machine-gun. His hand was just centimetres from the barrel when a single blast blew him a metre back through the air. He landed near Ketaki, bleeding from the chest. She threw herself onto him, pressing the heel of her left hand into the wound.

The crown prince fired at Dhirendra a second time. Ketaki felt the bullet smash through her left forearm. Strangely alert, she saw the king put up his hand. His expression was imploring, as if to say: 'Whatever mistake you've made, it can be put right. But take one more step and I can't help you.' She'd never seen such a stern look on his face. She saw his glasses fly off, and knew he'd been hit again.

Dipendra started retreating a second time but as he backed to the door he saw Kumar Khadga. The crown prince fired again, hitting his uncle in the right armpit.

Gorakh had earlier raced to his father-in-law's side with Dr Rajiv, intent on carrying His Majesty out of the room. Now he was standing near the billiard table, just beyond where the king's head lay, as Dipendra backed out. Their eyes met, and it was so cold. Gorakh's mouth formed into a half-smile that seemed to say, 'Shit, I don't have a gun or anything.'

The crown prince, who just twenty minutes earlier

couldn't stand up, grouped two bullets neatly into his brother-in-law's sternum. Then he threw the little machine-gun onto the floor near his father, and left the room for a second time.

Princess Shruti, who had been adjusting the volume on the stereo during the first attack, now headed to the king. 'What have you done to my father?' she called out to the gunman. Then she saw Gorakh. '*Baba*, you have been hit too.'

She knelt down, cradling her husband's head on her thighs. 'Looks like he's going to finish us all off,' Gorakh told her. 'Run.' He thought she should go for the glass door behind the billiard table, not knowing it was locked. But Shruti wouldn't leave him.

Prince Paras watched as the stricken king tried to get up and grab the little machine-gun, a Heckler & Koch MP5, which Dipendra had thrown on the floor.

'Leave this,' commanded his sister, Princess Shobha, tending to him. She grabbed the gun by the magazine, which came off in her hand. She tossed it away.

Maybe she thought it was Dipendra's only weapon, but Paras had seen the others: the 9mm pistol on his left side, a shotgun on one shoulder and an M16 on the other. There was plenty of firepower in reserve.

As she tossed the magazine aside there came a much louder concussion from just outside the door. The gunman wasn't through yet. Ketaki, still lying with Dhirendra, watched as a white light stalked the room. Dipendra's M16, the standard US military assault weapon, had a spotlight fitted under the barrel and telescopic sights above it. The light started landing on people, and they fell. Aim. Fire. Aim. Fire. The older women who had gathered near King Birendra were the first targets.

Princess Komal, the king's dumpy sister-in-law, fell, hit in the back. The king's sister Princess Shobha was next. Then another sister, Princess Shanti, collapsed over Komal and Shobha, splattering them with her blood.

Princess Sharada had run to her husband, Kumar

Khadga, and was lying over his body sobbing: 'What has happened to you? What has happened to you?' Ketaki watched as Sharada calmly put her body between the gunman and her husband. And she watched as the back of Sharada's head flew off.

Ketaki called to Jayanti, her sister: 'Rush for the billiard table. Get under it.' The diminutive Jayanti didn't move, she just looked straight back at Ketaki. Then her eyes shut, and Ketaki knew her sister had been shot, even before the sound of the blast registered in her brain.

Jayanti collapsed next to her. Ketaki could tell she was alive because she could hear her breathing. Ketaki then watched as the white light moved towards the billiard table and settled on Princess Shruti who was still cradling her husband on her lap.

Gorakh heard the shot, and simultaneously felt his wife's body go limp. Shruti fell from her kneeling position. Gorakh, lying there with two bullets in his chest, had a clear view of the room. He'd seen all the bodies dropping and the second burst of bullets being pumped into the king. Now the white light flashed across his eyes. God, I'm gone, he thought. More shots rang out. He felt an itch in his right leg and realised he couldn't move it – he'd been shot above the thigh. He saw his right thumb was gone. A bullet hit his toes, and one skimmed his hairline.

Prince Paras was watching from across the room. He had attempted to come to the king's aid with Rajiv and Gorakh at the very beginning, but his aunt, Princess Shobha, ordered him back. He had gathered the young princesses in the corner and got them to take cover behind the sofas.

Paras had shouted at the old general, Rabi, who was standing amid it all in wide-eyed confusion. He was able to prompt the retired soldier to come to the relative safety around the corner.

Similarly, M.K. Singh had stood there in the middle of the carnage. He would remember that it suddenly struck him: This is the Kot Massacre. He was mulling this over when Prince

Paras, at the far side of the room, shouted: 'You're standing in the line of fire. Duck!'

But Singh didn't drop, instead he walked across the room to Paras and hit the deck beside a lounge. He lay on his stomach, his arms crossed over his head, pretending to be dead.

'What happened to you?' Paras's sister Princess Prerana asked Singh.

'What? What's wrong?'

'You're bleeding.' He was drenched in blood but had no idea a bullet had gone through his forearm.

'I can't do anything about it. Let it be.'

Dipendra disappeared and silence returned.

Flat on the ground and bleeding profusely, Dhirendra told Ketaki she'd been hit.

'Yes, in the arm,' she answered.

'No, you've been hit somewhere else. Your face is covered with blood.'

She heard blood dripping onto the marble floor and looked down at her right shoulder. There was something white there. Bone. Her shoulder had virtually disappeared. She bundled her sari with her disabled left hand – hit when she'd first gone to Dhirendra's aid – and stuffed it into the gaping joint. The dripping sound stopped.

Dhirendra was feeling around with his hands. 'I can't reach my pocket,' he told Ketaki. 'Can you reach in and get my mobile?'

'Who do you think you're going to call?' she asked, expecting the ADCs to burst into the room at any moment.

'Who do you think's alive?' he asked.

The only person she had seen moving was M.K. Singh.

'Jayanti's stopped breathing,' Dhirendra said. Ketaki had heard it too. They knew her sister was dead.

Ketaki's mind raced with a jumble of thoughts. Okay, he wants to be king. Poor Nepal with this madman running it. She thought of those who had always told her that the Shahs were mad. She never thought the madness would show itself like this. Damn it, she thought, I've worn my best black bra and now it's ruined.

She couldn't understand why the ADCs weren't here.

Dipendra was suddenly back in the room.

Gorakh – still conscious despite two bullets in the chest – watched as the crown prince walked over to the king, kicked the body, then shot him again. He saw Khadga – shot in the armpit in the very early stages of the massacre – crawling away near the bar. Dipendra shot him again in the back of the knee. Gorakh wondered where the hell the ADCs were.

Dipendra was coming towards him. Gorakh's mind was strangely calm. The madman was so close, now standing over him, all Gorakh could see were his fat thighs and the barrel of his gun as he delivered the *coup de grace*. The hot metal burst into the base of Gorakh's throat – point blank, in the groove where the two collarbones meet.

Somehow Gorakh was still conscious. He watched Dipendra walk to the corner of the room where Paras was protecting the young royals. Dipendra pointed the gun at his favourite cousin's face.

Singh, face down on the floor, heard Paras imploring: '*Nai, dai! Nai, dai!*' (No brother! No brother!) 'It's me. Are you sure you want to kill me? We are the only ones here.' One by one, Dipendra stared at each of the huddled princesses with a hollow gaze. He was God, and they would live. He backed out of the room.

Ketaki saw him head towards his residence and presumed he was going to get more guns or ammunition to finish them all off. She was certain they were all dead. Especially after she saw him kick his father's body. There was no doubt in her mind that this was a power grab.

She watched as the doctor, Rajiv, climbed out a window. He'd bring help soon. Any second now. There was complete, horrifying silence. Lying with Dhirendra and her dead sister, she waited.

Although the sequence of events is unclear, both Ketaki and Singh saw the queen, wearing a red sari, reappear at some point, having left at the end of the first attack. It crossed Ketaki's mind that she hadn't seen her for the rest of the ordeal. It seemed so unlike Aishwarya to run away. Now, Aishwarya turned around and again headed out the door after her son.

Ketaki called to her, '*Bhauju, bhauju!*', 'Sister-in-law, sister-in-law!' She wanted to stop her, but she wasn't sure if any sound came out of her mouth.

'She's not going to turn back,' Dhirendra said. 'Did you see the look on her face? She's either going to get killed or disarm him.'

Prince Nirajan followed his mother out. Ketaki called out to try to stop him also.

'You can't do anything about it,' Dhirendra said.

There was more silence. A burst of automatic gunfire. Silence. Then another blast.

Huddled on the billiard-room floor, Ketaki looked at Dhirendra. 'He's killed them both.'

Exactly what happened to the queen remains a mystery. A kitchen boy saw the crown prince 'moving backwards' with a gun in each hand. A woman in a red sari was in front of him. 'The two were not talking,' the boy said later. 'They were running, shouting, screaming. I cannot say who was speaking.'

Another staff member also saw a woman in a red sari outside the billiard room. He said she ran away and Dipendra ran after her across the courtyard garden. Neither mentioned seeing Nirajan.

By now, the king's senior ADC, Colonel Sundar Pratap

Rana, had already stolen into the billiard room, assessed the king's condition and left. There was the sound of breaking glass as the ADCs kicked in the glass door behind the billiard table. The huddled royals gave thanks, but wondered where the hell the elite bodyguards had been?

chapter 27
the adcs

After ADC Colonel Sundar Pratap Rana had escorted the king to the billiard room, he had joined his colleagues in their office nearby. He took Major Gajendra Bohra, the crown prince's ADC, outside to show him the broken streetlight.

'All the guests are inside,' a junior ADC reported when Rana returned to the office, 'and the crown prince is in his room. He's a little bit drunk, so he went to bed.'

This didn't strike Rana as so unusual, and he sat down to work on the following week's schedule. Rana wanted to discuss his plans with the helicopter pilot and had just picked up the phone when he heard a vibrating sound, like a cupboard shaking. Birds screeched in surrounding trees.

'Go and check that,' he ordered the queen mother's ADC, Captain Chakra Shah.

The air-conditioning was on, the window closed. Absorbed in the television, Captain Shah hadn't heard anything. Major Bohra hadn't heard it either, but he got up from his computer and went outside to look. They were on his turf, after all.

He'd been gone only a few moments when a burst of gunfire cracked the night.

'Sir, I can hear shots,' Bohra called to Rana. But everyone heard them this time, either because the door was now open, or because at this point the crown prince had thrown down the small machine-gun, the MP5, and picked up the louder M16 assault rifle. At about the same time, the ADCs heard a female voice shouting: 'Call the doctors! Call the doctors!'

Rana's reflex was to push an SOS button on his mobile phone to alert the royal physician. He thought that perhaps Crown Prince Dipendra had accidentally shot himself while shooting birds or vermin from his room. Then more shots rang out. Colonel Rana didn't wait for the doctor to answer.

Dipendra's ADC, Major Bohra, went straight to the glass side door near the billiard table. It was thirteen metres from the office, a distance that would take five to ten seconds to cover. Bohra looked through the glass door across the room and claims he saw the crown prince leaving through the main door to the hallway.

Another ADC, Pawan Khatri, however, had remained in the office to call up the military guard on the radio. When he had finished, he ran to the glass door and says he saw the crown prince backing out of the door, scoping the room with the light on the end of the gun. The spot briefly flashed across Khatri's face.

So Major Bohra, who had arrived at the glass door many seconds earlier, may have seen more than he has let on. Bohra says he pulled at the door, which he knew would be locked. He ran another thirteen metres along the side of the building to the hallway, where he peered around the corner, but says he did not see anything. He turned back.

Bohra later told an inquiry that he'd moved cautiously: 'My aim was to protect the Crown Prince.' The ADC was in the deepest conflict of interest. His close friend, whose life he had been charged with protecting for the last decade, clearly needed to be taken out, but the rules forbade this.

As the queen's ADC, Ananta Simha, explained, protocol

applied a strict hierarchy to the lives of the people inside the billiard room: 'Even if I had seen the crown prince shooting other royal family members, I wouldn't have done anything. Only the queen or the king, then I would have shot him. Or, if he was shooting at other royal members, and the queen or the king gave orders, then I would shoot him down.' Asked what he would do if the crown prince shot at him, the ADC replied: 'Nothing. I would be dead.'

It is hard to imagine that Major Bohra did not see more carnage than he has told the world. We met him on two occasions and found him to be affable and impressive. Short and muscular, he'd once considered a career in professional soccer. We drank beer and ate Portuguese chicken, but he would not talk about the incident. We felt sorry for him.

As Bohra looked into the blood-splashed room, he later told the inquiry, he saw 'all had fallen, but . . . I was only thinking of how to get him [the crown prince] under control. No one knew where he was.' Then he saw the king's in-law, Dr Rajiv, escape out a window next to the glass door.

Clearly, Major Bohra didn't think the doctor was responsible for the carnage inside, because he chased him for a short distance and then let him go. That is to say, Major Bohra already knew exactly who was responsible but was helpless to do anything about it. (Rajiv ran all the way out of the palace grounds without any effective challenge from the guards. In a move for which he was later strongly criticised, the one person capable of giving further medical assistance to the fallen king hailed a taxi and was out of there.)

When the king's ADC, Colonel Rana, had put down his mobile phone and rushed to the locked glass door to the billiard room, he had seen Dr Rajiv standing over the king's body. The veteran ADC was relieved. If King Birendra was in trouble, at least there was a doctor with him.

Rana ran past Major Bohra to the hallway entrance, where he momentarily saw the armed crown prince cross the corridor and disappear into the darkness of the courtyard garden. Rana didn't know if Crown Prince Dipendra was the gunman or if he was trying to protect his family, but he knew that if His Royal Highness shot at him, he could not return fire. His training had taught him that his priority was not to remove the threat but to remove the king from the threat.

He had to get into the billiard room. Get to the king. He expected it would cost him his life. Handgun drawn, he went down the hallway and into the room. His mind did not register the bodies fallen in a tight group in front of the billiard table, blood pooling on the white marble floor. None of the other royals were his concern. The ADC only saw King Birendra in the middle of them all. He heard someone say, 'Catch the crown prince,' but it washed over him.

The monarch was snoring on the cold floor with blood soaking his white shirt. Rana was annoyed that Dr Rajiv had mysteriously disappeared. Suddenly, a burst of automatic gun-fire came from the garden. It was still a battle zone. As he bent over the king's body, he expected a bullet in the back at any moment.

See, think, act. ABC: airways, breathing, circulation. He couldn't carry the king out of the room the way he'd come in. That was where the firing was coming from. So he tried to break the glass side door, but couldn't do it alone. Instead he left the king and went back out the way he'd come.

Colonel Rana had been the only ADC to venture into the billiard room. All the others remained safely in the area of the glass door. Now Rana rejoined them and together they kicked the glass door in. They ran into the billiard room, picked up the king's limp body, and ran with him out over the shattered glass without any regard to the dead and dying all around.

They carried Birendra to his Jaguar, always parked closest to the gate. There was no time to wait for a driver. Colonel Rana thumped the overpowered vehicle through the clotted streets of Kathmandu on a mad, panicked dash. ADC Khatri had the king's head on his lap, one hand in His Majesty's neck wound and the other giving CPR. He was certain he could still hear faint breathing.

Rana was on the walkie-talkie, trying to alert the hospital.

Trying to contact palace officials. He had his head out the window, yelling at traffic. The siren was wailing. He yelled to God. His world had gone crazy.

Perhaps two minutes elapsed from the first shots to when King Birendra was raced out of the room. Some put it at more like three or four minutes, but time was warped by the events. It could equally have been just ninety seconds. No one could say for sure.

'People say the whole thing took two minutes, three minutes,' Colonel Rana told us. 'That's impossible. If it's two minutes, what were we doing? Maybe we didn't hear the first sound. As soon as we heard it, we ran in there.' He estimated that from the time the queen called for help until the king was evacuated was a mere seventy seconds.

But the ADCs' version of events is irreconcilable with that of the survivors. It is hard to imagine that some of the ADCs did not at least see Dipendra shoot Gorakh at point-blank range, then face off with his cousin Paras before backing from the room for the last time. Even so, their hands were tied. Unless they saw him shoot King Birendra or Queen Aishwarya, they were powerless to act.

Towards the end of the carnage, General Rabi had seen Dipendra throw down an empty magazine. As a military man, he listened for the metallic click that would tell him the gunman was reloading to come and finish them off. But all was quiet. It's finished, he thought.

He slowly got up. 'My God! Everyone is dead. Everyone is dead.' Then he saw Ketaki move.

'Uncle Rabi, I got shot here,' she motioned to her shoulder.

'Don't move, and don't talk,' the old man told her. 'Stay there. People will come and take you. Don't try to get up.'

Dhirendra was moaning.

'What happened to you, sir? What happened to you?' Rabi asked.

Dhirendra didn't reply.

As the survivors slowly emerged from their hiding places, Prince Paras took charge. 'Anyone with a gun, guard this door.' He motioned to the main entry. The ADCs had left to carry the king's body to the car.

Paras went to Dhirendra. 'Paras, my feet don't move,' his uncle said. 'I can't move my feet. Please move them.' Paras reached down and held them, but Dhirendra could not feel it. 'I can't see straight,' he said. 'Look after your Aunt Ketaki.'

Then, in the pile of bodies in front of the billiard table, Paras saw his mother, Princess Komal. He had not seen her get shot. Now she was trying to get up from under Princess Shanti, gasping for breath. He went to help her. 'I'm not well. I'm not well,' she said, holding her blood-splashed forehead. He felt around her scalp, but found no wound. He realised the blood was his Aunt Shanti's. But Komal did have a bullet through a lung.

The sound of another gunshot rang out. The danger was still very real. Paras thought it might have come from the sitting room where Queen Mother Ratna and Princess Helen were. He dashed there and found them chatting away, totally oblivious to what had just happened. The two old women had heard some shots. 'There he goes shooting cats again,' the queen mother had remarked. They had heard some shouting but presumed it was the youngsters playing in the garden.

'Dipendra shot King Birendra and all the others,' Paras informed them.

'Where is the king?' asked the queen mother.

'I have sent him to hospital already,' Paras replied.

'Where is the queen and Nirajan?'

'I saw the queen leave the room and Nirajan was following her. I don't know where.'

General Rabi also went in to see Queen Mother Ratna.

'Where is the crown prince?' she asked him.

'I don't know.'

'Tell the ADCs and the soldiers that the crown prince shall be arrested immediately,' the queen mother ordered.

When we asked Rabi if the queen mother appeared shocked, he replied: 'No, no. After all, she's a Rana girl. Coup and murder have been in our family for a long time. We hear about all these things, you see. We are not afraid of coup.'

The ADCs had heard the single shot as they carried the king to his car. The crown prince was still on the loose. Major Bohra knew that it was not going to be easy to bring his friend and principal under control. He proceeded with great caution.

After ADC Ananta Simha had helped carry the king, he turned back to the office to telephone the royal physician. He spoke to the doctor, then began searching for his charge, Queen Aishwarya.

Even though he'd been in Tribhuvan Sadan minutes earlier, it had been so shocking to see the king on the floor that he hadn't noticed all the other bodies. Now the full horror was there before him. He poked through the moaning jumble of saris and blood, but the queen was not there.

He went back to the office and phoned Her Majesty's maid to ask if she'd been seen back at the palace. She hadn't. And so Simha returned to Tribhuvan Sadan.

In all this time, Dipendra's ADC, Major Bohra, had not checked the shadowy courtyard garden into which the crown prince had disappeared, nor his bedroom. One family member who was not a witness would later say that it was only when the queen mother gave an order to 'shoot the Crown Prince' that the ADCs could do anything against him.

Major Simha, the queen's ADC, met up with Bohra on the edge of the courtyard. A few ornamental lights along the path did little to illuminate the scene. Then they heard loud moaning and followed the noise about twenty metres to the little bridge over the pond.

Dipendra was lying there in his camouflage gear, moaning, gurgling. A military guard who had just arrived picked up a pistol lying next to the body and tossed it into the pond. Prince Paras came over and supervised as the still-moaning crown prince was carried into the light. They saw blood on his head. So much blood.

ADC Simha turned from where the crown prince lay and saw another body less than ten metres away in the darkness. It was a pulp of flesh and lead. Prince Nirajan. Alerting others to his find, Simha continued to search for the queen.

He noticed something red on a doorway across the garden. He went through the door to the white-lit stairs leading up to the crown prince's sleeping quarters. A trail of brain tissue, red *tika*, earrings, broken glass bangles, teeth and part of a jawbone led the major up to the body of Queen Aishwarya on the seventh step. Several large blood splatters indicated she had been shot from above. It appeared she had chased her son into the searing neon light of the stairwell. In some accounts, it is claimed that she was saying words to the effect of 'You dirty rotten bastard.' He blasted her face off with a burst of seven rounds.

The evacuation of Tribhuvan Sadan was well and truly underway as the military guard arrived. 'Those who are gone, leave them,' Paras had ordered. 'Take their pulses. Those with signs of life, they should be taken first.'

Ketaki had lost consciousness. When she came to, she was still on the floor. She saw Queen Aishwarya being carried by her arms and legs and she thought they could have at least taken her on a carpet.

Ketaki knew no one would be able to lift her in the same way. Her right arm looked like it would fall off if anyone pulled it, but still she felt no pain. 'I can't sit, but if someone helps me sit, I can walk,' she told the guards.

Stretchers had been brought to ferry the wounded. A guard walked the barefoot Ketaki towards the glass door, but she didn't want to go through it because of all the broken glass. 'Can you get my shoes?' she asked him. 'They're back in there on the other side.' She thought the ADC was going to smack her, but he lifted her over the debris. Outside, Paras was ordering his sister and wife and some of the other eight who were un-injured to go and pick up Dhirendra's ex-wife, Princess Prekshya, and go to his place, lock the doors and stay there.

Dipendra's second ADC, Raju Karki, whom Devyani had phoned and urged to come in on his day off, had meanwhile arrived at the ADCs' office to find it empty. He changed into his military greens and found Major Bohra in the driveway, where the bodies of Princes Dipendra and Nirajan were being loaded into a vehicle. They soon set off on a frantic drive to hospital.

Ketaki got into the front seat of a van. Dhirendra was in agony on the floor in the back. She wanted someone to lift him onto the seat, thinking it would be too bumpy on the floor. As they drove, Ketaki used her feet on the dash to stabilise herself, both her arms being out of action. She warned Dhirendra to brace himself with each approaching pothole, but there was little he could do. She didn't know that he was paralysed.

They talked all the way.

'Who's alive?'

'I saw the queen. She is dead. I saw Nirajan. He is dead. I don't know about the king.' She hoped by some miracle he would be alive.

When Colonel Rana steered the king's Jaguar through the hos-pital gates, as far as he was concerned, Crown Prince Dipendra – or whoever had done this – was probably right behind, about to make sure he finished the job. Once inside the facility, Rana ordered the commander of the guard to seal the hospital. No one else was to be allowed in.

About ten minutes later, however, the order was counter-manded as the other wounded started to arrive, the crown prince among them. More royals turned up, walking, being carried or wheeled into the trauma hall.

Colonel Rana went outside for a breath of air and felt like he'd never felt before. Helpless. The man of action who had got to where he had purely on merit was suddenly confronting failure for the first time. A failure of the most far-reaching kind. He had his gun with him. He thought about using it.

chapter 28
the emergency ward

a young woman, Lieutenant Sadikshya Singh, was the duty doctor at Birendra Military Hospital. No sooner had she heard that an ADC had phoned from the palace warning that a VVIP was on the way, than someone in the trauma hall called to say the patient was already there. As Dr Singh rushed to the hall, she was met by Sundar Pratap Rana and another ADC. They told her the patient was the king.

Reaching the examination trolley, she noticed that blood was coming from each ear. Blood was everywhere. She checked for signs of life but there were none. Dr Singh started cardio-pulmonary resuscitation, pumping at the king's still chest, forcing air into his lungs. She called for help, dressing the wounds with compression bandages to hold the blood in. Nurses jabbed IV drips into both arms, and prongs into his nose for oxygen. Surgeons, anaesthetists, physicians, heart specialists and more nurses were all on their way. But as the young lieutenant pumped away at the king's heart, she knew it was all too late.

The king's son-in-law, Gorakh Shamsher Rana, appeared in the doorway. He was walking, with assistance, despite four bullets in his chest and four other minor wounds. In the car on the way to hospital, he had kept repeating to the driver, 'My blood group is AB positive,' worried that hospitals get people's blood types wrong. He was still talking as he was helped through the door.

The young doctor left the king to the nurses, who continued to pump at his chest and the ambu-bag, desperately hoping against all reason to spark some life. Dr Singh saw the bleeding on Gorakh's right thumb. 'It's gone,' he said. 'My chest hurts.'

She ordered the nurses to put him on a drip and oxygen, then rushed to his wife, Princess Shruti, who was on another trolley. Shruti had no obvious signs of injury, yet she was unresponsive, pale, her pulse barely there and her pupils not reacting to light. Dr Singh started CPR, and ordered IV lines, an adrenalin injection and atropine to increase her heart rate.

The royal physician, Dr Khagendra Shrestha, arrived and took over the king's resuscitation efforts from the nurses.

Crown Prince Dipendra was brought in on a stretcher and placed on the floor since all the trolleys were taken. Brain matter was oozing from his head wounds. He too was set up with IV lines and oxygen, and was the first to be carried upstairs to the operating theatre.

Prince Nirajan's body was carried in, but required little medical examination. Neither did Queen Aishwarya's. Eighty per cent of her brain was missing.

M.K. Singh walked into the trauma hall holding his bloodied right forearm. All the doctors were busy working on the king, then the crown prince and Princess Shruti, so Singh moved around the untended trolleys to see if he could help. Her Majesty was dead on one. Princess Sharada, Princess Jayanti, Princess Shanti and Prince Nirajan, all gone. He found Princess Komal alive and asked her how she was feeling. She grimaced, but didn't speak as she held her stomach and ribs, obviously in great pain. On top of the wounds inflicted by

Dipendra's shooting her in the back, Komal had broken three ribs as she fell.

Singh moved on to Gorakh's trolley. He was talking, but very slowly, very low.

He found Dhirendra in some difficulty. 'Could you pull my necklace down? I'm having trouble breathing,' the former prince said. Singh tried to loosen the heavy gold chain around his throat. Dhirendra looked in a bad state. He was turning blue. His breathing was shallow. Nurses dressed his wounds and the blood was sucked from his lungs. He was given oxygen and his colour improved.

Next to Dhirendra, Ketaki was still bleeding profusely from her right shoulder. She wanted something done immediately, but there was nobody there. Singh felt her frustration, but she just had to wait.

Princess Shobha felt cold, she said, and asked for a blanket. The king's middle sister had a small wound on her face and the top of her ring finger was missing.

Dr Upendra Devkota, Nepal's first and most renowned neurosurgeon, had just finished performing neck surgery at his private clinic. He was talking to a relative of the patient when one of his usually respectful deputies rushed in and asked the relative to leave.

The deputy shut the door. 'Sir, you have to rush to the hospital,' he told Devkota. 'The crown prince has a bullet injury.' At that moment a man in uniform stormed in: 'This way, sir.' It was Queen Aishwarya's ADC, Major Ananta Simha.

The doctor was dragged along in the soldier's wake, calling instructions to the deputy as he left.

The ADC barged his four-wheel drive onto the evening streets. Red lights flashed as motorbikes and cars did their best to get out of the way. The two men didn't talk, but Dr Devkota knew something was very wrong from the way the ADC was driving. They banged into another vehicle but sped off, arriving at Birendra Military Hospital in what seemed like moments. The doctor felt giddy. Soldiers swarmed the gate.

Dr Devkota was used to being something of a novelty when he visited hospitals. Such was his renown, he was always being pulled aside to see extra patients. So it was no surprise that voices came at him from everywhere: 'Upstairs, doctor', 'This way, doctor.' He was dragged into the trauma hall. It was full of people. There must have been a bus accident, he thought.

He was shown a grey-haired man on a stretcher. The man was extremely pale. Blood splattered his white *kurta suruwal*. A locket around his neck showed a picture of the afro-haired cult guru Sai Baba. Nurses were trying to resuscitate him, but Dr Devkota could see they were wasting their time. He felt for a pulse, looked at the man's eyes. 'He's gone. There is no point.'

The royal physician appeared. He took Dr Devkota through the hall, murmuring, 'Disaster, everybody has been shot,' as he pointed out the dead royalty. They stopped at a patient being resuscitated. 'Princess Shruti.'

The princess's heart was barely beating. Dr Devkota could not feel a pulse. He examined her quickly and saw no external injuries. Maybe it was internal bleeding, he thought. Since he could see no head injuries, there was nothing he could do.

Princess Shruti faded fast. There was later a suggestion that the modesty of the doctors hindered her treatment: she had been shot in the rectum as she bent over her stricken husband. The crown prince's sister died of internal injuries at 9.55 pm, about thirty-five minutes after arriving at the hospital.

The neurosurgeon still had no idea what had happened as Dr Shrestha hurried him back to the man with the Sai Baba locket. 'This is His Majesty.'

Devkota felt a surge of emotion. The shock of what he'd just seen caught up to him: the royal family was gone. The injuries he'd seen were bullet wounds and it began to sink in that whoever did this was trying to wipe out the whole dynasty. Possibilities raced through his mind. The military, the Maoists, an Indian invasion. Whatever it was, he saw a very bleak future for his country.

He paid his last respects to His Majesty and walked out, his mind in a whirl. His thoughts went to the time he met the king at an international neurosurgical conference in Kathmandu three years earlier. Three poster-sized photos of the two men in animated conversation graced Dr Devkota's lounge-room wall. In his heart, he felt as big a loss as when his parents had died. But he knew he had to overcome it. Devkota changed into his surgical uniform, and entered the operating theatre. There, the heir to the throne was waiting.

Princess Shanti's son Binod Singh, the Raja of Bajhang, was one of the cousins who had been excused from attending the family get-together at Tribhuvan Sadan just hours before it began. He was finishing his dinner a little before 9.30 pm when he was surprised to hear his mother's car driving into the family compound. He wasn't expecting her home until 10.30 or 11 pm.

His younger brother Pramod went downstairs to see why she was back so early, but then called up to Binod: 'Get ready. We have to go to the palace.'

'What happened?'

The driver answered. 'I don't know. I think I heard some bomb go off.'

Binod quickly changed and put on a *topi*. On the way to Narayanhiti Palace, he asked the flustered driver to tell him everything he'd seen and heard.

'I heard some shattering. Like a corrugated-tin sheet crashing down, or monkeys running around on it.' Binod knew they had a monkey problem at one of the palace's temples. 'No, but there were bodies being taken out,' said the driver.

The Maoists were foremost in their minds. Pulling up at the palace, Binod saw his uncle, Kumar Khadga, being stretchered out. Binod had grown up with guns and hunting. He knew the wound in his uncle's chest was from a bullet. He'd also been one of the first people on the scene when communists bombed the Annapurna Hotel in the early 1990s but there was none of the smell of a bomb here. Still, he presumed it was a bomb because nothing else made sense.

'Where's my mother?' he asked. He was pointed towards a pick-up truck, where he found Princess Shanti laid out on the back seat. He leaned in. She was cold. Then he checked his uncle's pulse. He was still alive. 'Get him to hospital,' he ordered.

Binod rushed home and called his cousins, Princess Sharada and Khadga's children, who lived next door. 'I have seen my mum dead,' he said. 'I've seen your dad. He is wounded but alive.'

Binod and his cousins were confused as they drove to the hospital. The military weren't on the streets, yet surely if the Maoists had attacked, the whole city would be shut down. And if it was a bomb, wouldn't they have heard it from their homes so close to the palace?

When they reached the hospital's front entrance, Queen Mother Ratna stopped them from rushing in. She made them sit around her. 'Dipendra did it,' she said. 'We didn't expect him to do this.' Then she sent them in.

The ward felt like a war zone. Doctors were running. Some were still working on His Majesty. Binod moved from stretcher to stretcher. All dead. His uncle Kumar Khadga, whom he had seen alive back at the palace, was now gone.

The cousins had to work hard to recognise their relatives. They noted the gunpowder burns on the skin of some of the victims, showing how close Dipendra's gun had been.

Princess Shobha, their aunt, lifted her arm. 'Thank God. Someone is alive.' Then Binod saw Ketaki move. She was pretty beaten up, but could talk. She started to tell him what happened. Gorakh, in a faint voice, filled in more details.

271

Binod felt anger at his exalted cousin the crown prince. Yet he was sad. The two conflicting emotions made it hard to feel much of anything. Everyone wore the same dazed expression – the doctors, the generals arriving on the scene and later the senior politicians as they walked in on the horror.

Binod used his mobile phone to call Alan Chester, Ketaki's English husband.

'Auntie has been shot,' Binod said, putting Ketaki on.

'Please come. I need you,' she told her husband. She had a fear of needles and knew there were plenty ahead.

'What happened?' he asked.

'I've been shot. We've all been shot. I don't know how many of us are dead.'

'Who shot you?' Chester wanted to know.

'You think about it. I'll tell you when you come.'

Dipendra had a hole on either side of his head, each oozing blood and brain tissue. He was naked except for his underwear. A tube ran down his throat. His blood pressure and heart rate were okay, but his pupils were fixed and dilated.

Dr Devkota pushed his thumb into the crown prince's sternum, causing the patient's arms to twist slightly. It was only a small movement, but the reflex action meant he was not brain-dead. On the Glasgow Coma Scale – where a score of 15 is a healthy person and 3 is brain-dead – the crown prince scored a 4.

The outlook was extremely poor. The entry wound was a one-centimetre diameter hole just behind the left ear. The larger exit wound was above the right ear. As a general rule, when a bullet enters and exits behind the hairline, it should be fatal. The bullet doesn't just bore a hole through the brain, it transmits perpendicular shock waves which cause invisible vibration injury. But Devkota felt he had to do what he could and hope for a miracle.

He asked the other doctors to paralyse and ventilate the patient. He would do the operation where he was. The hospital was less well-equipped than others, but moving the crown prince would almost certainly kill him. So, feeling the pressure of the whole world watching, he began.

For Ketaki, the wait for treatment seemed like forever. She heard Princess Komal complain to the hospital staff: 'It's been a long time. Aren't you going to operate?'

Dipendra had been the first casualty to be whisked up to the operating theatre, but Ketaki didn't feel any resentment at him being given priority. When you are brought up with proto-col ruling your every move, such an order was natural. And while Princess Komal, with a bullet in her lung and three broken ribs, might have had to wait now, in three days she would be queen and any future pleas for help would be met with a click of the medical heels.

Ketaki saw that Gorakh had stopped moving. She knew he wasn't dead yet because his face remained uncovered. His condition was steadily declining, though. As a mere in-law, he didn't get to an operating table until 4 am, despite being critically injured. He had eight bullet wounds in all.

When the doctor eventually operated on him, an inch or two of gold chain was removed from the wound at the base of his throat. As Dipendra shot him point-blank in the throat, the bullet had nicked a corner of his Krishna pendant and taken the chain into the wound. His left jugular had a tear in it, but it seemed that the chain carrying his pendant had taken much of the bullet's impact and may have helped save him. Various pieces of shrapnel were removed from his chest, but plenty of smaller fragments remained. His most serious injury, though, was to his heart. One of the first bullets to strike him had nicked his right atrium, where he'd need three stitches.

Not seriously injured, M.K. Singh had the gaping wound

on his forearm dressed around midnight. He went home at 12.30 am, but when he got there he realised he was still bleeding on the inside of the forearm. They had only dressed the exit wound and missed the smaller entry wound. His wife cleaned it up with Dettol, after which he had a cup of coffee and went to bed.

He got no sleep.

Through the long hours of the early morning, Dr Devkota worked on Crown Prince Dipendra. The operation took five hours. As the dawn approached, Devkota had time to go to the surgeons' room. It was only then, talking with his shell-shocked colleagues, that he heard the terrible story. The other doctors claimed that the person he'd just worked so hard to save had murdered all the others.

Outside, it was getting light.

chapter 29
long live the king

At least somebody from the royal family is alive, Dr Devkota thought, as he strode along the corridor to meet the dead king's brother, Prince Gyanendra. At least somebody can take charge.

In the warm, early morning light of 2 June, Gyanendra's helicopter had brought him from Pokhara and landed at the hospital. He had gone straight to intensive care to see his dead and wounded family. His brother Dhirendra was clinging to life. Gyanendra's wife Komal, Princess Shobha (his only surviving sister) and his cousin Ketaki were all recovering from surgery. Gorakh had deteriorated overnight.

Now Dr Devkota was on his way to brief Gyanendra on Crown Prince Dipendra. The neurosurgeon was accompanied by the royal physician, Dr Shrestha.

Gyanendra, ashen-faced but composed, looked up as the two doctors walked in. 'Tell me,' he said, 'how is the crown prince?'

Devkota gave it to him straight: 'Any through-and-through

injury of the brain behind the hairline is usually fatal. He is still alive, but the long-term prognosis is very, very poor.' It would take a miracle for Dipendra to survive.

This was a serious problem. The Raj Parishad (Nepal's privy council) could not announce King Birendra's death without declaring a successor. And that successor was facing almost certain death. Would he die within moments? Would he hang on a few hours? A few weeks? Was he already brain-dead?

With the crown prince heavily sedated, Dr Devkota had not been able to make an assessment since the night before. The doctors wanted to know, though, if he was brain-dead, should they turn off his life support? 'Well, given that we don't know if he's even brain-dead, let's find out first,' Gyanendra instructed. 'If he is brain-dead, then we'll discuss whether to remove life support. Let's meet again at 10 am.'

Devkota headed home to take a quick shower.

M.K. Singh had barely slept. He was dressed and out the door by 7.30 am. His bullet wound still needed seeing to.

The Saturday-morning traffic was unusually quiet. He noticed that at each intersection people were gathering. Talking. They had heard. All night, telephones had been ringing across Kathmandu. The two morning newspapers that carried news of the deaths had sold out instantly.

Singh arrived at the nearest clinic.

'What happened to you?' asked the doctor.

M.K. wouldn't tell him. He had served in the palace. He knew how these things worked.

Dr Devkota was just out of the shower when the phone rang. It was the hospital. His deadline to reassess Crown Prince

Dipendra had been brought forward to 9 am. The Raj Parishad had called an emergency meeting. The privy councillors wanted a definitive prognosis. Devkota phoned the doctors on duty and ordered that Dipendra's sedation and paralysis drugs be stopped, to enable him to carry out an assessment.

By the time he reached the hospital, he found the patient trying to move his legs. Trying to breathe and cough. His brain was alive. The message was conveyed up the line.

Dr Keshar Jung Rayamajhi, chairman of the Raj Parishad, had been at the hospital all night. The thin old man was not coping well. A former general secretary of the Communist Party turned staunch monarchist, Rayamajhi had wept over the lifeless body of his king.

Now he was responsible for declaring him dead and naming a successor. Tradition demanded that Birendra's body be cremated today, which meant a new king had to be decided on immediately. The pressure was enormous.

As he went into the council meeting, Rayamajhi received the latest news on Dipendra's condition. Constitutionally, it cleared the way to declare him king. Rayamajhi would later claim there was no further hurdle to the succession. While everyone else who'd been to the the hospital knew the crown prince was a murderer, and many of Rayamajhi's colleagues were discussing it before the meeting, Rayamajhi would insist he hadn't heard.

Dipendra's crimes were therefore never formally raised at the meeting. He was now immune from prosecution. Above the law. And, according to the rules of succession, so long as he was alive, the Raj Parishad could not declare another king. Thus, the seventy-odd members in attendance voted unanimously in favour of Dipendra. With His Majesty King Dipendra Bir Bikram Shah Dev 'physically unable to take care of the affairs of state', however, Prince Gyanendra was named regent.

Early that afternoon, almost sixteen hours after the massacre, Rayamajhi made the first official announcement that
Dipendra was king, following the deaths of King Birendra and
Queen Aishwarya. Struggling to control his grief throughout,
the politician made no mention of how they died.

The country was gagged, shackled by a news blackout. A
five-day period of national mourning was declared. The international media were already claiming the new king was a killer,
beaming the message direct to the middle class by satellite and
the internet. But Nepalese television and radio only rolled out
doleful music to the masses. And the rumours festered.

Throughout the afternoon of Saturday, 2 June, tens of thousands of mourners gathered on the streets for the funeral
procession. Riot police and soldiers surrounded the palace and
lined the funeral route. There had already been minor clashes
on Durbar Marg, as Nepalis flocked to the palace gates
demanding answers.

In her hospital bed, Ketaki was still groggy from surgery
but could hear the national anthem and knew they were taking
her family to their pyres. She was relieved she didn't have to
face it.

It was 4 pm when the procession left Birendra Military
Hospital for Pashupatinath. At the head of the cortege, 1000
soldiers carved a path through the flood of grief. Behind them
trailed a melancholy parade of royalty, politicians and generals.
Among them, devastated, was Pashupati Shamsher Rana. His
shattered daughter Devyani had already fled the country for
New Delhi.

On a simple bamboo platform borne by Brahmins in
white *dhotis* (loin-wraps) came the body of King Birendra. He
was wrapped in a saffron cloth draped in prayer scarves and
covered with flowers. Vermilion streaked his grey face.

Marching on the king's right was his devoted ADC,

Colonel Sundar Pratap Rana. Rana had never seen so much colour. Never imagined King Birendra was so loved. Through the narrow streets, desperate hands dismissed cultural taboos and reached out to touch the dead monarch. Overhead, mourners swamped rooftops and windows, tossing offerings and chanting 'Long live the king!' and 'Our king and our country are dearer than our lives!'

Flowers, incense and red powder rained down on Colonel Rana's head. And looming out of the colour were the wailing faces. It was too much to bear. Tears streamed down the soldier's cheeks.

Behind the king's platform came the shrouded Queen Aishwarya on the same gold palanquin that bore her to her wedding thirty-one years before. Her horrific head injuries were masked by the face of a large china doll. Then came their children, Prince Nirajan and Princess Shruti, and cousin Princess Jayanti.

As grief overwhelmed the crowd, their sorrow turned to anger. 'Hang Koirala!' some shouted as the prime minister passed. One group burnt an effigy. Then, as the procession wound by the Buddhist temple at Swayambhu (known to tourists as the Monkey Temple), a roar went up and irate mourners began stoning the prime minister's Mercedes. Police officers fired and the mob scattered in confusion.

The procession pushed on, wading through the shallow, black waters of the Bishnumati River and into the heart of old Kathmandu, squeezing through claustrophobic lanes as crowds continued to surge behind. Outside Narayanhiti Palace, the growing cortege paused for a moment, before moving on to complete its three-hour journey to Pashupatinath.

There, on the banks of the Bagmati River, the deceased royals were bathed in the sacred waters. One by one, the bodies were placed atop pyres of sandalwood and marigolds. Darkness fell and it began to rain. The pyres were lit. Brahmins recited holy verse, soldiers formed an honour guard and a volley of shots echoed through the Kathmandu Valley as flames engulfed the dead.

Early on Sunday morning, 3 June, Regent Gyanendra broadcast a statement in which, for the first time, he addressed the cause of the royal deaths. Their Majesties died, he said, following 'a sudden discharge of an automatic weapon' during a regular family dinner.

Across Kathmandu, shutters were drawn and the air was still. Barbers set up street stalls and shaved thousands of heads in a mark of respect normally reserved for the mourning of one's parents. Numbed Nepalis queued to sign condolence books outside the palace. Women wept over portraits of the king and queen. A young motorcycle mechanic in the Terai was so heartbroken he drank a bottle of poison.

At Pashupatinath, the royal cremations continued with the last rites of Princess Shanti, Princess Sharada and Sharada's husband Kumar Khadga. Later in the day, Khadga's mother would also be brought to the banks of the Bagmati. When told that her son and daughter-in-law had been killed, she had collapsed and died.

With little more than condolence messages and eulogies filling the newspapers, wild stories swept the capital. The Maoists cried 'conspiracy!' and whipped up the anguish. The simmering frustration erupted into riots. Gangs of young men roared around on motorbikes to the chant of 'Hang the murderer!' They blamed Prime Minister Koirala, Regent Gyanendra, Prince Paras. Even the CIA and Indian intelligence. Anyone but their beloved Dipendra. In one incident, an enraged mob burned copies of an Indian newspaper for publishing a front-page photograph of the crown prince holding an automatic rifle.

Meanwhile, Dr Devkota was working desperately to save King Dipendra's life. It had been a stressful day at the hospital. The surgeon hadn't even stopped to eat. Dipendra was rapidly slipping towards brain death, while his uncle Dhirendra was in a critical condition, with massive chest and spinal injuries.

That evening, when Regent Gyanendra returned to the hospital with the queen mother, Dr Devkota broke the news. Dipendra's chances of survival were now zero. They could turn off the ventilator, or keep treating him as long as his heart continued to beat.

'Keep treating him,' Gyanendra said.

At 3.45 am on Monday, 4 June, King Dipendra's heart stopped.

Another emergency meeting of the Raj Parishad unanimously voted to declare Gyanendra king.

In light of the changed circumstances, Gyanendra went on state radio to confess that, in his previous reference to 'the tragic incident at the royal palace' there had been 'constitutional and legal difficulties in expressing what had actually transpired'. That is, the truth would have been treason. He promised an urgent investigation.

Later that morning, in a stone courtyard in the old royal palace of Hanuman Dhoka, Gyanendra ascended the throne. The country's third king in four days. Beneath a drizzling sky, the royal priest placed the extravagant plumed crown atop the solemn king and offered him a gold coin, just as the priest's father had in 1950 when, as a bewildered child, Gyanendra was crowned by the Ranas.

King Gyanendra looked pale and drawn. His eyes welled with tears. A palm-reader had once predicted Gyanendra would twice be king. His family had laughed.

As Gyanendra retreated to the palace, violence broke out across the city. Rampaging mobs pelted stones at police, demanding answers. Rioters stormed the palace gates, hurling abuse and cries of 'Murderer!' at the new king and his son Paras. Police beat them back with batons and rubber bullets. Trees were uprooted and cars overturned. The stench of burning tyres and tear gas choked the streets.

When police started shooting live rounds, at least three demonstrators were killed and dozens injured. A curfew was imposed across the valley from 3.30 pm, ahead of King Dipendra's funeral. Anyone who broke curfew would be given one warning and then shot. Tanks rolled into the deserted, smoking streets.

In stark contrast to the majestic procession of his father, Dipendra's body was laid on the back of an open truck and whisked through the hospital gates. Thousands of protestors, despite the curfew, attempted to hold the truck back. At least three more were killed and hundreds of suspected Maoists arrested.

The military convoy, escaping any more violence, sped the corpse along the Ring Road straight to Pashupatinath. King Dipendra's cremation, with full state honours, was attended only by army brass and officials. A priest lit the pyre.

That evening, Dipendra's uncle Dhirendra died in hospital, bringing the number of dead to ten.

King Gyanendra broadcast another message to the nation in which he announced the committee that would investigate the massacre.

Ten days later, the two-man commission handed its findings to the king.

chapter 30

the romanovs
vs columbine

K ing Gyanendra untied the report's blue velvet cover and began to read. Three pages in, he handed it over to Prime Minister Koirala. 'Take this report to the people immediately.'

An hour later, probe committee member Taranath Ranabhat presented a summary of the investigation live on television. Flaunting a grisly display of camouflage gear, cartridges and guns, the verdict was decisive: the lone gunman was Dipendra.

Ranabhat and Supreme Court Chief Justice Keshav Prasad Upadhayay had worked around the clock for a week. They'd interviewed over 100 people and, with dozens of staff to assist them, churned out 300 pages of material. However the report, which made no mention of who shot Dipendra nor commented on his motive, came too late and raised as many questions as it addressed.

Prince Paras, in his statement to the committee, suggested the forbidden marriage was behind the massacre. For many ordinary Nepalis, though (and even many within the royal circle), this was not reason enough. And so the dissection of the report began.

The committee's reference to an unidentified 'black substance' in Dipendra's cigarettes sparked serious curiosity. While it was almost certainly hashish, the suggestion that it might have been cocaine, or amphetamines, or angel dust, grasped the public imagination. It somehow diminished Dipendra's responsibility – perhaps the cigarette had been spiked? – and would explain how he could revive himself from a drunken stupor, load up with guns and shoot his family with such accuracy.

That is, of course, if he was even drunk in the first place. The crown prince's boozy display was completely out of character. But there were no blood tests and no autopsy on Dipendra, nor on any of his victims. According to royal physician Dr Shrestha, 'It was not hospital practice.' As to whether Dipendra even smelt like he'd been drinking, neurosurgeon Dr Devkota only said: 'It's difficult to say when you are in the theatre with anaesthetic drugs around. I have never commented on that.'

So if indeed Dipendra was the killer, a sceptical public asked, how could he simply walk up to the most protected man in the land and pump him with bullets? The suspicious survival of the new King Gyanendra's entire immediate family continued to focus attention. Why exactly was Gyanendra not at the dinner? How was Paras the only person able to talk a homicidal maniac out of killing him? After all, they were the only beneficiaries of the massacre. Already despised, or distrusted at best, father and son were easy targets for the conspiracy theorists.

There was, of course, the matter of Gyanendra's wife's life-threatening injuries. But where, asked the cynics, was the proof? Where were the photos? The medical evidence? How were they expected to accept anything less from a palace that had fed them nothing but lies from the start?

Believers in the Gyanendra–Paras conspiracy needed to explain away the eyewitness statements, however, all of which identified Dipendra as the killer. Two explanations stood out: either the survivors had all been threatened, or (and it's a big 'or') the killer only *looked* like Dipendra. The assassin was really some sort of clone. A hired murderer in a Dipendra mask. It explained why his face remained expressionless throughout the rampage and why he never said a word, they said.

The idea was popular. And not just among the masses. Dipendra's close friend Tej seriously believed it. Others who knew him maintained that the crown prince simply wasn't capable of committing the crime. 'He's not the kind of guy who could have done it, emotionally, psychologically,' said his old geography tutor Dr K.C. Even if he did, they asked, why then would he kill himself? *Did* he kill himself? Mysteriously, Dipendra (a right-hander) had an entry bullet wound behind his left ear.

Those familiar with his shooting ability responded that the crown prince had been ambidextrous with a gun. 'Committing suicide, shooting yourself,' added M.K. Singh, 'there is no question of marksmanship. You just put it there and squeeze the trigger – which even a child could do, I would say.' Others weren't so convinced.

It had been naive to think that a week-long investigation into the deaths of ten people could provide all the answers. The commission failed to query contradictory statements, and in many instances just didn't ask the right questions. There was a second, internal palace investigation, but it was never made public.

Regardless of the facts, many Nepalis maintained it was impossible that their crown prince could murder his parents. He was too good. Meanwhile, those who knew that it was indeed possible were asking questions of their own.

During our five months in Nepal, we were welcomed into many elegant Kathmandu living rooms with the warmest of Nepalese hospitality, and given the same devastating account of what had happened on 1 June 2001. You simply could not sit across from these survivors, listening as they recounted the horrifying details, and doubt their story.

Many were still shell-shocked. Some were angry. 'I cannot refer to him [Dipendra] as king,' one relative told us. Other family members wouldn't even refer to Dipendra by name. He was, to different people, 'the idiot crown prince', 'the dickhead' or 'the murderer'.

For them, the mystery wasn't who but why. And unlike the conspiracies outside the palace walls, their questions struck at the soul of the tragedy. Why did Dipendra shoot King Birendra first when it was his mother he couldn't stand? Why did he fire the first round into the ceiling? Why did he go in and out of the room aiming at his aunties' heads? And why did he blast his beloved brother with such brutality?

Many we spoke to were grappling with just how much Devyani Rana knew. Why had she phoned Dipendra's ADCs, desperately concerned about her lover's welfare while he was still at the party playing billiards? Or was this just another instance of inaccuracy by the probe committee?

And why had the ADCs taken so long to respond to the gunfire? Their raison d'être was to protect the royals. There was a strong suggestion that Dipendra's ADCs were familiar with his threats to 'bring down the institution'. He had made the threat at his birthday party the year before, after all. So why hadn't anyone taken him seriously?

Then there were people like public intellectual Dipak Gyawali, who dismissed such suggestions altogether: 'There's just no political content to it. The parallel is not the Romanovs of Russia, it's Columbine High. You have these situations all the time: somebody runs amok, takes out a gun and starts shooting.' The real question, then, was whether the massacre was a calculated coup or a devastating explosion of madness. Or was it a combination of both?

If there had been any conspiracy, we were told time and again by family members, it was a conspiracy hatched by Dipendra.

Lying in her hospital bed, one arm smashed by Dipendra's bullets, the other badly damaged, Ketaki couldn't even smoke a cigarette. Her dear sister Jayanti was gone, along with all the others. How dare he leave her in this state. And then they'd named him king.

Ketaki wasn't the sort to just burst into tears. When you grow up in the royal family, you learn not to show emotion. But now she broke down and cried.

With nothing to do but contemplate what had happened, she figured Dipendra had set out to kill only his father. Then, forced to kill his favourite uncle, Dhirendra, when he intervened, Dipendra's plans unravelled and his descent into madness began.

But she couldn't understand why Dipendra had made the killing so open, so public. He could've killed his father in private, put a gun in the king's hand and said he committed suicide. Even if there were suspicions, nobody could accuse Dipendra. By then he'd be king.

The more Ketaki thought about it, the more she dwelled on the phone call she had received that Wednesday to check she was coming to dinner. Maybe the whole massacre had been planned.

When people asked Princess Shruti's widowed husband Gorakh what he thought, the young man would pull down his collar to reveal two neat bullet scars, just an inch apart, on the left side of his chest. Dipendra had shot the bullets from across the room. 'I'm dead sure he was faking being drunk,' he would tell them.

'He was sober,' General Rabi told us. M.K. Singh concurred: 'At eight o'clock, he's so sober he takes permission to pick up the queen mother, and [half an hour later] he's passed out.'

'He needed a reason to get up to his room,' concluded one survivor who didn't want to be named. 'Being the host, you can't just take off. People would have looked for him. The fact that he played drunk and had to be carried upstairs . . . It had to be pre-planned.'

In a small sunlit study, three young royal relatives, deep in mourning, explained their version of the tragedy.

'The only reason he came down with so many weapons was to cover his arse if anyone started shooting at him. It was so clear it was just his father he was after.

'His actions clearly show that he was power-hungry. He was planning to take over. If it was about the girl, he could have married her and lived outside the palace. He was a popular guy. After His Majesty died, the people would reinstate him. But he wanted power. He wanted the throne *and* the girl.'

'He had a weapon stashed in the garden,' another cousin pointed out, 'he had the pistol, fully clipped, he had his M16 fully clipped. The bullets alternated between full metal jacket and hollow point. Even during time of war we don't do that. Only for assassination. Shoot a full metal jacket first and then a hollow point for the maximum damage . . .

'His plan was just to shoot the king and blame Paras. It's so clear. So clear for us.'

The cousins claimed that after one of Paras's wilder moments, King Birendra had confiscated his 9mm pistol. The weapon was then deposited in the palace armoury.

'The gun that he shot himself with was Paras's weapon. This makes it clear to us that Paras was to be blamed. And the thing you've got to realise is: *the king is dead, long live the king.* A second later, the generals in the palace would have saluted the crown prince as His Majesty. The palace would have turned the facts around and he would have been king like that.'

We couldn't confirm that Dipendra had shot himself with Paras's old pistol, but it was not inconceivable that the inquiry would have kept quiet on such an incendiary fact.

'He knew that the people would never accept Paras as the crown prince,' one cousin said. 'Think about it – the country thinks Paras did it anyway. That's why he shot his brother [Nirajan] . . . sixteen shots into his back. That he shot his own brother, but not Paras, just goes to show that his brother was a bigger threat to him.'

As it turned out, Paras's actions that night turned him into a family hero. 'If Paras wasn't there, the rest of the people wouldn't be alive,' one cousin confirmed.

What the cousins couldn't explain was the slow reaction of the ADCs.

'Where the hell was the security? Dhirendra was down, Ketaki was down, and they had enough time to have a conversation. There was lots of time . . . We feel there has to be something more. That his own ADCs knew about it. You have to realise, in regard to firearms, we are in tune. We're not people who have no connection with weapons. If a gun goes off over there, we say: "It doesn't sound like a pistol, must be long-barrel. It's a shotgun, it's a rifle, it's this, it's that." So we can't register the fact that the security personnel did not react. Either it was planned or they feared for their own lives.

'I don't want an investigation on what bullets were fired, where they were fired. I want an investigation of the situations, emotions, conversations, attitude, that lead to all this. I mean, what we think is, he said: "I'm going to shoot my father, I'm going to become king." And the rest of them around him went: "Yeah, yeah, yeah."'

'I'm inclined to believe there may have been people behind the crown prince who pushed him to that extent,' echoed one of the king's senior aides. We were sitting in an empty hotel bar in Kathmandu, talking on condition of anonymity. The aide was not on duty during the massacre, but was involved in the investigation.

'It looked like he just wanted to shoot his father and declare himself king. As a king you have immunity from everything. Maybe some people had planted that in his head . . . I think he felt lots of internal conflicts and maybe there were people that were influencing him on this.'

Like who?

'Those who stood to benefit . . . when he became the king. Maybe some people would benefit directly out of that.'

Did the aide have anyone in mind?

'If I did I wouldn't tell you.'

Different versions of this theory were worming their way through the palace surrounds – that Dipendra, urged on by his friends, had decided to kill his father.

'You have all these sycophants saying you are going to be king,' an anonymous massacre survivor told us. 'There are even stories floating around [Dipendra and Devyani's] clique of friends that they were ready to offer him gold coins that night to acknowledge him as king.' While it was popular within royal circles, we found no evidence to support the theory.

Similarly, speculation that Dipendra's ADCs knew what was happening was tempting but flimsy. 'I can't help but wonder whether the king and queen's ADCs were somehow prevented from coming to the rescue,' said one survivor.

Someone else whispered: 'You know, the latest story doing the rounds is that when Devyani rang [ADC] Raju Karki that night she really told him, "Dipendra's going to shoot everybody." And Raju Karki said, "But he says that all the time."'

Following the secret palace investigation, four ADCs were fired. Three were on duty that night: Colonel Sundar Pratap Rana for the king, Major Ananta Simha for the queen, and Major Gajendra Bohra for Crown Prince Dipendra. The fourth man was Major Raju Karki, the off-duty ADC who received the worried phone call from Devyani.

While the army publicly cited negligence as the reason for their dismissal, none of the sacked ADCs faced any disciplinary action. The internal report could only have found, therefore, that there had been no dereliction of duty.

We met Dipendra's two ADCs, Raju Karki and Gajendra Bohra. They both seemed very charming, intelligent men. Aside from their statements to the probe committee, on which they were never cross-examined, neither has yet spoken about that night, nor their relationship with Crown Prince Dipendra. The ADCs for the king and queen, however, agreed to talk.

Colonel Sundar Pratap Rana, King Birendra's long-serving ADC, spoke in a low, even voice. He was finally talking, he told us, because he could no longer bear the question mark hanging over his actions that night. He couldn't stand the thought that some people believed he did not do everything in his power to protect King Birendra. 'When I got dismissed from my service, I felt I lost everything I had in my life,' he explained.

He likened his role to that of a shirt protecting a body. What happened on 1 June 2001 was like the heart exploding but the shirt wasn't designed to protect the body from itself. 'I did everything I was supposed to do.' The palace appeared to agree. When Rana was sacked, his commanding officer told him: 'You just happened to be there. We had to take some action. We know you didn't do anything wrong.'

The mild-mannered colonel was bewildered. 'Nobody blamed me. Nobody in the palace told me: "You messed up." I worked for the new king for one month and suddenly the principal secretary told me: "We have had an 'unexpected decision' to remove you from the army."' Dejected, Rana nevertheless remained a strong royalist.

He has never believed the massacre was planned. 'If there's a coup, a plan, there should be some evidence, some army men waiting nearby to take over. He might even have told us, "I'm doing this and afterwards you have to declare me king." There's no evidence . . . [Crown Prince Dipendra] was very angry at the time. He dressed up, got four rifles, and came down. That's what he did when he got angry. He used to get dressed, take a gun, and leave the palace. Driving and walking around. [This time] Instead of going outside the palace, he went into the billiard room.'

So, we asked, were Dipendra's ADCs, Gajendra Bohra and Raju Karki, aware of any plan?

'We had separate talks after the incident. They never expected that this would happen. There's no plan at all. I think it was just the marriage and alcohol. There is no evidence of a coup . . . If he wanted to kill the king, he should have killed us first. He could come with a machine-gun or with a cannon. We would line up to salute. It would be no problem.'

'We would die saluting him,' agreed Major Ananta Simha, Queen Aishwarya's ADC, a stocky young man with wire-rim spectacles. We asked Simha if he and Colonel Rana were prevented by the crown prince's ADCs from going to the rescue.

'That's not the case,' he said. 'They never stopped us.'

Did Devyani try to warn Simha?

'No. We were never in contact with Devyani.'

So what about the theory that one of the ADCs killed Dipendra?

'He was carrying an automatic rifle, I was carrying a pistol,' Simha pointed out. 'It was next to impossible that one of the ADCs shot him . . . The garden was dark. To shoot a person in the head you'd have to have night vision and be standing right next to him . . . People are saying that the ADCs came much too late. But the thing was, in those kinds of parties, you couldn't go in without being called. That was the normal custom. And when we heard the shots, then naturally we went inside regardless. But when we got to the room, the whole incident had already finished.'

Like Colonel Rana, Simha did not believe the massacre was planned. 'Because a person who has made up his mind to kill his parents will have some abnormal behaviours before that. To kill your parents is a huge thing. And the thing was, when he went to pick up his grandmother, I was there. When he came out I was there on the gate, and he was fine. He was normal . . .

'Everybody has their own theories, nobody knows for sure. But for me, it was that phone call which did it.'

The final phone call between Dipendra and Devyani remains a mystery. Much to the disappointment of many grieving royal relatives, Devyani has maintained her silence. Her patchy statement to the probe committee, sent from Delhi where she was receiving medical care, revealed her to be a broken woman. 'I never thought this could happen,' she wept.

There is no doubt she was also a victim of the massacre. But many of the other victims are looking to her for answers.

'So, the mystery deepens, you see,' said old General Rabi. 'The thing has come and gone. It's over. This is an act of God. We must forget this history and think of a new one. Forming the detail will agonise you.'

chapter 31
taming an angry spirit

k ali Bista lived by the highway. Her little house had a yellow-and-blue cigarette advertisement painted over its entire roadside wall. She was used to the river of life that wound up and over the hill into the Kathmandu Valley.

Despite the constant blaring of souped-up truck horns and the danger to her three little girls, the location had its advantages. Like when an elephant being walked to Kathmandu paused just a few metres up the road, on 10 June 2001. For all elephants are incarnations of the popular god Ganesh, remover of obstacles and granter of success.

A crowd of people were gathering around to touch it and offer it money, seeking good luck. Kali Bista had her baby girl, Shajana, on her hip and a few rupee notes in her hand as she approached to seek the giant's blessing. Her other two daughters, with diamond studs in their noses, stood back.

The elephant, a tuskless male called Moti Prasad, was tired and hungry. It had walked all through the cool of the night. Now, at 7 am, it was getting hot. It was a foul-tempered thing at the best of times.

About 100 metres behind Moti Prasad, another male elephant was following. Its *mahout* (driver) saw the woman approach the elephant and saw Moti Prasad charge at her even before she'd touched it for good luck. The elephant picked Kali Bista up and rolled her in its trunk, moving the young woman to its mouth and holding her there. Moti Prasad's *mahout* was beating the beast's head and ears mercilessly with his hardwood stick, but it would not drop the woman.

The baby Shajana fell from her mother's grip and some-body picked her up, bleeding from the temple, but okay. The tusked elephant at the rear was charging now too. Elephants are intelligent creatures and the tusked elephant knew it had to stop the other one. The second *mahout* urged it on, but the elephant seemed to act on its own. It rammed its long white tusks into Moti Prasad's leathery hide. It banged again until the bleeding beast finally smashed Kali Bista down.

Her husband of eight years, Raju Bista, a truck driver, ran out of their billboard house to find his wife's battered body surrounded by twenty or thirty onlookers. He picked her up and put her in his truck, charging off to Bir Hospital in Kathmandu. But the life slipped out of Kali Bista ten minutes before they arrived.

The *mahouts* remounted their elephants and continued their own slow journey to the capital. Soon, it would be too hot for the giants to move. The road would burn their feet. But they had to be there for an important ceremony the next day.

The tusked elephant would transport a Brahmin priest across the Bagmati River and symbolically out of the Kathmandu Valley. The priest would, in turn, carry the spirit of the departed King Birendra, smoothing his path into the after-life. The ceremony was always held eleven days after the death of a Nepalese king. Thus, three days later, Moti Prasad would carry King Dipendra's spirit from the valley.

Eleven days after the death of any person, their spirit is restless. Untamed. Some very serious *puja* is required over twelve months to domesticate that spirit, to turn it into a soul and allow the dead person to join the ancestors. But kings of Kathmandu going back to the Middle Ages have used this ritual, the *katto* ceremony, for a bit of extra shepherding.

As the chief royal priest, Ramesh Prasad Pandey, explained: 'We have to convince the soul that he no longer belongs to this world. He will be told to start his heavenly journey.'

King Birendra's *katto* ceremony went smoothly. Ramesh Prasad had found a poor old Brahmin willing to take on the onerous responsibility of delivering the king to the other world. The Brahmin, Durga Prasad Sapkota, aged seventy-five, partook of a meal of eighty-four small dishes representing the body of King Birendra. He mounted the tusked elephant at a temple near the Bagmati River and crossed the dirty stream, leaving the city of Kathmandu for the neighbouring city of Patan.

Traditionally, the old Brahmin would have continued out of the valley, never to return. And having eaten the dishes consisting of foods a Brahmin should never touch, he would have lost his caste and could not work as a priest again.

His rewards for doing this, however, would have been great. The last time the ceremony had been performed – for King Mahendra in 1972 – the Brahmin who'd eaten the *katto* had been given a house and land in the Terai.

But in the days after the ceremony for King Birendra, Sapkota was telling anyone who'd listen that he'd been given nothing but a few items of furniture and some clothes meant to have belonged to the king.

This gave the royal priest a big problem. Ramesh Prasad had forty names on a list of poor Brahmins who were willing to eat the *katto* and carry King Dipendra's spirit into the afterlife. But the man who had been selected for the job had since spoken to Sapkota and changed his mind.

By 7 pm on the evening before Dipendra's ceremony, Ramesh Prasad found his list of forty had disintegrated. No matter what he did to convince the thirty-nine other poor old priests that the ceremony was just symbolic, they wouldn't budge.

The belief that a part of the dead king's brain was included in one of the eighty-four meals was firmly ingrained in everyone's understanding of the *katto* ceremony, and that sort of thinking is hard to change. Ramesh Prasad assured the priests they would not really lose their caste, just their status. Even so, that was no small matter for the population of Brahmins who live in poverty around the Pashupatinath temple. Their revered status is all they have. They are old and looking forward to a better life in their next incarnation. By eating the *katto*, they are taking on the sins of the departed king, and that could cost them.

The whole country would be watching this ceremony. The coverage given to the first *katto* ceremony had been huge, but just as importantly, Ramesh Prasad had to do something for the spirit of Dipendra. The royal priest didn't for a moment believe King Dipendra had killed his family. But even so, anyone who has been murdered has an angry spirit. And dying young leaves a spirit with many unfulfilled desires. It is hungry and restless. Without a son to do the *puja* for him, Dipendra was going to be especially volatile. So unless they could ease him smoothly into the afterlife, he threatened to remain in this world to haunt them all.

Devi Prasad Acharya was a poor Brahmin in a humble little home in the Pashupatinath precinct when a royal priest arrived and asked him to come to the palace.

Acharya was told of the problem. According to his version of events, he said to the royal priests, 'If I get a house and other properties, I'm ready to eat the *katto*.' The palace priests agreed. Of course they did. They were desperate. That Dipendra was a mass murderer wasn't an issue for Acharya either. Like most people, he believed the crown prince was innocent.

He went home and told his wife of the offer. She was adamant he shouldn't do it. She feared becoming an outcaste and losing all their income. 'We will become beggars. I can't allow you to go.'

He told her what had been offered: a house, money, land. It was a tempting mix. His wife agreed, reluctantly.

On the day, a car picked him up and took him to a canopy set up by the river. Dressed in a white loincloth, he cooked rice and dahl; other curries had been prepared for him. It felt like he was the centre of the world. The prime minister, all the top government officials were there. Television cameras pressed in and cameras flashed. Riot police with shields surrounded them.

'Okay, you should eat now,' said one of the palace priests.

But Acharya was still unsure of the promises made to him. He turned to Prime Minister G.P. Koirala. 'All I want is a small house and some money to live on,' he said, live on television. 'Only then will I eat.'

'Everything will be taken care of,' the prime minister promised.

'Okay, I'm ready to eat the meal.'

For the next twenty minutes, Acharya devoured everything put in front of him on little silver plates. He didn't look around and his face never showed any expression as he defiled his earthly body with the body of the king. Acharya would claim that it was all symbolic. There wasn't even any meat in the meal. Others, however, have said it contained goat meat, bone marrow and ash from Dipendra's funeral pyre.

After eating, he was dressed in heavy gold and red brocade trousers with a matching coat. A silver bird-of-paradise crown, worn by Dipendra at his coming-of-age ceremony, was placed on his head.

'How are you?' the prime minister asked him. 'Are you happy?

'I am happy. I have everything now. I just don't have a house. I need a house.'

Again he was assured he'd get what he wanted. And so he mounted the tuskless male elephant, Moti Prasad.

Looking back, Acharya would claim that the elephant behaved the way it did because, being an incarnation of Lord Ganesh, it knew of the deception taking place: that the politicians were lying.

The dignitaries followed the elephant down to the river. As cameras flashed in its eyes and the path down the river bank crumbled at its feet, the temperamental beast trumpeted wildly before turning and suddenly charging back up the bank. Dignitaries and journalists scattered, 'leaving a trail of slippers and Nepali caps in their wake', Reuters reported.

The *mahout* beat at it with his stick and managed to turn the beast around, but again it shied from the water and swung around menacingly towards the dignitaries. A team of *mahouts* joined in, shouting and slapping, and dangling from its tail.

On top of the elephant, Acharya was terrified. He saw the *mahout* produce a small axe and bring it down on the animal's trunk. A 'river of blood' flowed down its head. At that, Moti Prasad seemed to settle and was coaxed into the swirling, monsoonal river.

Reuters reported that 'the elephant was finally encouraged to lumber through the polluted Bagmati followed by a fusillade of stones and rotten fruit thrown by a now vengeful crowd'. As it waded into the water, behind them was a retinue of porters, carrying the furniture which was meant to have belonged to Dipendra: a metal locker, a bed, a sofa, a television and a fan. The elephant carried Acharya up the hill south of the city to the place where his old acquaintance Sapkota, Birendra's *katto* Brahmin, was staying.

Sapkota told Acharya of his plight: that he'd been given nothing; that the few measly items carried by the porters were all Acharya would get. Acharya didn't quite believe him at first. He'd been promised a house on television, after all.

The other part of the deal was that both men got to keep the elephants. Such unwieldy beasts are too expensive to maintain and so both of the men quickly organised buyers to come and have a look.

Sapkota claimed he was offered 200,000 rupees for his. Acharya said he was bid 100,000 rupees for Moti Prasad. But early one morning a few days after the ceremony, Acharya's son took the buyer to the zoo where the beasts were being housed, and both elephants were gone. Their *mahouts* had been ordered to take them back to Chitwan, where they continue to be owned by the government. (Moti Prasad no longer carries tourists but does lifting work for the army.)

The two men staged a sit-in and became something of a sideshow. They were eventually persuaded by the police to go home to their old residences.

The Reuters account of Dipendra's *katto* ceremony ran in an Australian newspaper. Reading it had been the trigger for our trip to Nepal. The image of this priest, driven into exile under a barrage of rotten fruit fascinated us. The several accounts we read all said the *katto* Brahmin was to be exiled to some far-flung corner of the kingdom, where he'd be given a house.

We imagined, somewhat naively, that we'd follow the elephant tracks and dung pats to a spectacular hill village. We'd sit at the feet of this outcaste, perhaps with the Himalayas hanging dramatically from the sky, as he told what would surely have been an amazing story.

It didn't quite work out like that. After many enquiries, we found ourselves in a cab with our friend Dinesh, trailing a young journalist on a motorbike to the Pashupatinath precinct of Kathmandu. We met the first *katto* Brahmin, Durga Prasad

Sapkota, playing cards on a bamboo mat in the concrete court-yard behind his house.

He was angry. The government hadn't promised him a house, he admitted, but he was just a simple man. 'They all said, "You don't have to eat the *katto*." I didn't know I was going to eat the *katto*. They tricked me.' No sooner had he got to the ceremony, he claimed, than they were shoving dishes in front of him, telling him to eat faster.

We asked about reports that he'd been given a house.

'Everyone has their own opinion on what they gave us.' His grandchildren, sitting all over him, were laughing. 'They give us nothing at all.'

Not a cent?

'Just a little bit of furniture and clothes.'

We wondered if we could see the bird-of-paradise crown, and he asked if we wanted to buy it. Unwilling to insult him with a measly offer, we told Sapkota we'd think about it.

'Each and every thing is for sale,' the old Brahmin added.

Could he still act as a priest?

'Not since the ceremony. If someone is interested to call me to their home, I am ready to go. But nobody has called me.'

The mood shifted when his eldest son entered the court-yard and began to berate his father. We stood on the sidelines as barbs flew back and forth.

'My family is not known as a good family because of that ceremony,' his eldest son told us, summing up the heated exchange. 'It's put a bad mark over the whole family.'

Our journalist guide then walked us to a nearby house, but it appeared the landlord had evicted the other *katto*, Devi Prasad Acharya. Didn't want his property tarnished. Jumping into another taxi, we followed the journalist's motorbike up a hill, stopping near a man squatting by the road with a dirty cream shawl wrapped around his hunched body.

'This is him,' the journalist said. The Brahmin from Dipendra's *katto* ceremony seemed much older than the other man, yet at sixty-six was ten years younger. Acharya was cross-eyed with a thin face and a short grey beard. Standing to reveal bare feet and skinny legs, he led us down a steep, uneven path into his house, a one-room cement block. Religious images peeped out from behind neat piles of clothes and bedding.

The Brahmin squatted on his bed by the only window as we sat on an adjoining bed. A tiny child – his grandson – rampaged around, while his wife stood at the other end of the room.

As the Brahmin spoke of his life, he exhaled in rhythmic asthmatic moans, a low wheeze from deep in his chest.

What did he do with his life now? we asked him.

'The 200 kilograms of rice given by the government [for his role in the *katto*] was finished last month. The rent is 1400 rupees. We are just selling our things and paying the rent. My life is like that now. Selling the things . . . the things I was given. Next I'm going to sell the TV and those sofas.' He rested his head in his hands, moaning.

'Even if the government gave us a small house, we'd be very happy,' his wife said, 'but they didn't give us anything.'

How would they survive when the gifts were all sold?

'We don't know what to do,' the wife replied. 'Before that ceremony, I used to go to people's houses to wash clothes and do household work. But after the ceremony, people think we have lots of money, and now nobody calls me to their houses for work.'

We asked Acharya if he was worried about what would become of Dipendra's spirit.

'I don't think the spirit of Dipendra will get peace. And the present king, he will also get big difficulty and problems. The palace will have to face that.'

So the spirit of Dipendra would haunt King Gyanendra?

'Yes.'

Why?

'They don't make the spirit happy, so they will face many

difficulties. I was expecting to get the same as the person who ate the *katto* of Mahendra – he got lots of land in the Terai and he also built a house. But after the *katto* ceremony I lived in Jawalakhel [a suburb in Patan] for two or three days, and on the last day the policeman tried to get me out of there, but I wouldn't leave because I didn't get anything they promised. I was very strong: "I'm not going back home because I'm not so good priest now. My name is very bad after eating the *katto*." The police went back to the minister and after talking to him came back: "Okay, they'll provide you with a house, maybe in Kathmandu or just out of Kathmandu." They took me in a Jeep back to my house. I still expected to get something. But nothing. I went back to the chief district officer three times but nobody allowed me to see him.'

So if he got a house in the Terai, we asked, would that satisfy Dipendra's spirit? Would the ceremony be over then?

'If we got a house and some money, I will give my blessing to Dipendra.' Acharya held his hands together in front of his face as though in prayer, and dropped his head. Then he started to speak again: 'The sister of Dipendra, Shruti, came to me in my dream and she asked me, "Did you get everything to make you happy?" I told her: "No, I didn't get anything to make me satisfied. They threw me a fraud." Shruti told me, "Okay, I'll manage it for you." After that I woke up.'

epilogue

ONE YEAR ON

I t is May 2002.
The sun warms the worn cobblestones in Durbar Square and a hot wind blows in from the Indian desert. Soon it will be the monsoon again.

We lean against the old palace wall and watch a Newar priest perform his *puja* at the big red Hanuman idol. He sprinkles the god with rice and flowers. Worshippers approach and touch their forehead to the cloaked monkey. Others offer long prayers, and we wonder what it is they might be seeking.

Beside us, camouflaged soldiers guard the gateway to the stone courtyard where King Gyanendra was crowned last year. On the far side of the square, a new royal Kumari has been installed. The omens for the new king, the royal priest tells us, are good. The little goddess is always in a very pleasant, happy mood.

The first year of Gyanendra's reign, however, has been neither pleasant nor happy. The state of emergency has been extended yet again. The People's War has now claimed over 4000 lives, more than 2000 of those in the last six months.

With the throne thrust upon him, Gyanendra was crowned an uncomfortable king. Alone, with virtually no family his own age to turn to for guidance, he was accused by many of his subjects of being a murderer.

Gyanendra, his family tells us, didn't ask to be king. 'Who would like to take up the kingship at that age?' asks his sister-in-law Anju. 'The country's not running smoothly. It's no fun to become the king right now . . . He was such a handsome man, oh, he was such a handsome man. And in seven days he had all these wrinkles.'

Now, as King Gyanendra prepares to come out of the one-year mourning period, the Nepalese people are looking to him to pull them out of the gloom. Despite their suspicions, despite his son, he is their king. As for the new Crown Prince Paras, well, as one Kathmanduite put it, 'Compared to Dipendra, I think Paras is a saint.'

Next month, according to the astrologers, not long after the royal family emerge from their mourning, Saturn will move into a new constellation. The bad times, they say, will end.

Colonel Sundar Pratap Rana, the late King Birendra's devoted ADC, is only a shell of the dashing royal aide he was this time last year. Still bewildered by his dismissal from the army, Rana cannot yet see an end to the gloom.

Today is 1 June 2002, exactly a year since Crown Prince Dipendra went on his deadly rampage. Rana is at home with his family, but he is lonely. 'I feel like I lost a battle,' he says. 'I spent my life with His Majesty. Seventeen years with him, the last five as a senior ADC. And I worked hard for everything I got.' He clings to the hope that King Gyanendra will realise the injustice of his sacking and re-evaluate the decision.

'The culprit was the crown prince. He became king and he died,' Rana says. 'There is no one to blame . . . If I was guilty of doing something wrong, I'd be in jail.'

For him, the massacre was like an earthquake. A big building was felled by the quake and he was just the little building next to it that got taken out and nobody noticed.

The same could be said of Devyani Rana. A year after the tragedy, the shattered young woman still hasn't returned home.

'Devyani is finished in Nepal,' one relative says.

Betrayed by the web of deceit Devyani spun around herself and the crown prince, others feel the same way. In certain circles she has become persona non grata. Speaking to those people, you get an eerie sense that, for them, Devyani's life ended the night of the massacre. They speak of her in the past tense. When they encounter her family, her name doesn't come up.

Those closest and most loyal to Devyani, however, have formed a tight, protective circle around the grieving woman.

'There has been a lot of Devyani-bashing because she's the one who's still alive,' says one close girlfriend.

Devyani is now living in London, isolated and afraid. It may be a long time before she returns. She recently told a friend over the phone: 'You're better off than me. You're at least still in Nepal.'

Meanwhile, a small group of royal relatives wait for her return. One of them tells us: 'We have made it clear to her family that if we see her we're going to ask: "Did you know?" And: "How far in advance did you know?"

'Maybe she'll say, "He said it so many times I didn't believe it." And that's justifiable. The crown prince had even said it in front of us a year before and no one took it seriously . . . We have read it over and over in history books. It's not new, but nobody took it seriously.'

One year on, King Gyanendra and Queen Komal have not yet moved into Narayanhiti Royal Palace. The Friday night dinners haven't resumed, either. The family all know they will have to pick up and go on at some point, but still, every time they get together, the conversation comes back to that night when it went so wrong. They're not ready.

Much of the palace remains deserted. Queen Mother Ratna lives there alone. The past year has almost been too much for her. She has lost four children and three grandchildren. Her family has watched her age.

Her sister-in-law, Princess Helen, hasn't coped well either, devastated by the loss of her daughter Jayanti. And the brigadier-general, Rabi Shamsher, still hasn't come out of shock. The shuffling old man agonises over his failure to knock Dipendra down when the shooting started.

Ketaki is only now coming to see herself as very lucky. Only her wings were broken, and they are healing. It is awkward, but she can serve tea again, and smoke a cigarette. She will never be able to lift her right arm out to the side, though. For so long, she felt guilty that her arm took the impact of the bullet that went into Dhirendra's heart. The poor man clung to life for four days, suffering. Maybe if her arm hadn't been in the way he would have gone instantly.

Gorakh still has a bullet buried in his chest. His heart isn't as strong as it might be, and he doesn't have a lot of confidence about exercising. But he's started to run again, and he's getting used to living without his thumb. It's much harder learning to live without his beautiful wife Shruti.

Their two little girls are growing up. Girwani is almost four and Surangana will be two in October. It has been especially hard on the eldest. She remembers her mum. The Nepalese for 'gone to heaven' translates as 'gone to meet the gods' but, Girwani asks her father, 'People go to temple to worship the gods and they come back – why hasn't Mum?'

On 20 June according to the Hindu lunar calendar, the royal family will end their mourning as the dead join the ancestors.

That day, the family will gather at the palace to observe the sombre first-year anniversary. They will offer rice to the dead. King Birendra's spirit will move on.

The royal priest will repeat the ceremony for Queen Aishwarya, Prince Nirajan and King Dipendra. In royal homes across Kathmandu, the same ritual will be held for Princess Shruti, Princess Jayanti, Princess Shanti, Princess Sharada, Kumar Khadga and Dhirendra Shah.

Being royals and so close to gods, it would be expected that their souls have finished being reborn into this painful world. King Birendra, as an incarnation of Lord Vishnu, will take up residence at his heavenly abode, Baikuntha.

Dipendra's spirit, though, will be troubled. He will be punished by the agents of Yamma, the god of death. He will be reborn seven times into lowly, difficult lives, struggling to emancipate his restless soul.

As this first lunar anniversary approaches, the queen mother asks that her family visit the billiard room before-hand. She wants them to be prepared when they arrive for the ceremonies.

The room looks shabby in the daylight. The family has to search hard to find bullet holes in the walls and ceiling. They are so small. But they can still recall where the bodies fell.

The building will be knocked down, the horrible memory erased. But the survivors have promised each other a legacy: there will be no more family intrigue, no more protocol and whispers shadowing what matters.

As the family confronts the billiard room, Ketaki is struck with pity. She feels sorry for Dipendra now, brought up here in this haunted palace amid all its ghosts. But the room itself is nothing. Like an empty stage after the play has finished.

postscript

Soon after we left Nepal in June 2002, King Gyanendra moved back into Narayanhiti Palace. Then, in October, he reoccupied the government, sacking the elected leadership ostensibly for failing to organise elections. He installed his own prime minister and cabinet.

While this move added fuel to the conspiracy theories that blamed the king for the palace massacre, from what we could gather his actions were hugely popular. There followed stories of Maoist leaders being helicoptered into the palace for secret talks and, sure enough, a cease-fire was called in January 2003. The Maoists regrouped and turned out for mass rallies in the capital calling for a new constitution. The democratic parties turned out for mass rallies in the capital demanding the king heed the old constitution, but still he resisted.

The cease-fire broke in late August 2003 and the Maoists moved into a new phase of their campaign with assassinations and bomb attacks in Kathmandu.

Demonstrations were banned but the democrats kept turning up to protest and the police kept arresting them at up to one thousand at a time.

The death toll rose daily and King Gyanendra clung to his birthright.

glossary

baba	guru
bandh	general strike
chhang	homemade rice beer
chia	tea
dai	older brother
daura suruwal	traditional Nepalese dress for men – tight, pyjama-style pants and a cross-over top
dhoti	traditional loin-wrap worn by men
durbar	palace
foxho	literally 'lungs', a Nepalese term for a fat person
katto	food eaten by a priest at the traditional death ceremony reserved for Nepalese kings
khukuri	traditional curved Nepalese knife still carried by Gurkha soldiers
kurta suruwal	loose pants and matching tunic worn by men and women
lakh	100,000; 100,000 rupees
mahout	elephant driver
malla	floral garland
mandala	circular design symbolising the universe
namaste	traditional greeting, accompanied by palms pressed together and a bow of the head
panchayat	village or town council
prasad	the part of a consecrated offering returned to the worshipper
puja	ritual worship
rakshi	distilled rice spirit
saddhu	Hindu holy man
sati	ritual custom of a widow burning on her husband's funeral pyre
Terai	the semi-tropical lowland belt of southern Nepal
tika	religious mark placed on the forehead
topi	traditional Nepalese cloth cap, worn by men

authors' note

There was a phrase we heard over and over during our stay in Nepal. 'The guest is god.' And it was certainly the way Nepalis made us feel. We were shown exceptional hospitality by the many people who welcomed us into their homes and lives, particularly given that it was often to talk about very difficult times.

Despite the state of emergency, we felt safe in Nepal and we urge people who read this book to go. Be careful, but the country is worth it.

To everyone who appears in *Love and Death in Kathmandu*, we thank you all: for your time, your courage and for making our journey so fascinating.

Where requested, names have been changed. We can only send our most sincere, anonymous thanks to everyone who went off-the-record, sometimes at personal risk, to tell us their stories.

We must point out that the views we express in this book do not reflect the opinions of any one individual we met or interviewed. Indeed, in Nepal it is difficult to find one simple version of anything. Also, while this is a work of non-fiction, some points of chronology regarding our travels have been changed for ease of story-telling.

We were incredibly lucky to make some wonderful friends in Nepal who truly went out of their way to help us. To Dinesh Shrestha and his fiancée Shanti, and Pankaj Pradhananga and his wife Sharmila, we owe our greatest thanks. If it hadn't been for them this book may well not have made it to completion. Thanks also to photojournalist Min Bajracharya for his wonderful images and his warmth.

Kunda Dixit, editor of the *Nepali Times*, was extremely generous with his time and resources, as were Subodh Gautam and Gunarag Luitel from Kantipur Publications. Many thanks also to Major General Tara Bahadur Thapa, former prime minister Kirti Nidhi Bista, Radhe Shyam, Crispin Conroy and the Australian Embassy in Kathmandu, the wonderful staff at our home away from home, the Hotel Narayani, Bachan Gyawali and Four Seasons Travel, and Shanta Malla and his brilliant Lajana restaurant.

Thanks also to Phil Stafford, Shanie Atkinson, Mark Marin and Jacki Jameson for their help in the early days, to Mike Willesee and Barbara Adams for reading the manuscript (John, we know you would've if you could've), Bill and Alice Whittaker for the desperately-needed computer, to Maree Whittaker for the chiropractic work, Jo Willesee for the care packages, and our beautiful friends Anthony and Briony Schofield, as always, for nursing our computers through some traumatic moments.

To everyone at Pan Macmillan, a huge thank you once again for helping us do what we love. Especially Tom Gilliatt, who drove this project forward with enthusiasm and much appreciated guidance.

Finally, we would like to thank all our gorgeous family and friends who have supported us through the writing of this book, and in particular Carol Willesee and Tristram Miall, who have done it in more ways than we could possibly have imagined, or ever thank them for.

bibliography

Adhikari, Pushpa, 'A Himalayan tragedy – A parallel being drawn between king's death and 1806 plot', *Sunday Observer*, 10 June 2001.

Allen, Michael, *The Cult of Kumari – Virgin Worship in Nepal*, Mandala Book Point, Kathmandu, 1996.

Bagchand, Umid, 'Nation in Grief', *Nepali Times*, 22–28 February 2002.

Barton, Fiona and Buckland, Danny, 'The Eton shop girl who talked of love with Nepal's killer prince', *Mail on Sunday*, 10 June 2001.

Bernstein, Jeremy, *In the Himalayas: Journeys through Nepal, Tibet and Bhutan*, The Lyons Press, Guilford, 1996.

Bhattarai, Dr Baburam, 'The new "Kot massacre" should not be accepted', *Human Rights and People's War in Nepal* website, June 2001.

Bhattarai, Binod, 'Emergency Room', *Nepali Times*, 15–21 February 2002.

Bista, Dor Bahadur, *People of Nepal*, Ratna Pustak Bhandar, Bhotahity, Kathmandu, 2000.

Burbank, Jon, *Culture Shock! – Nepal*, Times Books International, Singapore, Kuala Lumpur, 1992.

Cavenagh, General Sir Orfeur, *Reminiscences of an Indian Official*, WH Allen & Co, London, 1884.

Constable, Pamela, 'After Massacre, Nepal Mourns – Prince Suspected in Deaths Listed in Coma, Named King', *The Washington Post*, 3 June 2001.

—, 'Nepali King's Unruly Welcome – Protesters Demand Information About Deaths in Palace', *The Washington Post*, 5 June 2001.

Dalrymple, William, *The Age of Kali*, HarperCollins, London, 1998.

Devkota, Dr Upendra, 'At Chhauni, 1–4 June', *Nepali Times*, 22–28 June 2001.

Finlay, Hugh; Everist, Richard and Wheeler, Tony, *Lonely Planet Nepal*, Lonely Planet Publications, Melbourne, Oakland, London, Paris, 1999.

French, Patrick, 'Guns, drugs and madness', *The Weekend Australian Magazine*, 3–4 November 2001.

Greenwald, Jeff, *Shopping for Buddhas*, Lonely Planet Publications, 1996.

Gregson, Jonathan, *Blood Against the Snows – The Tragic Story of Nepal's Royal Dynasty*, Fourth Estate, London, 2002.

—, *Kingdoms Beyond the Clouds: Journey in Search of the Himalayan Kings*, Macmillan, London, 2000.

Harder, Ann-Marie, 'Royal Tragedy', the-voyagers.tripod.com, June 2001.

Hilton, Isabel, 'Royal Blood', *The New Yorker*, 30 July 2001.

Iyer, Pico, *Video Night In Kathmandu – And other reports from the not-so-far east*, Bloomsbury, 1988.

Jansen, Eva Rudy, *The Book of Hindu Imagery*, New Age Books, New Delhi, 2002.

Johnsen, Linda, *The Complete Idiot's Guide to Hinduism*, Alpha, Indianapolis, 2002.

Khadka, Rajendra S. (ed.), *Travelers' Tales Guides: Nepal*, Travelers' Tales, Inc., San Francisco, 1997.

Koirala, Bishweshwar Prasad, *Atmabrittanta: Late Life Recollections*, Translated by Kanak Mani Dixit, Himal Books, Lalitpur, 2001.

Lall, Kesar, *Nepalese Customs and Manners*, Ratna Pustak Bhandar, Kathmandu, 2000.

Langan, Heather, 'Nepalese Dies as Rioters Try to Storm Royal Palace, Reports Say', bloomberg.com, 4 June 2001.

Liu, Melinda and Roberts, Patricia, 'Nepal's Maoist Threat', *Newsweek International*, 18 June 2001.

McCarthy, Rory, 'Nepal's royal upheaval gives cue to Maoists', *The Guardian* (UK), 11 June 2001.

Misra, Neelesh, *End of the Line – The Story of the Killing of the Royals in Nepal*, Penguin Books, India, 2001.

Nepal, Kiran, 'It was Dipendra: Probe team finds smoking gun', *Nepali Times*, 15 June 2001.

Nevers, Kevin, 'Life and Opinions', *Chesterton Tribune*, June 2001.

Oliphant, Margaret, *Memoir of the Life of Laurence Oliphant*, William Blackwood & Sons, Edinburgh and London, 1891.

Onesto, Li, 'Red Flag Flying on the Roof of the World – Inside the Revolution in Nepal: Interview with Comrade Prachanda', *Revolutionary Worker* #1043, 20 February 2000.

Pathak, Perina, 'First fumbling scrawl into the world of knowledge', *The Kathmandu Post*, 18 February 2002.

Perry, Alex, 'Showing No Mercy', *TIME Asia*, 4 March 2002.

Popham, Peter, 'Guards who witnessed royal massacre sacked as Nepal's crisis deepens', *The Independent* (UK), 4 July 2001.

Raj, Prakash A., *'Kay Gardeko?' – The Royal Massacre in Nepal*, Rupa & Co., 2001.

—, *Portraits and Photographs from Nepal*, Nabeen Publications, Kathmandu, 1994.

—, *Queens of the Shah Dynasty in Nepal*, Nabeen Publications, Kathmandu, 1997.

Raman, B., 'Maoists' Tet-like offensive in Nepal', *South Asia Analysis Group* website, 27 November 2001.

Rana, Pramode Shamsher, *A Chronicle of Rana Rule*, R. Rana, Kathmandu, 2000.

—, *Rana Intrigues*, R. Rana, Kathmandu, 1995.

Rana, Purushottam Shamsher J.B., *Jung Bahadur Rana – The Story of His Rise and Glory*, Book Faith India, Delhi, 1998.

Sanwal, B.D., *Social and Political History of Nepal*, Manohar Publishers, New Delhi, 1993.

Scindia, Vijayaraje with Malgonkar, Manohar, *Princess: The Autobiography of the Dowager Maharani of Gwalior*, Century, London, Melbourne, Auckland, Johannesburg, 1985.

Sever, Adrian, *Nepal Under the Ranas*, Oxford & IBH Publishing Co., New Delhi, 1993.

Shrestha, Aditya M., *Bleeding Mountains of Nepal: a Story of Corruption, Greed, Misuse of Power and Resources*, Ekta Books, Kathmandu, 1999.

—, *The Dreadful Night – Carnage at Nepalese Royal Palace*, Ekta Books, Kathmandu, 2001.

Shrestha, Brig. Gen. (Ret.) Dr Khagendra Bahadur, *Memories of Late King Birendra . . . in My Pictures*, Mrs Sita Shrestha, Reader, Tribhuvan University, 2002.

Smythies, Olive, *Tiger Lady*, William Heinemann Ltd, Melbourne, London, Toronto, 1953.

Stiller, Ludwig F., S.J., *The Rise of the House of Gorkha*, Human Resources Development Research Centre, Nepal, 1995.

Thapa, Netra B., *A Short History of Nepal*, Ratna Pustak Bhanda, Kathmandu, 1981.

Thapliyal, Sangeeta, 'Maoists in Nepal', *The Hindu*, 18 December 2001.

Vaidya, T.R., 'First National Movement of Nepal 1842–1843', *Voice of History*, Vol XIV, no. 2 (Dec 1999), Tribhuvan University, Kirtipur.

—, 'The Kot Massacre: A Critical Assessment', *Voice of History*, Vol XV, no. 1 (June 2000), Tribhuvan University, Kirtipur.

Verma, Somesh, 'Late Princess Shruti was an all-rounder', *The Kathmandu Post*, 8 June 2001.

Wright, Alison, 'Democracy Day', *Travelers' Tales Guides: Nepal*, Travelers' Tales Inc., San Francisco, 1997.

Yogi, Bhagirath, 'Royal Palace Killings – Loose Ends', *Spotlight*, 22–28 June 2001.

'A childhood tied up in knots', *The Himalayan Times*, 17 February 2002.

'Anti-Hindu plot claim in Nepal massacre', *Sydney Morning Herald*, 6 June 2001.

'Cocaine fuelled Dipendra's gun rampage', *The Assam Tribune*, 11 June 2001.

'Death toll: 523 Maoists, 97 security personnel', *The Kathmandu Post*, 27 December 2001.

'Dipendra and Devyani', *Jana Aastha*, 20 June 2001.

'Dipendra was shot in the back? – Nepal's new regent terms it a tragic "accident"', *The Daily Star* (Bangladesh), 4 June 2001.

'Four days, three kings', *Nepali Times*, 22–28 June 2001.

'Govt forces suffer heavy losses in Achham', *The Kathmandu Post*, 18 February 2002.

High Level Committee Report on the Royal Palace Incident (Unofficial translation), June 2001.

'His Majesty King Passes Away – Her Majesty, Prince Nirajan among the dead', *The Rising Nepal*, 3 June 2001.

'"I was hit. Sruti cradled me. Then Dipendra came and shot her."', *Nepali Times*, 22–28 June 2001.

'King Dipendra in "very critical" condition – Regent says shooting an accident', *The Kathmandu Post*, 4 June 2001.

'King Gyanendra's address: Full text', nepalnews.com, 4 June 2001.

'Late King Dipendra cremated', nepalnews.com, 4 June 2001.

Lonely Planet India, Lonely Planet Publications, Melbourne, Oakland, London, Paris, 2001.

'Maoists strike big, leave 106 dead', *The Himalayan Times*, 18 February 2002.

'Massacre a grave political conspiracy: Maoist', *The Kathmandu Post*, 4 June 2001.

'Mourning nation seeks the truth', *The Kathmandu Post*, 4 June 2001.

Murder Most Royal, BBC, produced by Donna Sharpe, Blakeway Productions, London, 2002.

'Nepal Emergency Declared', news.bbc.co.uk, 26 November 2001.

'Nepal: People's War Intensifies in the West – Bold Move in Mangalsen', *Revolutionary Worker*, 3 March 2002.

'One year of people's war in Nepal', *The People's Review*, 31 July 1997.

'Pledge to continue struggle on fifth anniversary of People's War', *The People's Review*, 15–21 February 2001.

'Prince named king as Nepal royal funerals begin', cnn.com, 2 June 2001.

'Rajpariwar in a Mess – Students Demonstrate Against "Wayward" Prince, Demand Action', newslookmag.com, 9 August 2000.

'Royal Funeral', nepalnews.com, 2 June 2001.

'Shocked people mourn the death', *The Rising Nepal*, 3 June 2001. *Spacetime*, 18 February 2002.

'Synopsis of the High Level Committee Report on the Royal Palace Incident' (unofficial translation), nepalnews.com, June 2001.